King of the Mountain

To Margaret & Tom Corry,

Everyone - everybody deserves to have

Wealth - deserves to have

their life & deeds evaluated fairly,

and that's what I've tried to do here.

I hope you enjoy it.

Jod McCahan

P.S.

Colleen did a terrific

job interning with me this

Semester - you should be

proud - as I'm sure

you are.

KING
OF THE
MOUNTAIN

The Rise, Fall, and Redemption of
Chief Judge Sol Wachtler

John M. Caher

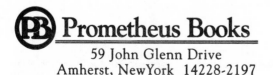
Prometheus Books
59 John Glenn Drive
Amherst, NewYork 14228-2197

Published 1998 by Prometheus Books

02 01 00 99 98   5 4 3 2 1

Library of Congress Cataloging-in-Publication Data

Caher, John M.
    King of the mountain : the rise, fall, and redemption of Chief Judge Sol
Wachtler / John M. Caher.
        p.   cm.
    Includes bibliographical references and index.
    ISBN 1–57392–197–1 (alk. paper)
    1. Wachtler, Sol. 2. Judges—New York (State)—Biography. I. Title.
KF373.W25C34   1998S
347.747'014'092—dc21
[B]   97–49303
                                                                          CIP

Printed in the United States of America on acid-free paper

For Kathleen, and forever

Acknowledgments

Several judges, former judges, staffers, and former staffers of the Court of Appeals and other courts were exceptionally helpful and candid, and their contributions were essential to this book. Many of them insisted on confidentiality and I, of course, will honor their wishes. Regretfully, then, I am unable to publicly acknowledge some of my most valued and cherished sources. They know who they are, however, and I trust they appreciate the depth of my gratitude.

However, there are several people whom I can publicly acknowledge, and do so with honor. At the very top of the list is my wife, Kathleen, and my daughters, Erin and Kerry. Their love and support made this book possible. Michael and Maureen McCarthy, who, aside from being two of my dearest friends, also happen to be my in-laws, contributed enor-

7

mously to this project, providing encouragement when it was needed most, and in the way it was most needed. My parents, James and Dolores "Fitz" Caher, instilled in me the confidence to pursue such an undertaking, but sadly died long before its conception. My brother Jim—a top-notch lawyer in Eugene, Oregon, and co-author, with me, of *Debt Free! Your Guide to Personal Bankruptcy without Shame* (Henry Holt & Co., 1996)—was an immense inspiration and help and, in fact, has been a guiding light for much of my life and career.

I first began thinking about this project at the urging of Henry M. Greenberg, former clerk to current Chief Judge Judith S. Kaye. Hank had the foresight to suggest, prior to Sol Wachtler's downfall, that I consider a biography of the chief judge, and I thank him for getting me started.

For their support, assistance, and encouragement, I also wish to thank: Brian, Kathy, Sean, and Brendan Caputi; Brian, Margaret, and Maura McDonald; Pat and Carol Caher; Bunny Burnes; Ray Fanning; Kate Donnelly; Michael J. "Mick" McCarthy III; Pat Maro; Theodore W. McCarthy; Jeff, Jeremy, and Joshua Winig; and Laura "X."

Several of Judge Wachtler's former clerks, particularly Michael Trainor, David Gould, and Thomas Gleason, shared their wealth of knowledge with me, for which I am grateful.

Members of the bar and the judiciary have been exceptionally helpful and patient with me over the years, taking the time to explain complex legal principles to a layman. Several provided specific assistance or insight for this book, including: David M. Cherubin, Veronica G. Dumas, Salvatore D. Ferlazzo, Eugene Z. Grenz, Louis Grumet, Michael J. Grygiel, Richard Honen, Michael Hutter, Kathryn M. Kase, Terence Kindlon, and Laurie Shanks. I owe a special debt of gratitude to the late U.S. District Judge Con. G. "Gus" Cholakis, who taught me a great deal about the law and life in our early morning discussions, and a great deal about courage and fortitude as his own life came to an end.

Current and former employees of the state court system have been extraordinarily helpful in nurturing my interest in the judiciary and the Court of Appeals especially: Paul Browne, Stuart Cohen, Matthew T. Crosson, Mary deBourbon, Hope Engel, Marjorie McCoy, Walt Mordaunt, Martin Strnad, Don Sheraw, and Dick Zander.

Scholars who have studied the Court of Appeals and continue to track the panel, particularly Vincent Martin Bonventre of Albany Law School, contributed significantly to my understanding of the court and the context in which the most secretive branch of government operates.

I would be remiss if I did not acknowledge the contributions of my colleagues at the *Times Union*. Its editors have always been supportive and encouraging, and its reporters thoroughly professional colleagues. A reporting career at the *Times Union* is as it could and should be for an idealistic journalism major, and I am grateful for the opportunities that have been afforded me by my editors. On this project Rob Brill and Mike Gormley were particularly helpful.

Sheree Bykofsky, my agent, believed in *King of the Mountain* from the minute she saw the proposal and worked tirelessly to convince the publishing world of its merit and value. A lesser agent would have given up long before. Sheree was instrumental in steering this book to an appropriate publisher, Prometheus Books, and a sharp editor, Eugene O'Connor.

Finally, I wish to thank the entire Wachtler family for the trust and confidence. Joan Wachtler openly discussed what remains a painful topic, and her children—Lauren Wachtler, Alison Braunstein, Marjorie Eagan, and Philip Wachtler—generously shared their memories and observations. Morton

Wachtler, the judge's brother, provided important insights into their early years. When I first approached Judge Wachtler about this project—which was solely my idea—I demanded three conditions, which I was in no position to make: (1) there could be no financial relationship between us, (2) he would cooperate fully, and (3) he would have absolutely no control over editorial content. Judge Wachtler quickly and readily agreed to each condition. I would not have undertaken this project under any other circumstances, and Judge Wachtler deserves immense credit for understanding that my credibility—and his, really—required an objective, straightforward, and, I'm sure, sometimes painful review of his extraordinary life and career. I can only hope that I have been as fair and just and considerate with him as he has always been with me.

Contents

Part II: The Mind

Part III: The Mystery

King of the Mountain

Introduction

O n Saturday night, November 7, 1992, a group of reporters with the Albany, New York, *Times Union* were
at a reception for the local symphony orchestra when editor
Harry Rosenfeld was paged for a telephone call. After a few
moments, Rosenfeld, a savvy and veteran journalist who had
spearheaded the *Washington Post*'s Watergate investigation
two decades earlier, and a man who long ago ceased to be
surprised by the transgressions and misdeeds of public officials, returned to the party quivering.

"You won't believe tomorrow's headline," Rosenfeld said
to no one in particular, sweating profusely despite the cool
fall evening. "What is the most bizarre, most unbelievable
story you can possibly imagine?" he asked, arms flailing,
nervously shifting his weight from one foot to the other.

Dan Lynch, the managing editor, quipped: "That Madonna had the pope's baby."

"No," Rosenfeld responded with a tinge of anger. "*More* bizarre."

One hundred and fifty miles away, in New York City, an associate judge on the state's highest court, the Court of Appeals, returned home from a speaking engagement to receive a call from an elderly relative that Sol Wachtler, the chief judge, had been arrested by the FBI for extorting money from his mistress, and that he was in the custody of federal authorities.

"Poor Uncle Ed," the judge said, hanging up the phone. "He's imagining things. We'll have to think about putting him in a home."

Another judge receiving a similar call that night barked, "April Fool's Day is five months off," hung up, and went to bed.

Hours earlier, shock waves had hit Court of Appeals Hall, an elegant fortress on Eagle Street in Albany, where a stunned guard was confronted on a quiet Saturday afternoon by FBI agents armed with a warrant authorizing a search of the chief judge's chambers. Weeks before, the U.S. attorney and the FBI refused to believe—until the proof was unassailable—that the man harassing socialite Joy Silverman was the revered Sol Wachtler.

"As soon as we realized Sol Wachtler was involved, I myself was reluctant to believe it," said James Fox, former head of the FBI in New York City.[1] Fox had met Wachtler just before the campaign of harassment began, on a yacht with a group of prominent businessmen who all but convinced the chief judge to run for governor. "I had a great deal of respect and admiration for him. Like everybody else, I thought he walked on water."

Over the next days and weeks, the court and the country would learn of the stunningly aberrational behavior of New

York State's chief judge—an adulterous affair with his wife's step-cousin, lurid phone calls and letters to Mrs. Silverman and her daughter when the affair crumbled, implied threats of kidnapping and extortion, bizarre costumes, and voice-altering devices—that resulted in a man with a previously sterling reputation spending thirteen months in a federal prison.

No one could believe it.

Movie-star handsome and loaded with charisma, Wachtler could surely charm and flirt, but he wasn't known to fool around. Politically astute and manipulatively clever, Wachtler knew how to get what he wanted; but after a quarter century in the public eye, there had never been so much as a hint of scandal. Intense and sensitive, Wachtler was known for compassion not cruelty, for consideration not contempt. He was a paragon of virtue, a pillar of the community, a judicial/political figure who stood above the fray —or so everyone thought. Even Wachtler couldn't understand what had come over him.

"How could I have written those detestable letters?" he asked in his diary. "How could I, in playing my mindless mind games with Joy, have been so insensitive, so indifferent to the pain I was inflicting on so many people, not to mention my court and my profession? How could my judgment have been so skewed as to blind me to the ruin I was bringing to a career, a profession and a marriage, all of which I had nurtured for over forty years?"[2]

At first, it was rumored that Wachtler had a brain tumor. How better to explain the apparent unraveling of a man who, to many, was a heroic figure? Then it was drugs that were to blame. Perhaps medication for the judge's back pain had affected him, people thought.

In the end came the stark realization that while Wachtler's behavior was certainly influenced by external factors—

both physical and psychological—the internal demons that led to his downfall are lurking near all of us, like a Shakespearean flaw.

Sol Wachtler was a giant not only in New York but in U.S. jurisprudence, and a jurist whose decisions on free speech, right-to-die, civil liberties, and criminal rights continue to shape both state and federal law. He was a public figure whose wit and insights are quoted in everything from popular fiction (such as *Bonfire of the Vanities*, authored by his friend and college classmate Tom Wolfe) to law reviews. Wachtler was a chief judge who manipulated his court and the judges on it through the power of his intellect and persuasive strength of personality, and a politician so engaging that he was touted as the first Jewish president. Some even referred to him as a "Jewish Kennedy." In 1986, *M* magazine included Wachtler in a photo array of the most stylish men of the year. (Others on the list included actor Laurence Olivier, Senator Robert Dole, bicyclist Greg LeMonde, pitcher Nolan Ryan, film star William Hurt, and musician Wynton Marsalis.) The magazine said Wachtler dispensed "justice with substance and style."[3] Wachtler had, and has, that elusive and almost undefinable star quality, a *presence* that would somehow make him stand out in a room full of total strangers, or allow him to have, at will, just about any audience eating out of his hand.

Yet the same qualities that led to his success as a judge and politician—the probing, analytical, and occasionally scheming mind; the aching desire for respectability; an ego that needed constant nurturing; and the insatiable quest to be king of the mountain—led to his destruction. So, too, did the fact that he was mired in a stale marriage; secretly taking a toxic mix of prescription drugs; grieving over the deaths of some close friends; consumed by fear that his violent headaches, limp leg, and hand spasms were the result of a rapidly growing brain tumor; accepting up to twenty-five speaking engagements a month; and embroiled in a bitter, very public feud with the man who had made him chief judge—a once dear friend named Mario Cuomo.

Like all of us, Wachtler had a need to be loved, but a heightened *politician's* need to be loved and respected. "He *had* to have adulation," said a former colleague. "He thrived on it. When he didn't get it, it was something he couldn't tolerate."[4]

Wachtler was used to having things go his way, used to being the wunderkind, the knight in shining armor, the judge in glowing robes, the rainmaker. He was Pygmalion, the kind sophisticate, and everyone else, particularly Joy Silverman, was Galatea. For seven years (four of them intimate), they would replay their familiar roles: Sol as the father-figure, basking in seemingly *unconditional*—but ultimately, very *conditional*—adoration; Joy as both the daughter-figure and mother-figure, and Sol as the son who needed her worship as much as she needed his attention. Sol as Henry Higgins, Joy as Eliza Doolittle.

"He made me feel loved," Joy said almost wistfully in Manhattan Supreme Court in May 1995, four years after the affair ended. The occasion was her divorce trial when she was called upon to testify about her infidelity. "He made me feel like a human being, like a woman . . . [providing] the comfort, the self-esteem, the love that I wanted so desperately from my husband, and that my husband would not give me."[5]

But after Silverman was through with Wachtler and replaced him with a younger, wealthier man, the judge concocted increasingly bizarre schemes to bring her back to him for comfort and security.

"Without Joy in my life, I felt no one needed me," Wachtler confided in his diary. "For seven years, I had been the one Joy turned to for advice—whether to deal with her own problems or those involving [her children] Evan and Jessica. I had been able to work with Evan to determine what college courses he should take to prepare him for law school. Jessica, who was very shy and reticent, had sought my advice on matters which affected her in a very personal way. I had come to think of all three of them as a vital part of my life. Their loss only added to my sense of decomposition."

Wachtler's wife, Joan, had largely outgrown him. His children were adults and on their own. The judges on his court, who once yielded to his experience, were becoming increasingly independent, far less reliant on the chief, far less deferential. And then Joy and, by extension, her children cast him aside. He needed desperately to feel needed. He needed to be someone's idol. He needed to be Joy's savior. And he would create a crisis from which to save her.

First, Wachtler resorted to hang-up calls. When that didn't work, he tried anonymous letters—increasingly offensive screeds designed to make her run back to him for comfort and safety and salvation. But Joy didn't run to Sol, she ran to the director of the FBI and, ironically, crushed Wachtler through connections he had established for her.

"I knew exactly who and what Joy was when I became involved with her," Wachtler recalls in his diary.

> Although I may have been . . . sexually naive, I was not a child. I was an adult who had lived an unsheltered life, someone who should have known better. I had known for years that Joy was capable of being avaricious and vengeful. Hadn't she told me of the time she called her first husband, while in a honeymoon bed of her second, to taunt him?

Hadn't I been the subject of her uncontrollable and profane rages? And what made me think when she told me in graphic detail how she had destroyed those whom she deceived as her enemies, including every man of whom she grew tired, that my name would not be added to the list? "When I finished with him, he was dead meat," she would say. Why couldn't I see that one day I too might meet the same fate?

If there was anything Wachtler loved more than the judicial process, it was politics, both in the partisan sense and the interpersonal sense. He was an extraordinarily gifted natural politician—astute, articulate, and cunning—but the kind of man people genuinely liked *and* admired, someone both fun and inspiring.

He remembered names and faces and birthdays. He took the time to chat with janitors and maids, and really seemed to care about what they had to say. With his attentive ocean-blue eyes and seductive baritone, he had a way of making one feel like the most important person he had talked to all day, and then made a hundred others feel the same way. Certainly, there was a politician's phoniness in some of that. Surely, at least in his subconscious, he knew he was currying good will and potential votes. Still, he could be extraordinarily thoughtful and kind and considerate when there was no apparent political benefit, seemingly nothing to be gained, except the affection of the recipient.

"He was a judge's judge, *and* a gentleman," said attorney Salvatore D. Ferlazzo, an Albany litigator who clerked at the Court of Appeals for Judge Bernard S. Meyer in the early 1980s, before Wachtler became chief. Ferlazzo was just another bright, young lawyer who would be gone within a couple of years, one of many. "I was a law student right out of law school and [Wachtler] treated me with great respect, and he didn't need to. He treated everyone with respect and dignity."[6]

Once, when Wachtler was an associate judge on the Court of Appeals, another judge lambasted a young attorney who had deluged the court with briefs. When Wachtler's time came to question the rattled counselor—after all, an appearance before seven of the sharpest legal minds in America is an intimidating experience for any lawyer, particularly one newly admitted to the practice—he softly said, "I, for one, found your briefs very helpful. Thank you."[7]

Another time, a former staffer recalls,[8] a lawyer arguing before the court seemed detached and distant. After arguments, someone mentioned to Wachtler that the attorney's mother was in the hospital and seriously ill. With no prompting from anyone, Wachtler quietly called the attorney's mother and told her that while he couldn't tell her how the case would come out, her son did a fine job and she should be proud of him.

He was also fun and mischievous, frequently playing tricks on his colleagues. He would hide a writhing mechanical hand in the bin where judges deposited their briefs, deposit a melting ice cream cake in a colleague's desk drawer (Cedric Faulkner, an assistant, got him back, though, leaving a slice in the judge's coat pocket), or place a rubber tarantula in a filing cabinet. In 1981, a third-year law student at Suffolk Law School in Boston spotted Wachtler's car—all the judges have specialty plates—parked in midtown Manhattan and left his résumé and a note on the windshield. "I thought a little *chutzpah* wouldn't hurt," the student said in the note. Amused, Wachtler wrote back: "Actually, I did not consider your method of delivery as demonstrating *chutzpah*. It would have made much more of an impression if you had broken the windshield and put it on my front seat. I shall keep your résumé on file—in the glove compartment of my car—and if you are still interested at some future date please communicate with me. I am enclosing an extra postage stamp just in case you can't find my car."[9]

Frequently, when an acquaintance was celebrating the birth of a child, Wachtler would send the newborn a letter, on his official, embossed stationery, welcoming the arrival into the world and offering a future job on his staff.

On at least two occasions, he quietly ran interference at Albany Law School—when the board was reluctant to name a Jewish dean and again when that dean, Martin H. Belsky, was under the gun for refusing to lower standards and admit the daughter of a powerful public figure. "Before I came here [Albany], there was some opposition to my becoming dean because of my ethnic background," recalls Belsky, now dean and professor of law at the University of Tulsa. "I've heard from others that Wachtler [who was on the board] squashed that quickly, with the statement: 'If he's not qualified, don't hire him. But don't say—directly or indirectly—that he shouldn't be hired because of his background.' "[10]

Wachtler could also be shallow and conniving, a chameleon in robes. A former clerk at the court recalls receiving Wachtler's seemingly heartfelt letter of regret, bemoaning that he was committed to some official function and would be unable to attend the clerk's wedding, and claiming that he would much prefer the nuptial ceremony. The clerk was touched by the gesture—until learning that Wachtler had used the exact same letter of regret to avoid several other weddings.[11]

Wachtler was only forty-two when he was elected to the Court of Appeals, the same panel where the legendary Benjamin N. Cardozo, his judicial hero, had presided a generation earlier.

He was elected after a controversial and bold—by 1972 standards—television campaign featuring the sound and sight of a slamming prison door, clearly pandering to fears about crime even though the high court has nothing to do with sentencing criminals. But on the bench, he was a far more liberal jurist, in the early years anyhow, than the one depicted in the ads. He wrote a landmark opinion permitting prosecution for marital rape, authored the decision that banned discrimination at many private clubs, dissented when the court voted against bestowing free-speech rights on folks wanting to distribute leaflets in shopping malls, held that the Xerox Corporation could not deny a woman employment solely because of her obesity, and expanded the rights of criminals. But in his later years, after he won the title of chief and the mantle of Cardozo, he led a retrenchment of the court on civil liberties issues, perhaps adopting a more pragmatic and less idealistic view of what the court could and should do. Former colleagues describe him as a good judge, although not necessarily a great one; an uncommonly persuasive man who, through the power of his intellect and persona, could have taken the court wherever he chose, but who sometimes lacked a compass.

"If he had his heart in it, he never ceased pressing for consensus," recalled one former colleague. "If you knew that Sol cared, you looked again and again and again at a case."[12]

But he didn't always have his heart in it, and tended, like a good politician, to choose his battles. Other jurists say that Wachtler, at times, seemed more interested in being viewed as a great judge than in actually being one. Wachtler's harshest critics say he was a mediocre judge, an ineffectual chief—and a political manipulator extraordinaire.

"Certainly, he was a wonderful speaker," said one former colleague. "Certainly, he came across as a masterful public servant, in the political sense. But I don't think he will be remembered as a great jurist. I don't think that was his chief interest. He was a very bright man, but I don't think he was a real student of the law or a deep thinker on legal issues. Quick, yes. Smart. Intelligent. But not a great jurist in my view."[13]

Some say Wachtler's philosophy shifted with the political winds. "I've never been able to discern a strong philosophical bent in Sol Wachtler," said longtime critic James T. Leff, a state Supreme Court justice in New York City. "He starts out slamming prison doors and then somebody explains to him that is not the way to go this month, so he becomes a big civil libertarian."[15]

Still, Wachtler was indeed both a dreamer and a schemer, and those qualities and defects are illustrated in his decisions on the bench and as the administrative leader of the largest court system in the western hemisphere. He led the nation's most important state appellate court and presided over a judicial system that handled 4 million cases annually; had a budget of over $960 million; and employed 13,000 people, including 3,500 judges. As an administrator, Wachtler worked tirelessly on his pet projects—the elimination of racial and gender bias in the courts, a more efficient case management system, cameras in the courts, legal services for the poor, modern court facilities, and the integration and melding of 120 local court systems into one huge state system—but in the end he grew bitterly frustrated with his limited reform powers in the judiciary, and plotted a challenge against his old friend and mentor, Governor Cuomo. After seven years, this politician at heart understood all too well that the chief judge, as the leader of one of the three co-equal branches of government, was politically impotent.

"I can't implement any of the initiatives that I want to," Wachtler complained to Silverman in a private June 8, 1992, telephone conversation that she secretly taped and in which he confides his interest in running against Cuomo in 1994.[15] "My community courts concept, all the things that I've been working so hard on, I can't get off the ground. . . . You know, honest to God, I feel I can make a difference . . . I just think this state is so hungry for some change. It's so anxious not to keep descending the way it has been. . . . Sometimes I get so enthused about this thing."

Just the rumor of Wachtler's return to politics after twenty-five years on the sidelines was enough to rattle the Republican establishment in New York in the fall of 1992, when he was under surveillance by the FBI and ultimately arrested. With Wachtler potentially in the picture, the party politic and the status quo—and nothing, but nothing, is more sacrosanct in Albany than the status quo—were in serious jeopardy. He was immensely popular and politically beholden to no one. No wonder, then, that after the downfall the pundits were quietly questioning the ferocity of a prosecution that seemed more intent on ruining the culprit than stopping him, and pointing out that the prime beneficiary of Wachtler's demise was his longtime political nemesis, U.S. Senator Alfonse D'Amato. With Wachtler out of the game, D'Amato, after decades of scrounging for power, was to become the most important and powerful Republican in the state of New York. The prosecutor who nailed Wachtler later secured a plum assignment, compliments of Al D'Amato.

But whether D'Amato or anyone else had anything to do with Wachtler's prosecution and harsh treatment is questionable, perhaps even doubtful, and maybe irrelevant. The fact of the matter is that it was Wachtler and Wachtler alone who orchestrated and carried out the campaign of harassment that would ruin his career. Without a doubt, D'Amato benefitted from it, but Wachtler caused it.

Regardless of the scandalous downfall from chief judge

and likely gubernatorial candidate to a criminal convict, Wachtler remains an endearing and engaging figure in American jurisprudence and an object lesson in the human condition. "Everyone," wrote Machiavelli, "sees what you seem, but few know what you are."[16] Wachtler's demise must be explained in the context of an entire public and political life, not in the vacuum of an aberrational year, and experienced not only for what it seemed to be, but for what it was.

"He should always be remembered as a great judge," said Mario Cuomo. "Everybody's life is a book, his a long and full one. This [the scandal] is a page. It is one he wishes he could rewrite, but he can't. But it is only one page. To judge the whole book by one page is unfair."[17]

Just days after dozens of FBI agents converged on Wachtler and scoured the judicial chambers where he had written some of the nation's most important decisions on search and seizure, the jurist's longtime clerk and confidant, Michael Trainor, pondered the frailties of the human psyche and tearfully asked: "If this can happen to a man like Sol Wachtler, what chance do the rest of us have?"[18]

This biography addresses that question, focusing on who and what Wachtler was and explaining what happened and why. It explores the depths of the man's heart *and* mind, explains both pragmatically and psychologically what led a person of such intelligence and integrity so far astray, and chronicles the unusually harsh pursuit and prosecution of an obviously disturbed man. This is the story of a judge who wrote decisions that opened doors for minorities, women, and the handicapped; who molded a renowned court; and who could and perhaps should have been governor, but made some childishly stupid mistakes which were possibly exploited, or even exacerbated, by an abuse of prosecutorial power.

"If this can happen to me," Wachtler told ABC television's

Barbara Walters on the ABC news magazine *20/20* on September 17, 1993, "it can happen to anyone."

Once, in happier days, someone introduced Wachtler in glowing terms, predicting that "one hundred years from today we will think of Sol Wachtler as today we think of Brandeis and Cardozo and Holmes." With typically perfect timing, Wachtler responded: "Yeah, as a dead judge."[19]

Today, he'd settle for that.

Notes

1. Interview with James Fox on May 22, 1995, with the author serving in his capacity as a reporter for the *Albany Times Union*.

2. Prior to the April 1997 publication of his own book, *After the Madness: A Judge's Own Prison Memoir* (New York: Random House, 1997), Judge Wachtler provided me with a copy of a personal diary. Although many of the quotes in this book mirror those in *After the Madness*, they were taken directly from Wachtler's diary, not the book based on that diary.

3. "Who Has Style," *M*, January 1986.

4. Interview with a confidential source on September 5, 1997.

5. Salvatore Arena, "Wachtler a Courtly Lover: Ex," New York *Daily News*, May 19, 1995, p. 5.

6. Interview with Salvatore D. Ferlazzo on September 3, 1997.

7. Interview with Michael Trainor on September 7, 1997.

8. Ibid.

9. Wachtler's archives.

10. Electronic mail correspondence from Martin Belsky in August 1997.

11. Interview with a confidential source, February 1994.

12. Interview with a confidential source on September 5, 1997.

13. Interview with a confidential source on September 7, 1997.

14. John Caher, "N.Y.'s Chief Judge Brings Leadership, Vigor to Job," Albany *Knickerbocker News*, January 28, 1988, p. 1A.

15. Transcript of June 8, 1992, conversation included as part of the court record.

16. Niccolo Machiavelli, *The Prince*, Great Book Site (Internet).

17. Interview with Mario Cuomo on November 10, 1997.

18. Interview with Michael Trainor in November 1992.

19. Wachtler told this story on several occasions at various public appearances.

PART I

The Man

CHAPTER I

Early Life

It was a defining moment in his eight-year-old life, the day Sol Wachtler learned to use his brains and his charm to save his head and his heart.

Blowing Rock, North Carolina, was a summer tourist mecca in the Great Smoky Mountains where Philip Wachtler, a kind but stern man with a Jewish name and a Puritan work ethic, moved his young wife, Faye, a Russian immigrant, and their two boys, Morton and Solomon. Philip was a salesman—and sometimes a jeweler or real estate speculator—who had up-rooted the family from Brooklyn during the Great Depression and was hopscotching the south, auctioning off the property of the dead and the destitute. Sol, the younger of the boys by three years, was a gawky, geeky Jewish kid with a strange Brooklyn accent. He was weak and scared, an easy and frequent target for the local bully, a beefy bumpkin named Jack.

33

"We got a question for you, *Solomon,*" Jack snarled, cornering his quarry and surrounded by his cowardly entourage. "Do you have *Jew money* in your shoes?"

Jack called him "Jew-boy" and punched Solomon in the nose. And Sol, for the first time in his life, fought back, although somewhat accidentally. With one awry punch, more a defensive effort than an offensive thrust, Sol caught the bully square on the throat and knocked him breathless. Jack bawled like a baby and Sol proudly wore the badge of a *real* man: a bloody nose.

The other kids were thrilled to see Jack dethroned, but they weren't so happy he was humiliated by an outsider, and a Jewish one at that. So, the next day a gang of young thugs pounced on Sol and were inflicting a severe beating when, suddenly, the thrashing stopped and the thrashers were being thrown around like rag dolls. Sol, cowering on the ground, looked up and saw an older boy named Claude, a thick but fair-minded youth who had come to his rescue. Claude became Sol's protector, and Sol—whimsical, paradoxical, and, by Claude's standards, worldly—became Claude's playful tutor. Claude kept the bullies at bay and taught Sol to milk cows. Sol amused Claude, charmed his beloved little sister, and taught him about oceans and boardwalks and Judaism. And they both learned that one hand washes the other.

Solomon Wachtler, born on April 29, 1930, spent the early years of his life living above a cleaning store in Brooklyn. When Sol was in third grade, the Wachtlers moved for the first time and would be on the road almost constantly for the next eight years as Philip brought his Reform Jewish family wherever auctioneering took him. By the time Solomon was fifteen his family had lived in Georgia, South Carolina, North

Carolina,* Mississippi, and four other states. By the time
Solomon was fifteen, he had lived in eight different states,
many of them in the deep South.

By adult standards, Sol must have appeared a lonely
youngster, lacking the stability of a permanent home. But he
recalls a happy childhood, an adventure-filled period when
he was old enough to be intrigued by concepts like justice
and discrimination, but too busy being a kid to really be
affected. There was a blissful naiveté to that period. "I grew
up believing that if you just brushed your teeth right, everything from sex to the worldwide food shortage would somehow work itself out," he said in his diary.

Sol recalled fondly the late-1930s drives from New York
to Florida along Route 1, passing through quaint towns and
hamlets, noting the northern smokestacks and the southern
cotton fields, and the Burma Shave billboards en route. There
was the occasional mishap—like when he got hit on the head
by an automobile chain hoist, an accident that Sol would
later blame for an imagined brain tumor that exacerbated his
campaign of harassment against Mrs. Silverman—but mostly
it was a time of fond remembrance and special times.

"We were in a motor cabin outside of Valdosta, Georgia,"
Sol recalled.

Morty, who couldn't have been more than ten years old at
the time, got out of bed. It was still dark. It was 5 A.M. and
Morty said he was going to the filling station next door to
inquire about a sign for an all-night pumper.

I watched him leave, and a few minutes later there he
was, pumping gas. And in those days pumping gas meant
literally using a pump handle to pump, much like well

---

*After leaving Blowing Rock, the next time Sol lived in North Car-
olina it was as a federal prisoner.

water was pumped for domestic use. He kept pumping for three hours, until it was time for us to go back on the road. He earned 25 cents for his labor. But the thing which moved me then, and moves me still, is that he spent the entire sum to buy me a doughnut and a bottle of chocolate milk. He spent not one cent of his hard-earned money on himself. . . . As soon as we were back on the road, Morty fell into a deep sleep. I remember looking at him and thinking that I loved him more than anything in the world.

The Wachtler boys had an education on the road as well as in the schoolhouse. Instead of just reading about chain gangs, they saw them. Instead of just hearing about ethnic intolerance, they experienced it, both in the deep South and back home in New York, where their peculiar accent, a mix of the southern drawl and Brooklynese, made them stand out. At first, Sol wanted nothing more than to be invisible, to be able to stray unnoticed. He learned quickly, however, that his charm, wit, intelligence, and disarming good-naturedness were valuable and exploitable assets. He ingratiated himself with others, combining a genuine sincerity with a knack for knowing how to please those who could help him. Sol was the type of child who would go out of his way to assist family, friends, and even strangers.[1]

He was also extraordinarily driven and ambitious, and determined to leave a mark, even if his stay in a region was brief.

Sol had an afternoon radio show—a comedy and variety hour—when he was twelve and started a little newspaper, *The Eternal Light,* for Jewish families when he was only thirteen. But sometimes his precociousness got him in trouble: after writing an essay for a local newspaper, the Wachtler family was deluged with anti-Semitic hate mail.

Sol's talents were apparent to his family. When Philip settled in St. Petersburg, Florida, and opened a jewelry store, everyone in the family was expected to work. Except Sol. Morty worked afternoons and weekends. Sol, destined in his father's eye to become the first Wachtler with a college degree, was ordered to concentrate on his schoolwork.

"We both knew what was expected of us," Wachtler said in the diary. "Morty had to prove himself capable of one day taking over the business and I had to wait for my turn to become the world's most gifted attorney."

When Sol was fifteen, he was sent to a boarding school in Milford, Connecticut, to prepare for college, arriving in January 1945. Although Sol was a lousy athlete, he was immediately recruited for the basketball team by an athletic director who noticed he had played hoops for the public school in St. Petersburg. Actually, Sol was elected captain of the St. Petersburg team solely on the basis of his popularity, since his athletic skills were nil. He got cut from the Milford team on the first day of tryouts, when the coach realized he couldn't run and dribble at the same time. Number 19 retired for good.

While Morty went into the jewelry business (he eventually opened the M. Wachtler and Sons jewelry store on 47th Street in Manhattan), Sol continued on to Washington and Lee University in Lexington, Virginia, where he was a classmate of novelist Tom Wolfe (who would later use Chief Judge Wachtler's most enduring quip—"A grand jury would indict a ham sandwich"—in his best-seller *Bonfire of the Vanities*) and NBC chief political correspondent Roger Mudd. He earned a combined bachelor's degree and law degree in five years, and got an early taste of politics and an early indication of his own political gifts. At a mock political convention, Wachtler's speech nominating Dwight Eisenhower was covered by legendary newsman Edward R. Murrow. The general himself was so impressed that when he heard the speech he called the young Wachtler to praise him.

Wachtler distinguished himself at Washington and Lee the same way he did in all of his life endeavors, combining his self-discipline and commitment to a goal with a personality that made others want him to achieve rather than resent his achievements. He was personable and warm, and a good problem solver. Sol was elected president of his fraternity, Phi Epsilon Pi, in his sophomore year, and became secretary-treasurer of the Literary Society and the Forensic Union. He was a member of the debate team and the scholarship committee and, in only his second year at the school, was honored as the student "who has contributed most to campus activities."

During his last year at Washington and Lee, Sol married Joan Wolosoff, a beautiful blonde Sarah Lawrence student and the daughter of millionaire developer Leon Wolosoff. Sol was unlike any boy Joan had met—sensitive yet strong, intellectual yet paradoxical. He could quote poetry with passion and without embarrassment. And, in contrast to Joan's other suitors, Sol didn't seem to care about the Wolosoff money and connections.[2]

Joan's cousin arranged their blind date. "I met Sol Wachtler when I was fifteen and he was seventeen," Joan recalls.

> It was exciting to be the "special person" of the most popular student on campus. He was elected by his university classmates as the most "outstanding" freshman, sophomore, junior and ultimately as president of the law school student body. . . . We were married five years later. I loved him because he was the kindest and gentlest human being I had ever known. He possessed a sensitivity that allowed him to talk freely about his emotions and feelings. He told me how much he loved his parents, his country, the English poets, and best of all, how much he loved me.[3]

Joan's family was loaded, and connected. They had built Manhasset's Miracle Mile and several federally funded housing projects, attracting the attention of Senator Prescott Bush, the father of President George Bush. Prescott Bush suspected the Wolosoffs were dipping a bit too deep into the federal well, but he could never prove anything.

"You wanted housing," Alvin "Bibbs" Wolosoff, Joan's uncle, sneered at Senator Bush at a 1954 hearing. "You got housing. I wanted money. I got money. If you ask me, this is one happy marriage."[4]

With Sol's charm and ambition and Joan's money, they were on their way. The newlyweds bought an eight-bedroom house and hired two maids, one of them Sally Dinkins, the mother of David Dinkins, who would later become the first African American mayor of New York City.

Wachtler continued studying law at Washington and Lee where he was president of the student bar association. Then he studied architecture at Columbia University School of Architecture, an experience that gave him enormous appreciation for Court of Appeals Hall, a beautiful edifice in Albany where New York's top judges hold court.

After school, Sol intended to join the U.S. Navy Intelligence Division during the Korean War, but he was drafted by the Army before his commission went through. Instead of "seeing the sea," Sol (he officially changed his legal name from Solomon to Sol while in the service) was a sergeant in the military police, instructing company commanders on how to pursue a court-martial. He wrote a monograph that was published and distributed nationally.

Sol was stationed at Camp Gordon, Georgia, when their first daughter, Lauren, with her father's ocean-blue eyes, was born on May 6, 1954. They were living in a development called Thomas Woods, located between Augusta, Georgia, and the army base in a district called the Sand Hills. Joan sterilized bottles in the 107-degree heat and Sol shooed the bugs—and, one time, a black widow spider—away from their baby. It was a far cry from the pampered Long Island life they would later take up, but both Sol and Joan recall the period fondly.

"Sol was never an athlete, had no hobbies—he spent every non-work-related hour with us," Joan recalls. "Ahead of his time in the practice of fatherhood, he bathed babies, changed diapers, stayed up all night with a croupy child, and spent Sundays at Kiddie City."[5]

After his military stint, Wachtler began private law practice with Austin and Dupont, a small law firm in Queens where Joan's uncle, Bibbs Wolosoff, an extremely rich entrepreneur, occasionally threw the fledgling lawyer some legal business. Sol impressed Bibbs with his intelligence and charm. They became good friends, with Sol taking care of more and more of Bibbs's legal needs. In time, Sol became Bibbs's confidant, advisor, and, ultimately, trustee for the millions of dollars he would leave to his spendthrift step-daughter—Joy Silverman.

Sol was introduced to Nassau County politics by a neighbor who called Joe Carlino, a state assemblyman and vice chairman of the Nassau Republican Committee, and put in a good word. Carlino met Wachtler, was impressed, and ran him for a council seat in North Hempstead. Rumor has it that Joan's family bankrolled his campaign. In any case, Sol won and, two years later, was the first Jewish supervisor in the history of North Hempstead. In 1967, Sol, under pressure from governor and future vice president Nelson Rockefeller, took on the popular Nassau County Executive, Eugene Nickerson (who later became a U.S. District Court judge). Wachtler lost a close race, but won a strong ally in Rockefeller, who appointed him to a State Supreme Court judgeship. After just four years on the trial bench, Wachtler was elected to the Court of Appeals, the highest court in New York State. He was only forty-two years old, one of the youngest lawyers ever elected to the court. Twelve years later, Democratic Governor Mario M. Cuomo made Sol the chief judge, the highest judicial office in the state and one of the most important and respected judgeships in the nation.

Meanwhile, Sol's family had grown, with the addition of three more children, Marjorie, Alison, and Philip. Sol played an active role in their lives, despite his increasingly busy schedule. They took adventurous family vacations every Christmas season to places like California, Florida, and Bermuda, or they'd yacht through the Virgin Islands or the Grenadines. Sol, as always, was the protector, the sage advisor, the one the children came to for comfort—their idol, as he would one day become Joy's. He would make up stories, parables really, of a little boy who encountered various moral dilemmas. He was the glue who held the family together.

"Once, in my younger years, I committed what I thought was an unforgivable offense," recalled daughter Marjorie D. Eagan.

> I had been caught shoplifting. The store manager released me with only a stern lecture, never telling the police or my parents. . . . Shortly thereafter, at the dinner table, my mother told us how proud she was of all of her children. Unable to hide my guilt any longer, I excused myself from the table in tears and ran to my room. My father followed. . . . I told him of the incident at the store, what a terrible person I was, and how I had deceived and betrayed my family. Vividly, I remember my father's face and words. He told me that there was no greater punishment he could inflict than the guilt and shame I had already felt during the past weeks.[6]

But as the children grew and left home and Sol's duties as chief judge began to require more and more of his time, his relationship with Joan grew stale and their marriage, like many, suffered from benign neglect. "The qualities that were once so attractive to me became the downfall of our relationship," Joan said. "He cared, and cared for, too many of his ideals [sic], and it was my perception that I was no longer a consideration in his newly restructured life. The rules of the marriage had changed. My work became my life."[7]

In time, Joy Silverman became Sol's life, and obsession. And he forgot the advice he gave to Alison when she left home and enrolled in Skidmore College in Saratoga Springs, New York. "Tootie," Sol told his daughter, "remember one thing: nothing is more important than self-respect. Once you do something, or allow something to be done to you, which diminishes your own self-image, then you have lost the firmest foundation of good character."[8]

Sol Wachtler is now living that lesson.

Notes

1. Interview with Morton Wachtler, September 19, 1997.
2. Interview with Joan Wachtler, September 26, 1997.
3. Undated letter by Joan Wachtler to the judge who sentenced her husband. The letter would have been written around May 1, 1993.
4. Linda Wolfe, *Double Life: The Shattering Affair between Chief Judge Sol Wachtler and Socialite Joy Silverman* (New York: Pocket Books, 1994), p. 30.
5. Joan Wachtler's undated letter to the court.
6. Marjorie D. Eagan, letter to the sentencing court, April 22, 1993.
7. Wachtler's diary.
8. Joan Wachtler's undated letter to the court.

CHAPTER 2

Politics

Nelson Rockefeller was an uncommonly powerful man, so much so that to him compromise meant he would, just maybe, wait a little longer to get exactly what he wanted. With a family fortune and a dictatorial hold on the New York State Republican Committee, "Rocky" did as he pleased, when he pleased, if he pleased. He was the ultimate power broker.

"Only three men in America understand the use of power," Richard Nixon once said. "I do. John Connally does. And, I guess Nelson does."[1]

"Nothing stands in Rockefeller's way," griped Jacob Javits, the Republican senior senator bumped off in a 1980 primary by Alfonse D'Amato. "Nothing. He always gets what he wants."[2]

Rocky treated the Republican party, and for that matter the New York State Legislature, as a wholly owned subsidiary of the Rockefeller empire. His family had repeatedly bailed out the party, paid off its million-dollar deficits, and bought Nelson the privilege of living in the governor's mansion for as long as he chose. He stayed for fifteen years and ruled with an iron hand before Gerald Ford made him vice president. Loyalists were rewarded, critics crushed.

When Rocky was at the apex of his power in the mid-1960s, Sol Wachtler was an up-and-coming Republican politician in the mode of Rockefeller, Javits, and New York Mayor John Lindsay—essentially, a rich liberal. Like Rocky, Sol was a master of the art of political manipulation, had a flair for friendships, and possessed a knack for spotting talent and a genius for recognizing the people and causes that could help further his career. He could also identify those who would derail it. He wanted to be a state senator,* and began his political career by winning a North Hempstead, Long Island, town council seat. Wachtler was thirty-three years old.

Only a year into his term, Wachtler had the luck to be in the right place at the right time, and the sense to know it. Supervisor Clinton G. Martin, a fellow Republican, had barely won the 1963 election for supervisor and his administration had been tarred by a couple of scandals, mainly involving the highway department. The Republicans were worried that the attractive Democratic candidate James H. Lundquist of Great Neck, who had nearly knocked off Martin, would capture the job at the next election. They needed a new candidate, and one who could get off to a running start. In a political brainstorm, Joe Carlino, the *de facto*

---

*Joan's uncle, George Blumberg, had been a Republican senator. Even though Blumberg was quickly ousted after making a wise crack about labor unions, everyone always addressed him as "senator." That appealed to Wachtler's vanity.

leader of the party, orchestrated Martin's ouster and Wachtler's ascension.*

"I had won very handily as a councilman," Wachtler recalled. "The Republicans had never before run a Jew in North Hempstead, ever. They felt that the demographics were changing and that my vote in the councilmanic race showed I could do very well. They knew Lundquist would run and thought that it would be a real battle."[3]

In February of 1965, nearly nine months before the election, Wachtler was appointed supervisor. He would have until November to make a name for himself, and the thirty-five-year-old politician didn't waste a minute.

Wachtler pledged to his constituents: "I promise to commit myself in mind, body, and spirit to the precepts of responsive and progressive government and I promise that along with the town board I will give you the type of dramatic and imaginative government which you expect and deserve."[4] He followed through by cutting taxes 17 percent, conducting public hearings throughout the sprawling township, improving the water and recreation systems, organizing a town beautification campaign, and successfully lobbying for new bus routes and commuter and shopper parking in the increasingly mobile suburban community. And he attracted establishment attention.

Just a month after his taking office, a Westbury *Times* editorial called Wachtler "a prepotent force with the magnetic attraction of a fresh approach and new programs."[5] The Great Neck *News* of February 16, 1965, called him "a striking example of the young-men-in-government policy fostered by his predecessor" and "the Nassau political community's brightest new star."

---

*Carlino got Martin a new, appointive job with the Nassau County Board of Elections.

During the campaign season, Wachtler was aggressive and ingenious in defending his brief record against the expected Democratic nominee, Lundquist, plus two minor party candidates, A. Werner Pleus, the Conservative, and Stephen Smolenski, the Independent.

Once, Wachtler went to a county board of supervisors meeting and publicly confronted County Executive Eugene Nickerson, who had praised Lundquist's diligence in serving on the county health board. Wasn't it true, Wachtler demanded of the county executive, with records in hand, that Lundquist had skipped eleven of the board's fourteen meetings? Nickerson, taken by surprise, shot back: "I would say, Mr. Wachtler, that you are getting a little nervous about the campaign." Wachtler quickly retorted: "No, I'm getting nervous about the county."[6]

Wachtler enlisted the aid of Javits, already a senior statesman, and Javits described Wachtler as "dynamic and progressive."[7] He won with 60 percent of the vote—the first Jew ever to hold a seat that many said a Jew could never win— and seemingly impressed everyone, even the loser. "You waged a forceful and obviously effective campaign—and, I might add, one that I felt was fair and honest," Lundquist wrote in a post-election note.[8] "I want you to know that I enjoyed being with you and appreciate and respect your acumen and ability." Privately, Wachtler thought himself to be the third-best candidate in the race—behind Lundquist and Pleus, and ahead only of Smolenski.

Once in office for his own term, as opposed to the remainder of Martin's, Wachtler picked up the pace. He took on the Port Washington Fire Department in the mid-1960s on behalf of a black constituent (who claimed he was denied membership), well before racial sensitivity was politically correct or even politically sensible. He struggled, unsuccessfully, to get the New York Stock Exchange to move to North Hempstead, which borders on the city line. In 1966, the day after Sandy Koufax, the All-Star hurler for the Los Angeles Dodgers, retired, Wachtler tried to get him to join the town of North Hempstead as a recreation specialist. "Few in America at this time have, as you have, the opportunity to reach impressionable youth with guaranteed success."[9] Koufax, a Brooklyn native and future Hall of Famer, turned him down.

Wachtler proposed commissioning helicopters to track down cars disabled on the major highways and hoisting them to the shoulder, literally picking up traffic flow. He opened a nursery in the Town Hall, so parents with small children could attend board meetings. He was so intrigued with gadgetry (a fascination that would, twenty-five years later, lead to voice-altering devices) that his code name on the town two-way radio network was 007, after James Bond. He was attracted to people like a magnet, and vice versa. Wachtler genuinely enjoyed mundane political duties like attending the the Sons of Italy picnic, the Nassau Detectives picnic, the Greek picnic, and judging Miss Palonia at the Polish-America club. Wachtler found he loved the limelight, and the limelight loved him. *Newsday,* on February 17, 1965, described Wachtler, with his gold elephant cuff links, as "always impeccably dressed. His dark, wavy hair is always combed. His shoes are always polished. And, at town board meetings, Wachtler always votes exactly as the others on the all-GOP board."[10] Indeed, things seemed to be going so well that when Long Island *Press* columnist Walter Kaner wrote a Christmas wish list for local dignitaries, he couldn't think of anything Wachtler wanted that he didn't already have.

But Wachtler had his eyes on a bigger pond than North Hempstead, and knew that he couldn't get anywhere without Rockefeller's blessings. So when Rocky approached the young upstart politician in 1967 and asked him to take on the near politically suicidal task of running against the immensely popular Democratic county executive (and potential gubernatorial rival) Gene Nickerson—and casually offered that he would reward his protégé if he ran and destroy him if he didn't—there really wasn't much choice. Wachtler ran, unhappily. "I was the only one left who hadn't said no. Gene Nickerson was such a high-quality guy, so bright and so competent. It was a race he deserved to win. The only reason they ran me is I was the last one out the door."[11]

But once in a race he was sure he couldn't win, Wachtler ran hard, spending $325,000 and fine-tuning the campaign tactics he had begun to develop in his town races. "They realized I couldn't win unless I got enormous exposure, because nobody had ever heard of me," Wachtler recalled.[12] While Wachtler was unknown, Nickerson was the incumbent, popular, and enjoyed the backing of Bobby Kennedy, then a U.S. senator from New York. "Our poll showed that only 18 percent of the voters knew my name. In the previous election, Nickerson won by something like 92,000 votes."

Wachtler rather crudely, but effectively, linked Nickerson to Lyndon Johnson when the president's popularity was at an all-time low, blaming Johnson, and Nickerson by extension, for failed policies and philosophies causing ghetto uprisings in 1967 and war protests. Later, Wachtler's campaign was snared in a trap when the campaign's chairman, Bill Nelson, was fed a phony document.

Wachtler's camp had been trying, unsuccessfully, to get hold of Nickerson's budget, but the county executive wouldn't turn it over. The county Democratic chairman, Jack English, a smart, crafty politician, orchestrated the sting. Nelson was contacted by an intermediary and told that he could have Nickerson's budget for $1,000. Nelson was shown three pages' worth, in Nickerson's own handwriting, as proof that the budget could be had, and approached Edward J. Speno, the county chairman, who wanted nothing to do with the deal. So, when the political operatives showed up to sell the fake documents, Nelson wasn't there. No matter. English still held a press conference in which he told the media that the Wachtler campaign had sunk so low that it was trying to pay off one of Nickerson's aides.[13]

Wachtler insisted he knew nothing about the scheme— and people believed him. Amazingly, he was able to use to his advantage what could, and perhaps should, have been the death knell of his campaign. Wachtler managed to put Nickerson on the defensive, forcing the county executive to admit to drawing up the fake document, in his own handwriting, to spread misinformation. The race became so high-profile, and so marked by similar shenanigans, that CBS eventually made a documentary of it, "Campaign American Style," with Eric Sevareid.

Wachtler lost the race, but came remarkably close. "It was shocking because I never, never in a million years thought I was going to win," Wachtler recalls. "Then, on election night, when the returns started coming in, it was stunning. You don't know what it's like until you've been there. I had hoped to lose by less than 20,000 votes."[14]

There was considerable speculation that Wachtler was undermined by a wannabe from his own party, Ralph Caso, the presiding supervisor of Hempstead and a Republican with dreams of someday becoming county executive himself. Caso unquestionably knew that if Wachtler beat Nickerson, he himself wouldn't be able to run for the top seat until and unless Wachtler stepped aside. Some pundits, noting that Wachtler's vote tallies had fallen off dramatically in Hempstead, theorized that Caso had worked against the party's choice. U.S. Senator Alfonse D'Amato asserted in his 1995 memoir: "Wachtler would have won that year, but his campaign was sabotaged by a rival Republican, Ralph Caso, the Presiding Supervisor of Hempstead. Caso didn't have the nerve to take on Nickerson himself, but knew if Wachtler had won, he would have been eclipsed by the good-looking young upstart."[15] Wachtler, however, never bought that theory and remains "very fond"[16] of Caso. (Caso did, by the way, become supervisor in 1970. However, he was knocked out in his own party's 1977 primary by Francis Purcell.)

Wachtler lost by fewer than three thousand votes, but won important supporters. In a November 16, 1967, letter to Sol and Joan Wachtler, Republican Chairman Ed Speno, who would become a crucial Wachtler supporter for years to come, wrote: "You conducted the best and most effective campaign in the history of Nassau County politics. . . . Ever since election night, I have racked my brain, I've cried, I've awakened twice in the middle of the night trying to think how I might have done the job better for you, what things I might have done differently, because I believe you deserved to win and I believe the majority of the people in this county wanted you to win."[17]

Immediately, Speno tried to get Wachtler to run for Congress, but Wachtler had other plans. He'd gained a powerful ally in Nelson Rockefeller, and fully intended to hold the governor to his promise and collect his reward. Rocky was well aware that Wachtler ran hard, and was even more aware that the close encounter prompted Democrats to drop Nickerson (who eventually was appointed by Lyndon Johnson to a lifetime job as a federal judge) as a potential challenger to the governor. If Nickerson had trouble with a young upstart on his home turf, the Democrats reasoned, he would get clobbered by Rockefeller. Rockefeller was grateful to Wachtler, and Wachtler knew he had an ace to play.

"I want to be judge," Wachtler told Rockefeller.[18]

Rocky frowned and changed the subject.

"You'll be governor one day," Rockefeller predicted. "You lost the election but won the race."

The judiciary is nice enough, but no place for a young man on the rise, Rockefeller thought. Once, at least, Rockefeller had muzzled a recalcitrant legislator by sending him to his "final reward"—the judiciary. Another time, he plucked a judge from the state Court of Claims, a man named Fred A. Young, to help run his abortive presidential campaign in 1964. Later, Rocky put him back on the court, as presiding justice, an outright reward that had little, if anything, to do with merit. In Rockefeller's mind, the judiciary was a retirement home for political has-beens, a limbo where he could stash annoying loyalists safely out of the way—and a dead end where a promising young politician like Wachtler would fade into obscurity, his talents wasted. Rockefeller's divorce had left lingering bad feelings about judges and the judiciary, and he didn't want to see a rising star like Wachtler stuck on the bench.

"After three years, you'll be bored or an alcoholic," Rocky scoffed. "Think it over and tell me tomorrow what other job you'd like."[19]

As ordered, Wachtler returned the next day.

"I still want to be a judge."

Rockefeller gave in. On the first of the year, there would be a retirement-related vacancy on the state supreme court—which, in New York, is the trial court, *not* the high court—and Rocky promised the job to Wachtler. What he didn't count on, however, was a severe grassroots backlash.

By pledging his support to Wachtler, Rockefeller undercut David Holman, a former district attorney and longtime party loyalist who, coincidentally, had helped Wachtler become the town supervisor. Holman, in the eyes of local politicos, had earned his robes; Wachtler, at thirty-eight, had not. Besides, the seat rightfully, from a political viewpoint anyway, belonged in Oyster Bay, not in North Hempstead. A Wachtler appointment would undermine years of political loyalties and deals. Regardless, Rockefeller announced in December that he intended to select Wachtler, who received a ringing endorsement from then Senator Speno.

"Sol Wachtler has had an enviable record of service," Speno said on the floor of the senate. "He has proven himself easy in the prosperity of victory and gentle in the adversity of defeat. The quality of his purpose has always been in keeping with an unalterable desire to do what is right and honest and what is best for his people, his party and his constituency. . . . This is a young man who is experienced beyond his years, a proven public official."[20]

But the Nassau County Bar Association's judiciary committee found Wachtler unqualified, ostensibly because of his relatively meager trial experience and a "gap" in his legal career, when he was working full-time as supervisor. Wachtler went before the committee again and spent an hour and a half trying to gain their support, and again he failed. But Marcus G. Christ, presiding justice of the Appellate Division and a man Wachtler refers to as his "guardian angel,"[21] came to his rescue.

Only after the matter went before the association's board of directors, which was conveniently packed with Rockefeller's friends, was Wachtler declared "qualified." Again, Wachtler had the support of the press. The Great Neck *Record* blasted the committee and praised the board of directors: "The director's decision counteracts the narrow-minded actions of the nine attorneys on the judiciary committee, men who were apparently stirred by personal vendettas and political sub-machinations. Their initial rejection of the former supervisor cannot diminish in any way the high regard, respect, appreciation and confidence that men of all political persuasions have for Sol Wachtler."[22]

In December 1967, the Westbury *Times* editorialized in support of Wachtler's nomination: "We are certain that Mr. Wachtler will, when his appointment to the state supreme court is confirmed by Governor Rockefeller, bring to the bench the same capability and understanding which were so much in evidence during his tenure as a councilman and supervisor, and the same insight which helped bring him within three thousand votes of becoming Nassau's youngest county executive."[23] The Great Neck *Record* opined that when Wachtler took the bench in mid-January 1968, the youngest supreme court justice in the state (making $37,000, which was $7,000 more than Nickerson), he would find himself uncommonly comfortable in robes, yet continually teased by politics.

Only a year after taking the bench, in 1969, Wachtler was being touted as a potential attorney general candidate. The speculation largely involved Kenneth Keating, of the Rochester area, who had been a fascinating figure in New York politics for many years. He had served in Congress from 1946 to 1958 and had been senator from 1958 until 1964. A year after losing his Senate seat to Robert Kennedy, Keating was elected to the Court of Appeals. Later, he served as U.S. ambassador to Israel and India. Joseph M. Margiotta, the increasingly powerful Long Island Republican political boss, was banking on Keating getting an ambassadorship and figured New York Attorney General Louis Lefkowitz would get Keating's seat on the Court of Appeals. That would leave the attorney general's position open to Wachtler. Wachtler, however, was lukewarm to the whole idea. "I never wanted to be attorney general," he said. "About two or three years into my judgeship, there was a judge named Howard Hogan, a dear, dear friend, and the administrative judge for Nassau County. He said to me that if you stay on the bench for four years, you'll die on the bench. Three years in, the idea crossed my mind of running for attorney general, but I never pursued it."[24]

He was equally cool to Margiotta's attempt to enlist him for another race against Nickerson. But in 1972, when Rockefeller again came calling, Wachtler jumped back in the political ring with both feet and fists.

Judicial races are typically low-key affairs, decided often as not by back-room politics as well as by a genuine electoral contest. Frequently, the major parties engage in a cross-endorsement deal, with each side trading seats more or less equally. The reason is simple: judicial races are expensive and the party doesn't get anything for its money and effort. Judges can't do anything, officially anyway, for the party while they are in office. Their terms tend to be long, so it is easy to forget the political boss. And there is little patronage—usually just a secretary and a clerk—available to judges. Better to spend the money on an assembly race.

In 1972, Democrats and Republicans agreed to cross-endorse candidates for several judgeships, including the state's highest court. But with three seats available that year, the pols couldn't simply split the bounty. State Democratic boss Joe Crangle from Buffalo, hoping to capitalize on anti-Republican sentiments during the Watergate scandal, figured the Democrats could take at least two seats. But he was eager to get one for the former Erie County district attorney, Mike Dillon. "They wouldn't give us two. So we decided to go for three," Crangle said.[25] Rocky was infuriated because the GOP had given up two of the seats in a previous year. He refused to allow the Republicans to endorse any Democrats, and forced an election.

"Crangle got greedy and I've never seen Rockefeller so angry, *so angry* at a person," Wachtler recalled. "He was just livid. He kept saying, 'The man gave me his word. He shook my hand.' He got mad and said, 'Then, we'll take all three.' Still, he said that if Crangle came around, he'd stick with his part of the deal."[26]

In April 1972, the state Republican Committee nominated Wachtler, Hugh Jones of New Hartford, and Dominick "Mike" Gabrielli of Bath. Jones, a Harvard Law graduate, had been president of the statewide bar association. Gabrielli had been a Steuben County district attorney, initially appointed by Governor Thomas Dewey, before his election to the state trial court. In 1965, Rockefeller had assigned Gabrielli to preside over an "extraordinary special and trial term" in Erie County dealing with a criminal conspiracy stemming from the purchase of property by the city of Buffalo.

"We weren't exactly picked for our judicial talent," Wachtler said. "I was picked because I was a downstate Jew who could get votes. Gabrielli was picked because he was an upstate Italian who could get votes [and because he had once presided over a corruption trial in Buffalo, Crangle's home base]. Hugh Jones had never been a judge. He had been president of the state bar association."[27]

Wachtler, only forty-two and with scant judicial experience, was rejected by the bar association, but Rockefeller ignored the bar and went with his political instincts, and Wachtler proved that he was up to the challenge, as a politician anyhow. He ran with vigor and passion. He aired commercials of himself slamming a prison door, even though Court of Appeals judges have virtually nothing to do with incarcerating criminals. "Let's put the thieves and muggers and murderers into those cells," he says into the camera. He called plea bargaining "a tacit form of blackmail," proposed computerization of courts, suggested increased use of arbitration in civil cases, outlined an individual assignment system in which the same judge handles a case from start to finish, and demanded more money to run the court system. He called for the use of court-appointed referees to dispose of "victimless crime" cases—like public intoxication, drug addiction, and prostitution. He traveled around in a twin-engine Baron Beachcraft airplane, making political visits to, of all places, state prisons.

"We are not going to have a complete society until we have a criminal justice system that works," Wachtler said in the campaign. "I intend to speak to this issue. We have a duty within the system to speak out and I intend to do so."[28]

Once again, Rocky's political instincts were sound: the Republican candidates swept the field.*

Crangle, a seasoned political pro, realized that the Republicans had in Wachtler a rising political star. "He would be governor today [but for the scandal]," Crangle said. "There is no doubt in my mind."[29]

Wachtler was sworn in on January 1, 1973—at forty-two, the youngest associate judge ever to sit on the court—by Chief Judge Stanley Fuld to a fourteen-year term. Despite the security and prestige of the judicial office, and his love of the judicial process, running for governor was a constant temptation during Wachtler's nearly twenty years on the Court of Appeals. He perpetually flirted with the idea of becoming

---

*Dillon, the man who caused Crangle to challenge Rockefeller in the first place, wouldn't run in a contested election and never made it to the high court, despite, ironically, Wachtler's later attempts to get him there. "I think Mike Dillon didn't get there because of the abortion issue," Wachtler speculated. "He was an outspoken opponent of abortion, and one of the finest human beings I have ever known." (Dillon was later considered, and rejected, as a Cuomo lieutenant governor candidate because of his anti-abortion stance.)

the first Court of Appeals judge to make it to the executive mansion since Nathan L. Miller, who served from 1921 to 1922, between Alfred E. Smith and Franklin D. Roosevelt.

As early as 1977, after only four years as an associate judge on the high court, Wachtler was touted as a dark horse candidate for governor in 1978. "It is very flattering to be considered for such a high office," Wachtler said at the time. "But I actually have absolutely no plans to do anything other than serve as a judge on the Court of Appeals."[30] Wachtler sat on the sidelines while Hugh L. Carey, a Democrat, was reelected governor.*

When Wachtler was named the Outstanding Jurist of the Year by the state Trial Lawyers Association in 1981, then lieutenant governor Mario Cuomo said: "Governor Carey and I sleep better at night knowing that Judge Wachtler is in the courthouse."

In 1979, Republicans and Jews wanted Wachtler to challenge Democratic Senator Daniel Patrick Moynihan, arguing that there should be a "Jewish seat" from the New York senatorial delegation. Margiotta wanted him to run for the seat held by Javits, assuming the senator would retire. But Javits didn't retire and was bumped off in a primary by D'Amato,

---

*The North Hempstead Republican Committee actively promoted Wachtler for vice president in 1988 over Dan Quayle, whom Wachtler later made jokes about. Joy Silverman had become close to George Bush and Quayle. In a June 8, 1992, conversation with Wachtler she secretly taped, Wachtler said: "Let's be honest here. The president has done some bad things, he's alienated a lot of Jews, he's alienated anyone that thinks about or is concerned about women's rights, he's devastated the legal profession with his last two appointments to the Supreme Court and he seems to be determined in his caving in to the conservatives to give away the presidency and I think one of his bad choices was, and I apologize for saying this, because I know you're close to him, Dan Quayle. A bad mistake."

Joy responded: "You're basically a politician at heart, you are."

something Wachtler never would have considered. Margiotta started pushing his name for consideration as Ronald Reagan's secretary of state. Others suggested Wachtler for U.S. Attorney General.

Governor Carey, obviously worried about Wachtler, took a cheap shot at the judge, suggesting that Margiotta was standing in the way of court reform. Margiotta, long a close friend of Wachtler's, was the leader of what was then the state's most powerful Republican political machine,[31] and he was already under indictment for municipal corruption. For years, Margiotta had been funneling portions of Nassau County's insurance commissions to politically linked firms and individuals through the Richard B. Williams & Son Agency.[32] A Second Circuit U.S. Court of Appeals, upholding Margiotta's conviction for extortion, noted that he had distributed over $500,000 to "numerous insurance brokers who performed no legitimate work, lawyers and other friends of Margiotta who rendered no services in return for their compensation, and Margiotta himself."[33] Margiotta was found guilty of inducing the Williams agency to "make the payments of the insurance commissions under color of official right and by means of the wrongful use of fear"—an offense known as a Hobbs Act violation. Stripped of the legalese, this means Margiotta used his clout to scare the Williams agency into going along with his plan. He was also convicted of mail fraud.

Margiotta proffered an interesting—and accurate, really —defense. He maintained that what he had done was simply common and legitimate local government practice.[34] The reform movement following Watergate clearly had not caught up to Margiotta and he was imprisoned in June of 1983, after two years of fighting his 1981 conviction.

Carey, knowing Wachtler couldn't respond publicly

because of judicial ethics constraints, was attempting to paint the judge with the same wide brush that had tarred his friend Margiotta. Privately, Wachtler seethed and plotted a run—for vengeance if for nothing else—for governor.

In 1981, while Wachtler was pondering his political future, four Republican members of congress from Long Island called on President Reagan to appoint Wachtler to the U.S. Supreme Court seat being vacated by retiring Justice Potter Stewart. "Mr. President," they wrote, "Judge Wachtler would bring to the highest court in the land superlative legal experience and knowledge, a brilliant incisive mind and a magnificent talent for expressing his opinions." It was signed by Norman Lent, John LeBoutillier, Raymond J. McGrath, and Gregory J. Carman.[35]*

Wachtler, deeply touched, responded with a personal note to each. "Dear Norman," he wrote to Lent, "with the American Civil Liberties Union saying I am too conservative and with the Conservative party saying I am too liberal, it is nice to know that someone out there thinks I am good for something."[36]

To LeBoutillier he wrote: "Pretty sly—here you are priming me to run for governor, while at the same time, behind my back, you try to get rid of me by trying to put me on the Supreme Court. Pretty sneaky."[37]

To McGrath: "I know, since you left me behind in Albany, you thought the only decent thing to do was to get me to Washington. Very clever—but somehow I don't think it will work."[38]

But the most telling note was addressed to Carman. "Although we both know the impossible nature of the situa-

---

*Conspicuously absent from the supporters was D'Amato, although D'Amato did later promote Wachtler for attorney general in 1988 when Edwin Meese abruptly resigned. But the job went to former Pennsylvania governor Richard Thornburgh.

tion, it was a great honor to have members of Congress submit my name for such an exalted post."

Later, Wachtler described his Supreme Court aspirations as "a great dream,"[39] but an unreachable one: "When the Republicans were in, I was perceived as far too liberal, and when the Democrats were in I was a Republican. My mother used to tell me about a rabbit who envied the birds. God gave him wings so he could fly, but the birds wouldn't play with him because he had big ears. So he went back down and the rabbits wouldn't play with him because he had wings. That's what I was in the political matrix."[40]

While the Supreme Court was probably out, in 1980, Wachtler was on everyone's short list as a potential 1982 gubernatorial candidate, along with then Rep. Jack Kemp, state controller Edward V. Regan, Senate Majority Leader Warren Anderson, former Rockefeller chief of staff Alton Marshall, and Assembly Minority leader James L. Emery. Wachtler spoke of the governor's mansion so often that his friend Mario Cuomo—then lieutenant governor—speculated in his diary : "I think Sol is really eager to run for Governor against Carey. He'd make a good candidate, too."[41]

Wachtler and Cuomo had become close friends and soulmates. Both were often in Albany away from their families. Neither was interested in the womanizing and cocktail parties that generally occupy the spare time of out-of-town politicians. They shared an intellectual love of the law and legal principles (Cuomo had clerked at the court in the 1950s for Judge Adrian Burke and had enormous respect for the institution), as well as a fascinations with politics, and discussed those issues at private dinners. In one of their standing jokes, Cuomo would urge Wachtler to run for governor so he could appoint him chief judge, and Wachtler would urge Cuomo to run for governor and appoint *him* chief.

"You know, Mario, the governor is really where it's at," Wachtler once said to Cuomo, revealing his interest in power. "I mean, just think of the awesome power of the executive branch to accomplish things and get things done."

Cuomo responded: "Are you kidding? If I have an idea for a program, first it has to be formulated, then it has to go through sixteen committees, then it has to go to the floor of the Assembly and Senate, and maybe it gets enacted. Whereas you judges, with the stroke of a pen, in one conference—bang!—can change the law altogether. You can rule that a law is unconstitutional or you can interpret a law in such a way as to change its meaning. You can establish a precedent that is binding on every citizen in the state. *You're* the ones with the power."[42]

Wachtler flirted seriously with running in 1982, but the timing was wrong. He did have the support of Joe Margiotta, whose Nassau County Republican organization was the most powerful in the state, but Margiotta was an outcast because of his conviction and Wachtler had, under subpoena, been a character witness. Further, he had written or supported decisions opposing the death penalty, seemingly favoring kiddie porn,* and potentially shifting the real property tax burden from businesses to homeowners. "I am not ashamed, nor do I apologize for anything I've written or participated in on the Court of Appeals," Wachtler said. "A judge must decide cases free from the passion of the moment."[43]

There was real doubt that the conservative wing of the

---

*Actually, despite comments from politicians, the case had next to nothing to do with kiddie porn. All the court said in the 5–2 unsigned opinion, with Wachtler in the majority, is that a provision banning promotion of nonobscene sexual performances is unconstitutional. Essentially, the court said that medical texts depicting naked children aren't pornographic.

party would support Wachtler and real doubt that he could win a primary without strong backing from the right, if necessary. On the other hand, Carey was acting odd—he had dyed his hair orange, married a much younger woman and, according to published sources, offered to drink water laced with PCBs[44]—and Cuomo was thinking seriously of waging a primary. That could have split the Democrats and distracted those who would have challenged Wachtler as the Republican candidate.

When Margiotta pushed D'Amato to run against Javits, he angered many Republican leaders—fifty-five of the sixty-two county chairmen—and there was speculation that it would came back to haunt Wachtler in 1982.

Regardless, Wachtler was willing to give it a go, even though he would have to resign from the bench. He secretly told his colleagues on the court that he was going to run when, abruptly, he changed his mind. The moment of truth, Wachtler said, came at the 1981 U.S. Open tennis match in Flushing, Queens, when he was approached by Donald Trump, who suggested the two could do business.

"I was ready to run for governor and even told [chief judge] Larry Cooke that I was going to run," Wachtler recalled. "That was on a Friday. On a Sunday, I went to the Forest Hills tennis matches and Donald Trump was there. Donald Trump was just emerging, no one had ever heard of him. He came over to me, pointed his finger in my face and said, 'People say you're running for governor. We're going to talk.' I went home to Joan and I said, 'I just can't do this. I can't go around raising funds and having people like him pointing their finger at me.' "[45]

The next morning Wachtler held a press conference at the Capitol, where reporters were certain he would announce his candidacy. "I have decided not to run for governor because I love being a judge and being a part of our Court of Appeals and of our state's judiciary," Wachtler said. His announcement shocked a veteran press corps, in the same way that Cuomo's would in 1992 when, with a plane waiting to take him to New Hampshire for the presidential primary, he balked. And as if to dispel any notion that he was stepping aside because of controversy, Wachtler added: "And make no mistake about the fact that I am very proud of my contributions to the law and of the substantial contributions that our courts have made and continue to make towards stability, civility, fairness and goodness in our society."[46]

At the time, Wachtler truly thought that he was swearing off politics for good. Margiotta was crushed: "Let's face it, I think Sol is the finest candidate coming out of this county that I've known since I've been in politics."[47]

In a 1981 editorial, just after Wachtler announced he would not run for governor, *Newsday* opined: "The world has never suffered from an excess of intelligent, competent public officials. So when one comes along, there are stirrings of optimism and appreciation among people who are concerned about such matters. Judge Sol Wachtler is a man who possesses both intelligence and competence. His decision not to run for governor in 1982 comes as a bit of a disappointment; he would have elevated the contest."[48]

Shortly after Wachtler dropped out of contention, Carey announced that he would not seek reelection. Cuomo, the Democrat, won a tough primary against New York City Mayor Ed Koch and then faced Rite Aid drugstore magnate Lew Lehrman, narrowly defeating him. Two years after taking office, Cuomo named Wachtler chief judge and gave him a new fourteen-year term (the court was changed from an elective body to an appointed one in the late 1970s). Immediately the political pundits smelled a rat. By naming

Wachtler chief judge, Cuomo had neutralized his most serious future opponent. A deal? There was plenty of speculation but no proof (Wachtler points out that at the time he withdrew, Cuomo wasn't yet a candidate, although the future governor was mulling over a primary challenge).

As chief judge, Wachtler had a lawyer's dream job. He ran the largest court system in the Western world, presided over the most respected state court in the nation, and was secure in his position, never having to run again. But by the early 1990s, he was frustrated with his lack of practical power (he couldn't institute his most important reforms without the support of the legislature, and the legislature ignored him) and feuding annually with Cuomo over the court budget. The money battle reached an apex in 1990 when Wachtler sued the governor for more funding and the two titans battled ferociously, and very publicly, until Cuomo blinked and partially gave in. Many figured the stage was set for a Wachtler-Cuomo contest in 1990, despite their long friendship.

Cuomo was in a bit of a bind, declining in popularity, and would have had a tough time with Wachtler. For one thing, he couldn't have very well claimed that the man he appointed chief judge lacked ability, intelligence, or integrity. For another, Wachtler was seemingly the only man on the horizon who could match Cuomo's intellect and oratory. It was widely speculated that Cuomo had been avoiding speaking at events where Wachtler was also on the agenda, knowing that the judge could, and probably would, steal his thunder. Republicans were virtually begging Wachtler to run. "We are waiting for Thor to descend from heaven," bemoaned one GOP leader, adding that Thor could still be found "if only Sol Wachtler would run." Again Wachtler— finding the speculation "heady stuff, very flattering" but unpersuasive—demurred, and Cuomo clobbered the weak challenger Pierre Rinfret, who, among other things, suggested he would fire the Court of Appeals judges if he didn't like what they were doing.

But two years later, Wachtler was ready. Cuomo was clearly on the decline politically. Wachtler was as well known and seriously under consideration. In September 1992, just two months before his arrest, Bill Powers, the chairman and organizational mastermind of the state Republican party, referred to Wachtler as a "dream quality" candidate for governor. Powers knew Wachtler could get votes, and he knew the judge would not be intimidated by Cuomo's rhetoric. "He seemed to be a very popular guy. He came from that great base, Nassau County. I don't know of any statewide official who could win without that boost from Long Island, to offset the Democratic votes of New York City."[49]

The glitch, however, was Wachtler's perceived liberalism. A Republican candidate for governor in New York simply cannot win without the support of the Conservative party, and Conservative Chairman Michael Long had not yet signed off on Wachtler, who was carrying dual political baggage from the right-wing standpoint: he was both pro-choice and anti-death penalty.

Notes

1. William Safire, *Before the Fall: An Inside View of the Pre-Watergate White House* (New York: Doubleday, 1975), p. 498.

2. Richard Reeves, "The Nationwide Search for Nelson Rockefeller," *New York*, September 2, 1974, p. 8.

3. Interview with Wachtler on April 14, 1997.

4. Wachtler's archives.

5. "A Prepotent Force," *Westbury Times*, March 4, 1965.

6. Myron S. Waldman, "Wachtler Attacks Rival's Poor Attendance," *Newsday*, October 19, 1965.

7. "Javits Here Friday in Full Support of Wachtler," *The Great Neck Record*, October 21, 1965.

8. Wachtler's archives.

9. Ibid.

10. William Spiegler, "Profile: Sol Wachtler," *Newsday*, February 17, 1965.

11. Interview with Wachtler on April 14, 1997.

12. Ibid.

13. Wachtler's archives.

14. Interview with Wachtler on April 14, 1997.

15. Alfonse D'Amato, *Power, Pasta and Politics: The World according to Senator Al D'Amato* (New York: Hyperion, 1995), p. 57.

16. Interview with Wachtler on April 14, 1997.

17. Wachtler's archives.

18. Wachtler's recollection, as conveyed in an August 1995 interview.

19. Ibid.

20. Wachtler's archives.

21. Interview with Wachtler on August 15, 1997.

22. "Sol Wachtler's Vindication," *Great Neck Record*, December 1967.

23. "Mark of Greatness," *The Westbury Times*, December 7, 1967.

24. Interview with Wachtler on April 14, 1997.

25. Interview with Joseph Crangle on November 11, 1997.

26. Interview with Wachtler on April 14, 1997.

27. Interview with Wachtler in February 1997.

28. Howard Clark, "New Appeals Judges Speak Out," Associated Press, November 16, 1972 (Albany *Knickerbocker News*, p. A4).

29. Interview with Crangle on November 11, 1997.

30. Frederic U. Dicker, "Wachtler Seen GOP Dark Horse," Albany *Times Union*, October 23, 1977.

31. Paul A. Smith, "A State of Politics," *New York State Today*, eds. Peter W. Colby and John K. White (Albany: State University of New York Press, 1989), p. 29.

32. Tim Beidel, "Grand Jury Arouses Political Speculation," Albany *Times Union*, August 2, 1992, p. A1.

33. Ibid.

34. Smith, "A State of Politics," p. 29.

35. Wachtler's archives.

36. Ibid.

37. Ibid.

38. Ibid.

39. Interview with Wachtler on August 21, 1997.

40. Ibid.

41. Mario M. Cuomo, *Diaries of Mario M. Cuomo: The Campaign for Governor* (New York: Random House, 1984), p. 66.

42. Duncan Christy, "Law, Order and the Judge," *M*, July 1985, p. 82.

43. Eric Freedman, *Empire State Report*, July 20, 1981.

44. E.g., Mark McIntyre, "Calculating the Risks of PCBs," *Newsday*, April 12, 1987, p. 15.

45. Interview with Wachtler on April 14, 1997.

46. Dick Zander, "Wachtler Rejects Governor Race," *Newsday*, September 14, 1981.

47. Ibid.

48. "A Judge's Decision to Remain on the Bench," *Newsday*, Nassau edition, September 17, 1981.

49. Interview with Bill Powers on September 3, 1997.

CHAPTER 3

Judicial Career

In his *Democracy in America* (1835), Alexis de Tocqueville observed that there is hardly a political issue which arises that is not ultimately a judicial question. Tocqueville, who had visited Albany just before writing his now famous work, considered the American proclivity for letting judges settle not just legal but social, political, and moral matters unique in the annals of history.

Unique it is.

On the one hand, the Constitution makes the third branch of government the weakest, or as Alexander Hamilton said, the "least dangerous."[1] The judiciary, he said, "has no influence over either the sword or the purse; no direction either of the strength or the wealth of the society; and can take no active resolution whatever." He added: The courts "may truly be said to have neither FORCE nor WILL, but merely judgment; and must ultimately depend upon the aid of the executive arm for the efficacious exercise of even this faculty."

At the same time, the judiciary is insulated from direct political pressure: A politician works primarily in the arena of influence, a judge primarily in the arena of ideas. James Madison wrote in the *Federalist Papers* that "justice is the end of government. It is the end of civil society. It has ever been and ever will be pursued until it be obtained, or until liberty be lost in the pursuit."[2] But he warned that justice is perpetually subject to "gradual and silent encroachments."

Sol Wachtler understood both the political *and* judicial realities.

As a politician, he was accustomed to handling political issues in an audacious manner, and he understood well how to orchestrate a devious attack and strategic retreat. He had a sense of political realities and had developed a skill in exploiting them. With a mind both agile and open, and an intellect and personal charm that won extraordinary loyalty and allegiance, Wachtler, at only thirty-eight years of age, was a rare addition to the judiciary. He was temperamentally suited for the judicial role and brought to the bench the wisdom of a jurist, the instincts of a trial lawyer, and the chutzpah of a Long Island politician. He even looked like a judge, dignified and suave.

But fellow judges were often skeptical of Wachtler and his motives, leery of his political savvy and ability to attract cases that kept his name in the news. Reporters have said he was the one of the few judges who leaked stories about himself. Political writers opined that if there was ever a man running for the Court of Appeals, it was Wachtler. He was pushing all the right buttons. Even his first rulings, while they certainly brought the spotlight to an unknown judge, reveal a certain vision and willingness to use the law to address social concerns. He ordered a municipality to grant a parade permit to Veterans against the Vietnam War—an early indication of his commitment to free speech—and shot down as unconscionable a contract that required a poor family to pay $900 for a $300 refrigerator, plus shipping, noting that the law is "beginning to fight back against those who take advantage of the poor and illiterate."[3] The young jurist forced the Nassau County Department of Social Services to go beyond their normal rent ceiling to keep roofs over the heads of two families, and expunged a juvenile's arrest record because the charge was withdrawn. He was well ahead of his time in advocating arbitration rather than litigation, and suggested that police and black youths—who were fighting over a poster depicting police officers as swine—"sit down and resolve the issue through intelligent discussion."[4] Later, as chief judge, Wachtler promoted arbitration and mediation as a solution to court congestion and, after getting out of prison, formed a company offering such services.

"Today, we have more criminals, more crime, and more victims than ever before. Our system is not punishing, or deterring, or rehabilitating, and a system which accomplishes none of these things cannot justify its own existence or long endure," Wachtler said in his typically outspoken fashion.

His victory in the Court of Appeals race was a great personal triumph, but it began the slow disintegration of his marriage. "When Sol was elected to the Court of Appeals, we were all elated," said Joan Wachtler, "but our lives changed dramatically. He spent two weeks a month in Albany, three hours from our home. I was lonely. . . . We all eventually learned to adjust our lives to the rhythm of Sol's schedule. One by one our children left home for college, careers and the establishment of their own families. Sol and I structured a mutually acceptable lifestyle. . . . Everything was in balance."[5]

At first, Wachtler was viewed on the bench with skepticism as a Nassau County political hack who lacked both the intelligence and fortitude to serve on the high court. But he immediately began to counter that image, hiring an odd-couple pair of clerks to pave the way: David Gould and Michael Trainor. Wachtler was immediately blessed with two trusted aides, both exceptionally intelligent, but in different ways.

Trainor was a Vietnam veteran, a former cop and straight-shooting, self-doubting, excitable Irish Catholic who wasn't at all sure he deserved to work at the high court since he had barely survived law school. Yet he had a steel-trap mind that rivaled Wachtler's, and Wachtler quickly sensed the quiet young man's innate intelligence and drive.

Gould, the brilliant son of Morton Gould, a famous composer who would later win the Pulitzer Prize, was a tear-gassed veteran of the anti-war movement, a smart-aleck philosophical bomb thrower, and a Jew. Gould had grown up around famous people, was pretty impressed with himself, and was hardly star-struck by a forty-two-year-old freshman Court of Appeals judge. But immediately Gould sensed that Wachtler was something special.

During Wachtler's first term on the court, he was eager to dispel rumors that he was nothing more than a pretty face, and asked Gould to come up with some dynamite material so he could display his brilliance on the bench at oral arguments. Gould found an old case that he thought was perfect, and Wachtler quoted from it in questioning an attorney from the bench—an attempt to show that he, the new judge, really did his homework. One problem: The case had been reversed some sixty years previously and had no bearing whatsoever on the matter at hand. Wachtler was embarrassed, and Gould was certain he would be out of a job as soon as the judge came off the bench. A clerk does not ever, *ever* publicly embarrass a judge, even the newest judge on the bench, even by accident. The sin is unforgivable. Oh well. Easy come, easy go.

"Any other judge would have fired the clerk on the spot," Gould said. "Sol called me in, put his arm around me and said, 'I hope you don't feel bad about this.' Actually, I felt awful. When Sol embarrassed himself, I turned to the person next to me in the courtroom—he didn't know who I was and certainly didn't know I was responsible—and said, 'Can you believe this new judge? The guy's an idiot!' "[6]

The Wachtler-Trainor-Gould triumvirate made an exceptional team: Trainor would tame, or at least reign in, Gould's more radical impulses; Gould seemed to ignite a spark of passion in Trainor, adding a healthy dose of irreverence; and Wachtler, serving as something like a chairman of the board, drew the best from each. Although Gould remained on staff for less than two years, he remained a trusted advisor for twenty years and ghostwrote many of Wachtler's most popular quips. Trainor stuck around for two decades, perfectly content working in relative anonymity and drafting many of the judge's most cited decisions. Maybe the public had no idea of the crucial role that Trainor played, but Michael, Sol, and the other judges knew it—and that was enough for Trainor. In the outer office was Dorothy (Dottie) Young,* the protective, motherly woman Wachtler chose as his secretary.

Over the next twenty years, Wachtler, with Michael Trainor at his side and Dottie Young guarding the fort, carved his place in New York law and national jurisprudence. He wrote the decision striking down a state law which

---

*Dottie died shortly before the scandal, which quite possibly wouldn't have occurred if she had been there with her eagle eyes trained on Sol.

exempted married men from prosecution for raping their wives, authored the majority opinion that banned discrimination at many private clubs, and dissented strongly when the court refused to extend free-speech rights to citizens wanting to distribute leaflets in private shopping malls. His decisions protected New Yorkers, to a greater degree than people in any other state, from intrusive police confrontations; forced "subway vigilante" Bernhard Goetz to stand trial for shooting four teenage muggers in a New York City subway; and prohibited the Xerox Corporation from denying a woman a job on the grounds that she was obese. He established an abnormally high standard for New Yorkers in right-to-die cases, walked a fine line between coddling and condemning criminals, and wrote forcefully about free expression. Ironically, he wrote prophetically about the horrific ramifications of solitary confinement. He relished his reputation as a judge who could be pigeon-holed neither as a liberal nor as a conservative and when, in 1982, a state Legal Aid Society report said Wachtler was becoming increasingly influential as he shifted from a "middle-of-the-road jurist to a strong, prosecution-oriented judge," Wachtler was furious.

One of his most difficult, and potentially problematic, decisions was a technical tax matter that, a colleague advised, would destroy any political ambitions. In 1975, Professor Jerome Hellerstein of New York University sued the town of Islip, challenging the assessment of his home on Fire Island. Until then, assessors simply ignored a 200-year-old statute requiring property to be taxed at full value. Instead, local assessors had levied taxes on businesses and commercial properties at a far higher value than private homes. Wachtler wanted to strike down the practice as unconstitutional, but was warned by his friend and colleague, Chief Judge Charles Breitel, that if he wrote such an opinion, he could forever forget about the governor's mansion. Bravely, Wachtler went ahead regardless.

"It was one of the most difficult tasks I ever undertook because I knew it would be extremely unpopular—not only with the public but at home, where I was living in a very large house on three acres, assessed value of $21,500," Wachtler said in a private letter to *Newsday* columnist Bob Wiemer. "But when judges decide cases because they want to be popular, then our society is in very serious trouble."[7]

The predictable backlash from *Hellerstein v. Islip*[8] seemed only to embolden Wachtler, to bolster his nerve to take on unpopular or controversial issues.

He wanted the government out of the bedroom, even if the sexual partners were two men or two women. "Sexual acts between consenting adults should not be criminal offenses, unless they violate the rights of others to be in a public place without fear or solicitation or embarrassment," Wachtler said in a 1979 speech at Hofstra University, long before gay rights was a politically correct viewpoint.[9] "Victimless crimes which are sexually related should be governed by the right to privacy. . . . We should distinguish between private conduct and public solicitation or displays and direct our attention to curtailing offensive public conduct."

In May 1980, Wachtler quit the University Club in Albany, with much fanfare, along with Chief Judge Lawrence H. Cooke and Bernard S. Meyer because it denied membership to women. He understood the electorate, yet did everything in his power to take the voters out of the loop when it came to selecting judges, and eventually succeeded. Although Wachtler got to the high court purely because of his ability to garner votes—his qualifications at the time were relatively meager—once there, he tried to put an end to judicial politicking. The straw that broke the camel's back on that issue was a man named Jacob Fuchsberg.

Fuchsberg, a wealthy New York City lawyer, had no judicial experience and no bar support, but got himself on the 1973 ballot by spending a fortune on a glitzy media blitz. Fuchsberg won the Democratic primary and forced Breitel to campaign vigorously and expensively to maintain his seat. Fuchsberg lost, but tried again the following year and won, bumping off a popular incumbent named Harold A. Stevens, the first black man to serve on the court. Stevens had been on the high court only a few months when Fuchsberg's victory returned the panel to an all-white group of men. It would be another decade before another black jurist, a deliberative, thoughtful judge named Fritz Alexander, got appointed, with Wachtler's help.

Fuchsberg seriously undermined the status quo of both politics and the judiciary. "Fuchsberg's ability and will to take on the partisan political leaders . . . upset the established patterns for who would serve on the Court of Appeals. . . . The ability of the organized bar to lend credence to established candidates with judicial experience was seriously jeopardized. Consensus and congeniality were things of the past. A new path to the bench, through the vigorously contested primary route by those without traditional support or experience, seems to have been established,"[10] said Luke Bierman, a legal scholar and veteran court watcher.

Fuchsberg had been an abrasive and combative trial lawyer, but the feistiness that served him well at the bar only made him immediately and immensely unpopular on the bench. Fuchsberg irritated the judiciary for the way he ran for the bench, and his bullying and often obnoxious behavior inside the genteel traditions of the Court of Appeals only widened the rift. Wachtler and the other judges were appalled at the demeaning way Fuchsberg treated his law clerks—some of the best and brightest newly minted lawyers in the nation—and considered such behavior beneath the dignity of the court.

Wachtler disliked and distrusted Fuchsberg from the start. But the incident that deep-froze an already icy relationship involved one of Wachtler's most important decisions. The court was about to issue a major ruling on search and seizure, in the 1976 case of *People* v. *DeBour*,[11] and Wachtler, by the luck of the draw, was chosen to write the main opinion. Fuchsberg wanted to dissent, but didn't know how. So he out farmed Wachtler's draft opinion—which had not been released—to a New York University professor to write the dissent. The professor, however, agreed with the decision and gave it to his students to study. Word inevitably got back to the court, and the judges nearly went berserk. A probe eventually revealed that Fuchsberg was routinely enlisting outsiders to write his opinions.

The court learned that he had farmed out to law professors at least twelve different cases. Sometimes he simply consulted by telephone. Other times he sent briefs to professors and asked academics to suggest outcomes. Three times Fuchsberg actually had professors write opinions, which he published as his own. Fuchsberg claimed he didn't know there was anything wrong with consulting with experts, and argued that there was no expressed rule prohibiting such conduct. The court responded:

> We are mindful that law clerks often contribute substantially to the preparation of opinions. There are, however, important distinctions between a law clerk and an outside expert. The law clerk is a sworn court employee [citation omitted]. He is a recognized figure of the judicial institution, familiar to the litigants and fully exposed to the submissions of both parties to the adversarial proceeding. We cannot

accept respondent's explanation that he looked upon the law professors he consulted as "ad hoc" law clerks.

We are equally disturbed by respondent's breach of the court's confidentiality. No Canon specifically prohibits transmission to non-court personnel of unpublished, draft opinions formulated by Judges and circulated as part of the collective decision-making process. However, the adverse impact of transmitting such draft opinions to those outside the court system is so obvious that condemnation of it need not be based on an express Canon or Rule. Confidentiality is crucial to the success of the deliberative process, but it is of utmost importance for the proper functioning of a collegial court.[12]

Fuchsberg was called up on charges on September 6, 1977, when then Chief Judge Breitel convened a special court specifically to investigate Fuchsberg's financial dealings.

Before taking office, Fuchsberg had purchased a fortune in short-term New York City bonds and, when assuming the bench on January 1, 1975, was holding $3.4 million worth of notes. He continued to trade in bonds, even though the court was hearing cases that could affect his holdings. The court found Fuchsberg's behavior ill-advised. "The fact that a particular action may be prudent from a business standpoint must never distract a Judge from his obligation to promote public confidence in judicial institutions," the court said.[13]

The court condemned Fuchsberg, but refused to throw him off the bench, prompting a sharp dissent from Judge Richard D. Simons, who would join Fuchsberg on the high court five years later. "His investment practices led inevitably to tangled conflicts between his private affairs and his judicial obligations, and his breaches of the court's confidentiality and use of law professors was a serious intrusion upon the rights of his colleagues on the Court of Appeals and the litigants appearing before him," Simons wrote. "Respect for the courts cannot be maintained by minimizing errant judicial behavior and finessing constitutional procedures. Respect is maintained by performance which assures the public that misconduct does not exist because it will not be tolerated."[14]

To be fair to Fuchsberg, however, he was not without his credentials or achievements, nor was he totally undistinguished as a jurist. At the bar, Fuchsberg was the first lawyer in the nation to win a jury verdict of $1 million.[15] On the bench, he was noted for his strong defense of civil rights and liberties. He was a consistent—critics say rabid—advocate for criminal rights and also a strong proponent of personal privacy, due process, and affirmative action.

In any case, the Fuchsberg-*DeBour* incident further convinced Wachtler and Breitel of the flaws of the elective system for picking judges, so they began a furious lobbying effort to establish a system based on "merit selection" rather than popular election. They convinced Governor Carey to embrace their plan and in 1977 the elective system was abandoned. Instead, a panel of twelve appointed by the governor, chief judge, and legislative leaders was delegated the authority to review candidates and submit a list of qualified candidates to the governor. Within that framework, Cuomo, a few years later, was able to ensure that a minority, Fritz Alexander, and a woman, Judith S. Kaye, both lacking serious political connections, would join the panel.

When Breitel retired in 1979, Carey was pressured by so-called Borscht-belt Democrats, a powerful contingent of Jewish politicians in the Catskill resort area, to appoint Cooke, who lived in that region. Carey needed their votes and their money. Cuomo, meanwhile, was lobbying for Gabrielli, a Republican but a man who had earned the respect of his colleagues and was suited both temperamentally—

Gabrielli was so popular at Court of Appeals Hall that staffers wept when he retired—and intellectually to serve as chief. But Carey, suspecting that Gabrielli was quietly supporting his gubernatorial opponent, Perry Duryea (and he was), wasn't inclined to promote someone he viewed as disloyal.

Meanwhile, neither Wachtler nor Jones, two popular Republicans, had bothered to apply. The senior associate, Matthew Jasen, a Democrat, lacked support. So Carey went with Cooke.

Cooke had been a municipal attorney before his 1955 election to a county court post in Sullivan County. Five years later, he was elected to the state supreme Court , and later (1968) placed on the Appellate Division by Rockefeller. When he ran for the Court of Appeals in 1974, two years after failing to finish in the top three in the six-way race that brought in Wachtler, Jones, and Gabrielli, Cooke got the highest vote of any of the five candidates. Five years after that, Carey made Cooke chief judge.

Intent on establishing himself as an administrator, Cooke imposed, by fiat, a new regulation that required a random rotation of judges to New York City. Some upstate judges were livid—most notably Rensselaer County Judge M. Andrew Dwyer Jr., a colorful character from Troy sometimes characterized as an erratic genius. "I won't go," Dwyer said publicly when he learned that Cooke wanted to send him, having been elected by the folks in largely rural Rensselaer County, to deal with the problems in metropolitan New York City. "They can't make me. And they don't have the gonads to try."[16] Dwyer was right on all counts.

When Cooke retired in 1985, he handed Cuomo a chance to name his first chief judge. It was politically and logistically a tough choice.

Three sitting Court of Appeals judges applied for the job:

Wachtler, Bernard Meyer, and Matthew Jasen. But Meyer and Jasen were sixty-eight and sixty-nine, respectively, and didn't make the list of seven from which the governor must choose. The list included: Wachtler; Bronx Surrogate Bertram R. Gelfand; U.S. District Judges Neal P. McCurn and Abraham Sofaer; and Appellate Division justices E. Leo Milonas, Joseph P. Sullivan, and Milton Mollen.

Mollen, a World War II hero taken prisoner by the Germans after his plane was shot down in July 1944 over occupied France (he escaped from a Nazi prison camp and joined advancing British forces), had studied law at St. John's University, just as Cuomo had. But one of the governor's attorneys, Matthew Crosson, was pushing hard for Wachtler.[17] Crosson, who would later serve as Wachtler's chief administrator, knew little about the judge when Cuomo told him to evaluate the candidate. Crosson went home one weekend with one hundred of Wachtler's decisions and found himself astonished by the combination of substance and style. Most judicial opinions read like gobbledygook, even to a lawyer like Crosson. Wachtler's, however, were different—clean, concise, articulate, reasoned, practical. Wachtler, Crosson realized, understood that he was writing not only for lawyers and legal academics, but the citizenry, and that his job was to resolve real problems, not engage in academic debate. He reported back to Cuomo, firmly in Wachtler's corner.

Cuomo was in a touchy spot. He thought highly of Mollen, who, aside from being personal friend, was also a Democrat and fellow St. John's grad. Yet if the governor, who had once worked as a law clerk at the Court of Appeals and had enormous respect for its legacies, named Mollen, he would break with tradition by appointing a chief from outside the court. The day of the appointment, nobody knew what Cuomo would do, not even his wife, Matilda.[18] At the absolute last minute,

Cuomo called Wachtler at his home outside Albany just before midnight. "Sol," Cuomo said, "I am going to do something for you that I have always wished someone would do for me."[19]

Publicly, Cuomo said: "In every category, I think Wachtler scored as high or higher than anybody else. Milt Mollen I know better than any of them. I could have done it on the ground that I knew Milt better, but that's an unworthy criterion. I could have said that Milt is a Democrat, but that's even less worthy."[20]

Cuomo was attracted to Wachtler's combination as a scholar and statesman. "No one ever gets faulted for choosing excellence," Cuomo reasoned.

> I don't think that the political registration, or even the political history of a candidate, is a relevant criterion. What I looked for is not how they decided the cases, whether I agreed with the decision, whether they're conservative or liberal or whether they're a strict constructionist or not. I read each of their opinions and decided whether they were competent, thorough, logical, clear. . . . [Wachtler] is uniquely respected among his colleagues on the bench, lawyers familiar with his work and litigants whose cases he has judged. Now he is in an excellent position to use his gifts of collegiality and judicial wisdom to lead this court to the stature and preeminence that it has enjoyed and deserves.[21]

Cuomo ultimately decided that Wachtler, with his intelligence and charm, could mold a cohesive, nationally respected court.[22]

In contrast to the controversy that resulted when Wachtler was appointed to Supreme Court and when he was nominated for the Court of Appeals, the now veteran appellate jurist (with twelve years on the high court) was universally lauded when Cuomo chose him for chief.

Gabrielli, by then retired, called Wachtler "a great human being." State Bar Association president Henry G. Miller called him "an outstanding judge and an outstanding human being." Women praised him for the *Liberta*[23] marital rape decision, which permitted the prosecution of men for raping their wives. Defense attorneys loved him for *DeBour.* Prosecutors liked his pragmatic approach to law enforcement, his ability to combine constitutional theory and common sense.[24]

Before the judiciary committee for confirmation, Wachtler boldly told the panel that the court system was standing "at the threshold of a crisis,"[25] and laid out his plans for reform. He charmed the Senate and was confirmed unanimously. Cuomo was delighted, Wachtler and his family elated.

Wachtler's mother, Faye, was well into her eighties when her son became chief judge and attended the formal announcement by Governor Cuomo. Cuomo, who enjoys repartee as much as anyone, immediately hit it off with Mrs. Wachtler.

"What year were you born?" the governor asked innocently as they made their way to the press conference.[26]

"Can you keep a secret?" Mrs. Wachtler asked the governor.

Cuomo assured her he could.

"So can I," she responded.

In one stroke, Cuomo rewarded an old friend and neutralized a possible opponent. But Cuomo, a student of the classics, failed to heed the wisdom of Emerson. When you strike at a king, Emerson had warned, you must kill him. Wachtler was alive and well—and politically ambitious.

Notes

1. *The Federalist*, No. 78.

2. *The Federalist*, No. 51.

3. *Jones* v. *Star Credit*, 59 Misc 189 (1969).

4. *Henry* v. *Looney*, 65 Misc 2d 759 (1969).

5. Undated letter by Joan Wachtler to the judge who sentenced her husband.

6. Interview with David Gould on September 7, 1997.

7. Wacthler's archives.

8. *Hellerstein* v. *Islip*, 37 NY2d 1 (1975), 332, NE 2d 279.

9. Shirley Armstrong, "Judge Urges Court System Reforms," Albany *Times Union*, January 17, 1979.

10. Luke Bierman, "Institutional Identity and the Limits of Institutional Reform: The New York Court of Appeals in the Judicial Process," unpublished doctoral dissertation, 1994, p. 85.

11. *People* v. *DeBour*, 40 NY2d 210 (1976), 352 NE 2d 562.

12. In the Matter of the Proceeding Pursuant to Section 22 of Article VI of the Constitution of the state of New York in Relation to the Honorable Jacob D. Fuchsberg, Associate Judge of the Court of Appeals, 426 NYS 2d, 639 (1978).

13. Ibid.

14. Ibid.

15. Dean Howard A. Glickstein, "A Tribute to Jacob D. Fuchsberg," Touro Law Center, 1995.

16. Interview with Judge M. Andrew Dwyer, 1985.

17. Interview with Matthew Crosson, September 1997.

18. Interview with Mario Cuomo on November 10, 1997.

19. Interview with Wachtler on September 7, 1997.

20. Marc Humbert, "Why Cuomo Chose Wachtler," Associated Press, January 8, 1995.

21. David Margolick, "Republican Judge Is Named by Cuomo to Top Court Post," *New York Times*, January 3, 1985, p. 1.

22. Interview with Cuomo on November 10, 1997.

23. *People* v. *Liberta,* 64 NY2d 152 (1984), 474 NE 2d 567.

24. John Runfola, "Lawyers Praise Wachtler," Albany *Knickerbocker News,* January 23, 1985.

25. "Senate Confirms Wachtler to Lead N.Y.'s Court System," Associated Press, January 23, 1985.

26. Wachtler commentary during the spring 1997 seminar of the National Association of Criminal Defense Attorneys.

CHAPTER 4

Downfall

J ust before becoming chief judge, Wachtler was called
upon to mediate a bitter, interfamilial dispute centered
around the estate of Joan's uncle, Alvin "Bibbs" Wolosoff,
who had developed into a wealthy, self-centered, and vindictive old man. Wachtler could hardly say no; Bibbs had
thrown legal work Sol's way when he was a fledgling lawyer.
And Sol's deft handling of the matter only solidified his reputation as the family legal genius—and brought him together
with Joy Silverman at the very time his marriage was
comatose. Joy was Bibbs's stepdaughter.

Bibbs, thrice married, had two sons, James (Jimmy) and
Van Warren from his first wife, and two stepchildren, Bruce
and Joy, from his second wife. Late in life, and with a third
wife, Bibbs seemed to spend his time drawing and withdrawing various wills, writing in or out whoever happened

to be in his favor or disfavor at the moment. About the only thing the various wills had in common was that they excluded Jimmy, who had successfully sued his father over a business deal. Bibbs died on July 21, 1984, at the age of eighty-one, leaving an estate of $24 million, with instructions that it be administered by Sol Wachtler. Apparently, Bibbs perceived that his will would be challenged, and perhaps assumed that nobody could mount a successful challenge against an estate managed by a judge on the state's highest court.

Jimmy, denied an inheritance, took initial steps to challenge the will, which put Wachtler in a position of defending Bibbs's right to disinherit his own son. "He said he dreaded the day he was ever conceived," Wachtler testified when Jimmy and his attorney, Allen H. Weiss, tried to get the judge removed as executor.[1]

Judges in New York state are allowed to serve as executors of the estates of family members or other people with whom they have a familial relationship—such as that between Bibbs and Wachtler. However, they cannot, under the Code of Judicial Conduct, serve as a fiduciary of an estate which "becomes involved in adversary proceedings in the court on which the judge serves or one under its appellate jurisdiction." In other words, Wachtler would have no business becoming a litigant in a matter where a judge under his jurisdiction was called upon to assess the credibility of the chief judge, or where his own court could conceivably be asked to review a ruling. But if the matter hasn't quite gotten to the litigation stage—as occurred in this case—the rules are less clear. So, rather than step aside, Wachtler sidestepped.

Weiss questioned Wachtler during a proceeding on February 8, 1985, and the judge volunteered that he consulted with his colleagues "to see whether they would have any objection or discomfort with my serving."[2] Wachtler said his colleagues had no problem, and he refused to disqualify himself. (Seven years later, however, *Newsday* tracked down five of the six judges who had served with Wachtler when he supposedly consulted with them about the propriety of handling Bibbs's estate—Bernard Meyer, Matthew Jasen, Lawrence Cooke, and Dominick Gabrielli—and none of them recalled him ever having brought it up.)[3]

Weiss ended up challenging the will on the grounds of monomania—a difficult claim based, essentially, on the argument that Bibbs was so consumed with hatred for his son that he couldn't think clearly and objectively. Wachtler hired the politically connected (and now defunct) firm of Shea & Gould, which made over a half million dollars in legal fees from the case (and, in 1988, hired Wachtler's daughter Lauren as an associate), to defend the will. Nassau County Surrogate Raymond Radigan, a longtime Wachtler friend who had a son working for Shea & Gould, presided over the case. But it never got to trial. Jimmy, who had initially been offered $200,000 by Wachtler, settled for a tax-free $400,000, and Wachtler remained executor, taking a commission of $525,000, and earning about $13,000 a year for managing the trust.

Bibbs had decided to leave the bulk of Joy's inheritance in a trust fund, to be administered jointly by Wachtler and Honey Wolosoff, Bibbs's third wife. He clearly wanted to ensure that Joy never got her hands directly on the entire bounty. Joy was thirty-nine years old at the time the trust was established and she wasn't even included in the line of trustees. If Wachtler declined or relinquished the job, he had, under the terms of Bibbs's will, total authority to appoint his own successor. If Sol died or became disabled prior to appointing a successor, his daughter Lauren would take over. If Lauren was unable to serve, a bank would serve as successor trustee. Bibbs suspected that Joy was incapable of managing the fortune, and attempted to assure that she would never get the opportunity.

Joy didn't mind having Wachtler in control, but she despised the idea of having Honey involved. She asked Wachtler to find a way to get her removed. Wachtler succeeded—ceremoniously presenting Joy with the papers making him sole trustee on April 8, 1985, her birthday—and becoming, in her eyes, a heroic figure who could achieve anything.[4]

Years later, when Wachtler was a criminal defendant guilty of harassing Joy and her teenage daughter, and awaiting sentencing, the issues regarding Bibbs's estate and the trusts reemerged in an ugly way, with Joy claiming Sol was using the trust in an attempt to control her and with Sol claiming that Joy was a spendthrift who could and would waste the fortune in a matter of days. Regardless, it was the trust that thrust together an odd couple: Joy, the thrice-married college dropout whose life had always lacked focus; Sol, the suave and sophisticated judge and family man whose life seemed a perfectly choreographed production. Sol brought focus into Joy's life, and she brought him affection and adoration.

Joy was married for the first time in 1969 to a man named Richard Simons (no relation to the judge who would serve with Wachtler on the Court of Appeals), who had been a friend of her stepbrother, Van.[5] Bibbs set him up developing land in St. Petersburg, Florida—ironically, property Bibbs had purchased from Wachtler's father.[6] The marriage lasted only a few years before Joy moved back to Kings Point— F. Scott Fitzgerald's "West Egg"—where she met a man named David Paul.[7] Joy and David eloped, but their marriage lasted only ninety days. When Joy met her third husband, Jeffrey Silverman, he was married and had two children. Jeffrey left his wife and married Joy in 1977. But by the time Bibbs died, Joy was unhappy in the marriage, convinced that Jeffrey was cheating on her.[8] At the same time, Sol and his wife, Joan, were growing apart, their long marriage stale from neglect on both of their parts.

Joy began to show up regularly at Wachtler's chambers in Mineola, at first to discuss the trust, but eventually to talk about her personal life. He became her advisor, her friend, her confidant, as did Sol's oldest daughter, Lauren. Wachtler, clearly flattered by the attentions of this attractive woman seventeen years his junior—he was fifty-six, she thirty-nine—was a tad baffled, and a bit scared. In his view, Joy was openly courting him, but he had always been true to Joan. Nevertheless, a relationship blossomed between the two: Sol, the wise, father figure, basking in the unconditional adulation of an adoring daughter; Joy the dutiful daughter and pupil, who would take the teacher places he would never have gone on his own. "My own father, he abandoned me after my parents' divorce, when I was three, and my first stepfather—I loved him so much—he died of leukemia when I was twelve, and my second stepfather, that was Bibbs Wolosoff, he left me a lot of money but he never would legally adopt me," Joy said. "So I guess Sol was Daddy. I guess he was just the perfect daddy. And he was starved for my affection—he hadn't really been touched by a woman for years. We were both so lonely."[9]

They met secretly, traveling together on what were ostensibly business trips, or spending nights at Sol's house outside Albany. But often, Sol needed to find something, anything, to keep Joy busy. He had an extraordinarily active professional life; she had nothing to do, except shop. Sol encouraged Joy to get involved in politics. "She reminded me that she had no college degree and no business skills or experience," Wachtler noted in his diary. "It occurred to me, in an instant, that she had more than enough qualifications for a political career."

Joy liked the idea of politics and, with Sol's encouragement, joined the Bush for President Campaign in early 1988. Joy enthusiastically joined up, but a week later called Wachtler in a panic: Al D'Amato had told her she was making a mistake; that Bob Dole, not George Bush, would be the 1988 candidate. Wachtler told her to stick with Bush, convinced that the vice president would get the nod, and equally convinced that the candidate would well remember an early supporter named Joy Silverman.[10] As usual, Wachtler's political instincts were right.

"Although I had known Sol since I was a child, he now became the guiding force in my life," Silverman told New York magazine. "He introduced me to Republican politics."[11]

When Joy grew impatient with her menial role as an obscure campaign aide, Sol reminded her that money was the lifeblood of politics and suggested that she get financially involved. She did. Joy got her husband to give Bush $100,000 in her name and another $100,000 from his company, Ply Gem, making them part of a select group of contributors.[12] That raised Joy's value and she began to garner more active roles in the campaign, as a true insider and organizer. Around the same time, Wachtler was looking for a way to end the dangerous liaison and had his secretary, Carol Mason, reserve a spot at a Westchester County restaurant, where he planned to put a stop to their relationship; but he could not bring himself to do so and continued the affair, though consumed by guilt.

After Bush won the 1988 election, Wachtler was eager for Joy to maintain the contacts she had made, in part because he was still hoping for a Supreme Court appointment and in part because he was seriously eyeing the governor's mansion. He had her write a proposal—actually, *he* wrote the proposal—to Lee Atwater, chairman of the Republican National Committee, suggesting ways to bolster the Republican party in New York and perhaps knock out Mario Cuomo. But when Atwater simply encouraged Joy to keep raising money, Wachtler told her to go directly to the president.

Bush, who had included Joy in a strategy session at Camp David, offered her an ambassadorship to Barbados in March 1989. Wachtler spent weeks learning, and then teaching Joy, everything imaginable about the Caribbean island. Regardless, Joy took a beating from Senator Paul Sarbanes, a Maryland Democrat, who publicly pointed out that her only real qualification was raising money for Republicans, and she was forced to withdraw. With Joy depressed over the Sarbanes incident, Sol was reluctant to leave, and the relationship continued.

Wachtler finally decided to leave his wife and told her he would be doing so after Labor Day of 1990. Sol had been so distracted for so long, and it had been years since they had made love, so Joan agreed a trial separation might be a good idea. Wachtler planned to live at his house outside Albany and, after a while, allow himself to be seen publicly with Joy. But that summer, Joan got sick and was confined to the house for an extended period. When the doctor suggested that Joan get out of the city for a while, so Sol brought her, not Joy, to the East Greenbush house. Joy was livid.

At the end of the summer of 1990, Sol's life really began to unravel. One day, as he was out walking, his left leg collapsed beneath him and he fell to the ground. When he attempted to walk, he noticed that the left foot drooped and wouldn't respond. Terrified, Wachtler feared he had a brain tumor. Although Sol sought medical assistance, he refused to undergo a magnetic resonance imaging (MRI) test (he suffers from claustrophobia and cannot tolerate closed spaces) which would have alleviated his concerns.

Convinced he was dying a slow and undignified death, Wachtler pictured his life deteriorating. At dinner one night, Sol told Joy that doctors at the Mayo Clinic had discovered an inoperable brain tumor—a lie—and that they should stop seeing each other so that he would not burden her. Joy, however, did not want to leave him in that condition and their relationship continued.[13]

Meanwhile, Sol managed to convince himself, as well as Joy, that the brain tumor was real. He called a neurologist friend, Dr. Ronald Cranford, and told him about a hypothetical friend with a brain tumor. Later he called radiosurgeon Itzhak D. Goldberg and oncologist Kanti Rai, telling them that he needed information related to a case to be decided by the court. All of them confirmed that the symptoms—Wachtler's symptoms, of course—were consistent with a brain tumor. Wachtler read everything he could get his hands on about brain tumors and became profoundly depressed. He scheduled an appointment for an MRI at UCLA Hospital in San Francisco, but was more terrified of the test than the possible result, consumed with a claustrophobic fear of being buried alive.

"I can still feel the panic that seized me—having the hinged lid closed, fighting for breath and then hearing the clumps of earth, one at a time, landing on my coffin," Wachtler noted in his diary. He wouldn't go through with the MRI. The same thing happened at another hospital in California and at Johns Hopkins University medical center in Baltimore.

Over the next several months, Wachtler continued in private torment, unsure of himself for the first time in his life and feeling useless. During the summer of 1991, Sol's life was in turmoil as he was unable or unwilling to make a commitment to either Joan or Joy. Joy, growing tired of his vacilla-tion, started to date David Samson, a lawyer and partner in the Roseland, New Jersey, firm of Wolff and Samson. Sol didn't know the identity of the new lover, only what Joy had told him one night at the Stanhope bar—that he was richer and more handsome than Wachtler.

At the same time, Wachtler was fighting with Governor Cuomo over the budget; fretting about the fact that he had to lay off five hundred new employees, mostly minorities hired as part of his work force diversity program; and wondering how long it would be before the suspected brain tumor reduced the chief judge to a mental incompetent in diapers. Meanwhile, his beloved mother-in-law and the wives of two close colleagues were dying of cancer, thus adding to his own sense of morbidity. In addition, he was making up to three public speaking appearances a day—lunches, breakfasts, dinners, editorial boards, commissions. It was endless.

That July, Wachtler was invited by Jerry Finkelstein, owner of the *New York Law Journal*, to spend an evening on his yacht, a stag outing that included Jim Fox, head of the New York office of the FBI; U.S. Attorney Andy Maloney of the Eastern District of New York; Bob Price, chief executive officer of Price Communications; New York City Council President Andy Stein; and Jim Finkelstein, editor of the *New York Law Journal* and the *National Law Journal*. The group vir-tually convinced Wachtler to run for governor in 1992.[14]

"Let me tell you something," Wachtler told reporters shortly after, speculating on a possible race between the chief judge and Cuomo, and eager to know something about Wachtler's personal life.

It would be very dull. If you ever looked into my back-ground you would find that I have lived a life that the media would find boring. I served in the military. I did not dodge the draft. I adore my family. I have never used drugs, here or abroad. I do spend time smelling the roses—and I do inhale [an obvious reference to then presidential candidate Bill Clinton's assertion that he had experimented with marijuana but had not inhaled]. I paid for my own headboard. None of my children have yet written a book about their childhood called *Judgie Dearest* or *There Was a Justice in Court But No Justice at Home*. And the club I belong to is so unrestrictive that our president is a cross-dressing African-American female named Murray Farkas.

Classic, witty Wachtler.

In private, however, Wachtler was coming unglued, consumed with fears over his suspected tumor, tormented by Joy's new love, and taking a host of over-the-counter medications: stimulants to keep him awake, sedatives to help him sleep, pain medications to combat headaches, plus various prescriptions.

By October, he had lost had lost fifteen pounds. Joan noted in an October 31 diary entry: "Something is terribly wrong. He's acting strangely. Very depressed, irritable, emotional. Moves his clothes in and out. Spending weekends away. He feels he's dying. Loves me but can't live with me until he gets his head together. Doesn't understand what's happening to him. Feels disassociated with himself. Feels a beautiful day is ugly. Hasn't slept in weeks. . . . Doesn't eat at all—drug related?"[15]

Wachtler's clerks, too, and Matt Crosson, his chief administrator, were growing alarmed. The chief stopped preparing for cases and no longer even read Michael Trainor's handiwork; Trainor the clerk had become Trainor the judge, writing full opinions that Wachtler barely reviewed. He began telling off-color jokes in public. He became furious when he learned that a favorite colleague, Judith Kaye, would be addressing a bar group, and perhaps stealing some of his thunder. He berated staffers whose memos were too long. He was obsessed with his appearance, and would occasionally flex his biceps to show off his physique to other judges.[16] Once, he summoned the entire court staff into the courtroom, spoke to them for an hour, and said he loved them. They left, scratching their heads and not knowing quite what to make of the chief's performance. Several figured Wachtler had called the meeting to announce he was resigning from the court to run for governor, but when push came to shove he got emotional and couldn't do it.

Joan pestered Sol to see a psychiatrist. He refused—again, fearing news leaks—but did give in enough to see an internist, who quickly diagnosed depression. The internist (not knowing that another doctor had prescribed Tenuate, an amphetamine-like drug that can cause mania; codeine; and Celestone, a steroid used for headaches) prescribed an antidepressant called Pamelor, and Halcion, a sedative, with strict instructions not to take anything else. The toxic and unrestricted use of these drugs would have a profound impact on Wachtler's behavior.

By the end of 1991, Wachtler was miserable. His relationship with Joy was over. His marriage was in rigor mortis. He was concerned about his health, convinced he was dying, and taking a dangerous mixture of drugs. He had to fire several hundred newly hired employees of the court system because of budget constraints and "found himself ruminating over the fate of people who, he felt, had trusted him and had gone forward to purchase homes, cars, consummate relationships and make changes in their lives. He felt personally responsible for what he believed to be their predicament and disappointment."[17]

For the next year, Sol was lost in space, ensconced in a world of bizarre fantasy in which he imagined all would be right if only Joy needed him again. He devised a plot to discredit Joy's new boyfriend, David Samson, and to scare her back to his embrace. He exploited friendships and abused the power of his office to further his scheme. In mid-October, Wachtler had the deputy clerk of the court, an honest and decent man named Stuart Cohen, dig up articles about Samson. Cohen assumed the chief judge had a legitimate aim and didn't inquire as to his reason. Likewise with Leonard A. Weiss, the presiding justice of the Appellate Division in Albany. Since Samson had been admitted to the bar in Albany, Weiss, as presiding justice, had access to his confidential file. Wachtler asked for it, and Weiss dutifully agreed to retrieve what should have been a sealed file.* "When the chief judge of the state asks you for something, what are you going say, 'what do you want it for?' "[18]

Wachtler also began and maintained a file of materials relating to Samson's representation of a company attempting to build an incinerator in Linden, New Jersey. He poked through Department of Motor Vehicle records, real estate recordings, and other materials, all in an effort to destroy his adversary. He became a one-man good cop/ bad cop routine, sometimes adopting the persona of "David Purdy," a fictitious ornery Texan and the toothless, diaper-clad victim of diabetes, and other times playing the role of "Theresa O'Connor," a devout Catholic. Wachtler appropriated "Purdy's" name from the son of a former secretary, and borrowed "O'Connor's" name from one of his cases.

---

*The file had been stripped and contained nothing that Wachtler could use to further his scheme except a copy of Samson's signature, which he later forged. Wachtler insists he did not abuse his office since virtually nothing in the file furthered his scheme, but the fact remains that he never would have received the file had he not been chief judge.

Using the "David Purdy" character, Wachtler posed as a private detective and called Samson's wife, offering to sell her information on his husband's new girlfriend. She hung up on him but he called back the next day, providing Joy Silverman's unlisted home telephone numbers in New York City and on Long Island. He told her about Jeffrey Silverman and his business, and he told her that he had spied on Samson and Joy and had seen them making love in front of Joy's teenage daughter.[19]

In February of 1992, Wachtler repeatedly sent Samson's wife notes, forging her husband's signature (which he got from the bar registration form) and hoping that she would become reconciled with David. By April, he was calling an activist against the incinerator plant in New Jersey, Beatrice Bernzott, claiming to be Samson's associate, and then he called Samson's office, claiming to be Bernzott's husband and accusing the lawyer of threatening her. Finally, posing as Samson, he made a series of collect calls—all unaccepted—to Bernzott.[20]

Three weeks later, Wachtler turned on Joy. Forging Samson's signature, he began sending obscene and threatening notes to Joy and her fourteen-year-old daughter, Jessica. On May 11, 1992, Wachtler mailed a condom to Jessica and a note that read: "I look forward to visiting you this summer . . . school should be great fun for you. BUT YOU MUST BE CAREFUL. The enclosed should be used by your boyfriend before you do "IT." . . . P.S. I have a picture of your mother doing "IT" which I well send you soon."[21]* Around the same time, Wachtler contacted Joy's divorce lawyer, Norman Sheresky, and suggested that she would get a larger maintenance award if he suddenly cut off her trust payments. Then, in a June 8, 1992, telephone

---

*This letter, for which Wachtler has been most criticized, was never received by Jessica Silverman. Wachtler has always claimed he sent it at a time and in a manner in which he knew that it would be intercepted by Joy, as, in fact, it was.

call to Silverman, which Joy taped, Wachtler responded with uncharacteristic arrogance to her query whether that scheme would work, whether the divorce judge would think she was finagling for more money.

"And if he points to the trust—let them ask me, let the judge, heh heh, let the presiding judge over the trial say to me, 'Are you doing this collusively in order to prevent her from getting money so she gets more by this, is it collusively?'

"Absolutely not, your honor."

"And you think they're going to believe me? You're damn well right they are going to believe me."[22]

At the time, Joy was receiving $9,000 weekly in tax-free income, $5,000 that she was getting from Jeffrey and $4,000 from the trust. Since she wasn't spending all the money, Wachtler figured a court would find that she didn't need the entire $5,000 from Jeffrey. The idea he bounced off Sheresky was designed to cut Joy's income to her needs, and force Jeffrey to pay for her "needs."

Two weeks later, Wachtler's behavior became even more bizarre. He posed as "Theresa O'Connor," the devout Catholic opposing the New Jersey incinerator project. In letters to federal and local prosecutors in New Jersey, "O'Connor" reported that "she" had hired "Purdy" and also Arthur and Irene Seale, who had just been charged with the kidnapping and murder of Exxon executive Sidney Reso. The letter revealed that the Seales, who had deposited Reso in a coffin-like box where he died of heart failure, were blackmailing Silverman and Samson, an effort by Wachtler to divert suspicion from himself. Wachtler became so fascinated with the character of "Theresa O'Connor" that he eventually drove to the town of Linden, where he imagined she lived, visited the church where he imagined she prayed, and mailed a letter from a mailbox from which emanated her "aura."

Meanwhile, the state court system was careening out of Wachtler's control. On the Court of Appeals, there were more dissents, more split cases, and far less leadership. Additionally, Wachtler was unable to concentrate on his administrative initiatives.

"He was completely unable to focus," Crosson recalled. "And his behavior became more unfocused as that year, 1992, went along."[23]

The diabolical plot against Silverman continued throughout the summer and fall as Wachtler became obsessed with convincing Joy that he was not responsible for the threats and that "Purdy" actually existed and was the one harassing both Silverman and Samson. Wachtler went to Samson's apartment in New York City on August 7 wearing a cowboy outfit, and told the doorman to report that David Purdy from Houston, Texas, had been by to see him. He made a similar visit to Silverman's apartment on September 12, 1992, delivering a typewritten blackmail letter. He became paranoiacally suspicious that Joy knew he was the culprit when his mother-in-law died in his arms on September 27, 1992, and Silverman, uncharacteristically, failed to show up at the funeral or even send a note. Wachtler was certain that was a sign that she knew.[24] Whether she did or not, the incident that brought the FBI into the picture was "Purdy's" threat to kidnap Joy's beloved daughter, Jessica.

Alarmed, Joy called FBI Director William Sessions, who initiated an investigation out of New Jersey. The note threatening to kidnap Joy's daughter, and its similarity to one written by Arthur Seale in the Reso case, commanded the attention of U.S. Attorney Michael Chertoff, who had a new, tapped telephone line wired into Silverman's apartment. On October 3, 1992, the FBI intercepted a call from Wachtler's mobile phone. But Chertoff had to be certain that it was

Wachtler, and not an aide or someone else with access to his phones, or an accomplice, who was making the threats.[25]

"Here's the problem: I think it was sometime in October, late September or October, when we first tracked a call back to his car," Chertoff said.

> But given who he was, you had to exclude the possibility that it was a staff person or somebody who had access to his telephones. You really had to have an ironclad case, because the one thing you can't afford to have happen is go in, make an accusation, have him deny it and then not be able to prove it. Then where are you at? One thing, hopefully, a decade of experience prosecuting cases tell you is if you are going to go in a case that is going to be, let's be honest, a very visible, controversial case, with someone who has got a strong presumption of innocence because of who they are and their status, you better make sure you are 100 percent there on the evidence, because if you are 70 percent there on the evidence, you are going to have a very big problem proving your case.[26]

Meanwhile, Wachtler seemed to be losing control professionally. Although he had always had difficulty remembering and reciting statistics—and tended to make them up when he couldn't recall them—his speeches on the court system and court initiatives took on a surreal quality. "A week before he got arrested, he convened this group," Crosson recalled. "He didn't get a fact correct. After it was over, I said, 'Were you talking about *our* court system? Sol, you weren't even in the parking lot of the ball park.' "[27] Still Crosson chalked it up to stress, and didn't think much of it.

"He was acting oddly," Crosson acknowledged. "But I attributed it to—and I regret this—fatigue, stress. It just never occurred to me that Sol Wachtler could be experiencing severe mental illness. He was acting strange, talking about running for governor, unable to focus. At that level of government, you eat fatigue for lunch. You are exhausted all the time. You are under stress all of the time. I attributed it to that."[28]

Desperate for "Purdy" to scare Joy back into his arms, Wachtler dangerously escalated the level of harassment by making extortion threats. Using a voice-altering device, Wachtler demanded $20,000 and reiterated his threat to kidnap Jessica. "You're gonna get a letter from me," he growled in a 10:00 A.M., October 7, 1992, call, "you better listen to every word of it and do what it tells you to do or you're not gonna see your daughter again, you hear me? I'm a sick and desperate man. I need the money and you'll be hearing from me."[29]

On October 9, 1992, "Purdy" called Silverman: "I'm wearing a diaper now. I've lost my teeth. I weigh over two hundred pounds. I'm a dying man." Wachtler's longtime secretary and close friend, Dorothy Young, had recently died after suffering from diabetes and having to wear a diaper. Her son-in-law was named David Purdy.

On October 28, 1992, "Purdy" called from a pay telephone outside a Boy Scout complex in Roslyn, New York. He again demanded $20,000 and told Silverman to deposit the money in a Manhattan stairway. "If you don't do that," he threatened, "if you fuck up . . . I promise you, it will cost you over $200,000 to get your daughter back. How does that suit ya?"[30] After five weeks under FBI surveillance, Wachtler had finally committed a potential felony, attempted extortion.

The FBI, tailing the judge, lifted his fingerprints from the telephone used to place the call. Still, they held off on making an arrest. Agents trailed Wachtler to Louisville, Kentucky, where he was speaking in early November, and followed him around for two days as he made repeated calls to

Silverman and Samson's wife (offering to sell her revealing pictures of her husband with Joy). They watched him buy two adult movies and two decks of Raunch-O-Rama pornographic playing cards in Louisville and tailed him back to New York.

On the night of November 6, 1992, Wachtler appeared at a dinner at the New York State Bar Association, delivering a characteristically witty and knowledgeable 35- to 45-minute speech before heading over to his chambers at the Court of Appeals. In the seclusion of his chambers, "Purdy" emerged again, typing three letters: one to be delivered to Joy if she left the money, one to be delivered if she failed to leave the money, and an anonymous letter to New York tax authorities suggesting they look into David Samson's finances.

The next morning, Saturday, November 7, Wachtler left his home outside Albany and drove toward New York City. He stopped at a pay phone and, with the FBI watching, placed several calls to European Hair Designers in New York. He identified himself as David Samson and asked the hairdresser to retrieve an envelope for him (the envelope containing the $20,000, put there by the FBI) from the basement steps next to the salon. At 10:15 A.M., Joy's doorman delivered the envelope. Fifteen minutes later, the hairdresser retrieved it. Shortly after that, Wachtler called, learned the envelope had been delivered, and told the hairdresser that a "Miss Heather" would be in for it later.

Wachtler continued on toward New York City, stopping at a supermarket in Scarsdale, where he discarded one of the two contingency letters, the one prepared in case Joy did not leave the money. It read: "YOU STUPID LOUSY CUNT. I'M GOING BACK TO TEXAS NOW. YOU BETTER HOPE I DIE SOON BECAUSE [IF] I DON'T YOU'LL WISH YOU WERE DEAD. YOU BETTER KISS YOUR DAUGHTER GOOD NIGHT EVERY NIGHT."[31]

He enclosed a photocopy of the back of a Raunch-O-Rama playing card. The FBI retrieved the note from the garbage.

After a visit with his daughter Lauren (who knew about the affair) and his grandchildren in Scarsdale, Wachtler drove into the city. He parked his car in Manhattan and, after dressing in a cowboy hat and dark, full-length coat, hailed a taxi. He gave the driver $10 and told him to deliver an envelope to Silverman's apartment. The FBI intercepted the "Purdy" letter, which read: "Are you stupid or do you think I'm stupid. I may be a shitkicker but I'm not a dumb shitkicker." He informed Joy that he was going back to Texas and taking the blackmail pictures with him. Although dying, "Purdy" said he might be back, and if he returned he would demand another $200,000 for the pictures.

A short while later, while he was driving home—in the opposite direction of where the money was deposited—teams of FBI agents pulled Wachtler over on the Long Island Expressway. At first, he thought they were terrorists or kidnappers, but he quickly learned he was in the custody of federal agents.

"Do you know what the worst part is?" Wachtler stated. "The judges! What will the judges think? They looked up to me. . . . Oh my God, oh my God. I could have been governor."[32]

At that exact moment, Joan was in Saks Fifth Avenue buying a new dress, the one she intended to wear when Sol announced his candidacy. That dream, however, was never realized.

Three days later, Wachtler called the senior associate judge and, sobbing uncontrollably, resigned from the court. "I told him I forgave him for what he had done," Judge Simons recalled. "If there was a man alive who could've listened to him and not forgiven him, I don't want to know that man."[33]

There was such a man. And his name was Michael Chertoff. The son of a rabbi and a Harvard Law School graduate who had clerked for Supreme Court Justice William Brennan,[34] Chertoff, only thirty-eight, had handled organized crime cases for U.S. Attorney, and eventual New York City mayor, Rudolph Giuliani, before switching parties and getting the top job in New Jersey. He was tough and experienced and was credited with nailing the Seales in the Reso case and negotiating a $15 million settlement with Exxon for a 1990 oil spill. Although most of the crimes Wachtler committed occurred in New York, authorities feared that the "good old boy network" would spring to his rescue, and so they diverted the case to Chertoff. Chertoff hung on to Wachtler like a pit bull.

Chertoff wanted Wachtler locked up in the Metropolitan Correctional Center for the weekend, arguing that the chief judge was a danger to Joy and her daughter. Paul D. Montclare, attorney and Wachtler's son-in-law—he is married to Lauren—worked out a compromise whereby Wachtler would be confined to the psychiatric unit of Long Island Jewish Hospital. At the hospital, where he was on the board of directors, Wachtler was confronted by his wife.

"My wife embraced me," Wachtler recalled on the *Oprah* television talk show of April 3, 1997, "and said, 'I love you very much.' I did not deserve that.... My family was victimized by me beyond measure."

On Chertoff's insistence, Wachtler was shackled to his bed and guarded by two armed marshals. "The very worst moment was when I was taken in chains through the corridors of a hospital where I was a trustee and then brought into a hospital room where my family was and chained to a bed," Wachtler said. "I once said to my children: 'I will never be able to leave you a lot of money because you don't make money in public service. But the one legacy I have is my good name and reputation.' And there I was, standing before them in chains."[35]

After three days in the hospital, Wachtler was led into a

lower Manhattan courtroom in handcuffs. Under the terms of a two-page detention agreement insisted upon by Chertoff, Wachtler could leave his condominium only for visits to his attorney and doctors and for court appearances. He was required to hire a private guard to watch him and report to prosecutors any visitors outside of his family. He could have no contact with Silverman or her daughter. With the government camping out in his house, Wachtler began to plot his defense.

Wachtler hired as his lead defense attorney—though son-in-law Paul Montclare would remain involved—Charles Stillman, a name partner in the thirteen-lawyer firm of Stillman, Friedman & Shaw and a dignified and experienced defense lawyer who would represent his famous client with as little fanfare as possible (Stillman had earlier represented Reverend Sun Myung Moon, who was convicted of federal tax charges). Stillman spent weeks having Wachtler evaluated by teams of mental health experts in an attempt to prove that his client, if not legally insane, was incapacitated. He attempted to negotiate a plea bargain under which Wachtler would plead not guilty by reason of insanity and escape a jail term by promising to undergo counseling and perform community service. Chertoff refused to consider any deal that didn't result in a prison sentence, and took his case to a grand jury. He subpoenaed Lauren Wachtler (not ruling out the possibility—since dismissed—that she was somehow involved in the plot[36]), the court's deputy clerk, and Wachtler's secretary and aides.

On February 1, 1993, Chertoff secured an indictment charging Wachtler with one count of interstate travel to promote an extortion scheme, three counts of mailing threatening communications, and one count of making false statements to a federal agency. With those charges, Wachtler was looking at sixteen years in prison.

Stillman and Chertoff worked feverishly for an angle and, when both had one, a plea bargain was finally reached. Chertoff threatened to subpoena the entire Court of Appeals to testify to Wachtler's lucidity, a scenario the now former judge found intolerable. Stillman, in turn, threatened to bring forth evidence that Silverman knew all along that Wachtler was the culprit, diminishing the image she and Chertoff tried to cultivate of an innocent, ignorant, and terrified victim.

Elaine Sheresky, the wife of Joy's divorce lawyer and her close friend, said in an interview with Jack Newfield of the *New York Post* that Silverman wasn't quite the scared bunny she pretended to be.

"In the first half of 1992, Joy told me she knew Sol was writing the harassing letters," Newfield wrote, quoting Sheresky.

> Joy told me this in a phone call she made to me. She knew it was Sol because the letters made reference to the contents of her apartment and Sol had been there and they had just broken up. Joy is being vindictive. She is used to getting her way. She did the chasing of him. She was the predator. She followed him to Albany.
>
> Joy is enjoying the scandal of it. She loves the excitement and glamour. She told me she might write a book about the case. The day Sol Wachtler was arrested she called me and was all excited. The next day she called me and asked if I thought the pictures of her in the newspaper were flattering enough.[37]

Meanwhile, Joy and her attorney, Carl Rauh, were demanding that Sol resign as trustee—an entirely reasonable demand given the circumstances. However, Joy wanted sole control of the money, and Wachtler felt that was contrary to Bibbs's wishes. Wachtler was unwilling to give her total control, a move Chertoff characterized as an attempt to maintain power over Silverman.[38]

Various proceedings ensued, with Lauren Wachtler called to testify. In an affidavit, Lauren told the court in no uncertain terms that Bibbs was "uncomfortable" with the notion of Joy controlling the money. "He stated that Joy's profligate spending was of extreme concern to him," Lauren wrote, asking that she, as the successor next in line, be named trustee. She in turn planned to follow the succession line established by Bibbs, resign, and place the trust in the hands of Chase Manhattan Bank.

Silverman objected to using the bank because the bank's fees would be double that of a private accountant. Her attorneys stepped up the effort to get the Wachtlers to give up control of the money, publicly releasing copies of the lurid letters and cards—including the infamous "condom communication" to Jessica Silverman. Eventually, the bank and Joy's accountant, Bernard Lippert, were named co-trustees.

At precisely 11:42 A.M. on March 31, 1993, the Associated Press flashed a "NewsAlert" bulletin announcing that Wachtler was pleading guilty to a single count of "transmitting in interstate commerce threats to kidnap." In other words, he sent a threatening letter through the mail. "Your Honor, I am pleading guilty," Wachtler told Judge Thompson in clear tones on the morning of March 31, 1993. He went on to explain what he did and why he did it.

> After my relationship with Joy Silverman ended in the summer of 1991, I began a course of activity aimed at causing Ms. Silverman to seek my help and protection. To do this, I hoped to put Ms. Silverman in fear that her reputation would be ruined by publicizing her relationship with David Samson. In addition, I began to attempt to find

ways to discredit David Samson, so that Ms. Silverman would seek out my help instead of his in coping with the threats to her reputation. . . .

My activity began with a series of hang-up calls to Ms. Silverman in the fall of 1991. When that did not cause her to contact me for help, I called Elaine Samson [David Samson's wife] and stated that I was "David Purdy," a private detective, and that I had information about her husband and Joy Silverman. Later, the Purdy character conveyed to Ms. Silverman that there were compromising pictures of Ms. Silverman and Mr. Samson. . . . I also sent letters to Ms. Silverman and her daughter. I signed some of those cards and letters with a signature similar to the one David Samson used to his attorney registration form to try to better convince Ms. Silverman that there really was a Purdy and that he had compromising pictures. I also had Purdy write about certain details of Ms. Silverman's daily life which were, based on my recollections.

Wachtler told the court that in the early summer of 1992, when he became convinced that Joy suspected him, he invented the "Theresa O'Connor" character and wrote two anonymous letters to authorities blaming "Purdy" and the Seales for the threats.

In August 1992, still not having been contacted by Ms. Silverman and believing that she still suspected me and in order to remove that suspicion, I began escalating the activity, eventually demanding $20,000 for the supposedly compromising pictures and ultimately . . . I conveyed threatening communications in interstate commerce to kidnap her daughter if she did not comply with my request. I at no time intended to kidnap or harm in the slightest way Ms. Silverman's daughter and I never wanted to nor did I take any money from Ms. Silverman. . . . At the time I made the threats . . . I was conscious and aware of my actions. . . . I am deeply ashamed and sorry for what I have done to others—Ms. Silverman, my family, and those who entrusted New York State's court system to my care. I know that I cannot ever make up for these acts.

After the plea, the various parties engaged in a chess match: Wachtler's attorneys filed documents in an attempt to minimize his conduct and his penalty; Chertoff filed documents in an attempt to maximize his conduct and penalty.

Chertoff's memorandum portrayed Wachtler as a scheming fraud who abused his power and the trust that had been placed in him. He ridiculed Wachtler's claims of mental instability.

From the beginning, Sol Wachtler sought to portray his campaign to torment Joy Silverman as if he were merely a passive instrument in the grip of mysterious forces. In fact, Wachtler's conduct was cold, calculating, and fully explicable in terms of a rational—if wrongful—desire to manipulate Ms. Silverman while concealing his identity. . . .

That Wachtler's crime was motivated by profound jealousy and the pain of involuntary parting does not mitigate or excuse the crime, or constitute a mental illness deserving of consideration by this court. Law and morality exist precisely to moderate and restrain emotional appetites and desires. The lust for Ms. Silverman no more mitigates this crime than the lust for money mitigates a pecuniary offense.[39]

Stillman responded forcefully, asking the court to take into consideration Wachtler's lifetime of good works, dedication to his family, and efforts to eradicate racial and gender bias in the court systems. He included testimonials from family, friends, employees, neighbors, clergy, educators, law-makers, philanthropists, and judges. He pointed out that Wachtler immediately took full responsibility for his conduct, resigned from the bar, and "already paid dearly for his crime" by the wrath he had brought upon himself and his family. Stillman wrote:

> Given the circumstances of this case, the loss and punishment that he and his family have already suffered as a result of the one and only wrongful act in this 63-year-old man's life, his previously unblemished record, his devotion to his family and community, his lifetime of good works, both private and public, which have comforted, improved, and inspired the lives of so many . . . society's interests will best be served by leniency. We ask not for special treatment of this man because he was a judge, we simply ask for fair treatment for a special man.[40]

Under federal sentencing laws, Wachtler was facing a sentence in the range of twelve to eighteen months. On September 9, 1993, Judge Thompson split the range, imposing a term of fifteen months. Wachtler's request to serve the time at a minimum-security prison in Florida was denied and, two days before his surrender date, the Bureau of Prisons ordered him to report on September 28, 1993, to Butner, North Carolina, a stone's throw from where he had lived unhappily as a child.

The Federal Correctional Facility at Butner is a medium-security facility about thirty-five miles north of Raleigh. The former chief judge of the highest court in New York state was given a new title, Prisoner No. 32571054, and ordered to strip for the mandatory search.

Understandably, Wachtler was miserable, but soon settled into a more or less comfortable routine; that is, until a bizarre incident on November 21, 1993, shattered his relative peace: he was stabbed in the back.

According to Wachtler's version, he was resting on his cot, half asleep and listening to his radio with earphones when an unknown assailant stabbed him twice. Initially, authorities accused Wachtler of stabbing himself since they couldn't identify the culprit, but eventually backed off that hypothesis. Regardless, he was transferred out of Butner five days later and flown to a medical facility in Rochester, Minnesota. Initially, Wachtler was kept in solitary confinement for observation, but later he was moved to the general population and locked in a small cell with three other prisoners.

"Maybe God will reward me as he did Job, with 14,000 sheep, 6,000 camels, oxen and mules," Wachtler wrote from prison. "Just my luck, he'll deliver them to me in my 12 × 14 cell."[41]

After thirteen months in prison, Wachtler was released to spend the final two months at a halfway house. He completed his term doing five hundred hours of community service by counseling offenders associated with the Education and Assistance Corporation of Brooklyn, knowing that the best years of his life—his years as reigning monarch of the Court of Appeals—had passed him by.

Notes

1. Court documents filed in connection with the case of *James K. Wolosoff* v. *Alvin B. Wolosoff*, 1975–76.
2. Ibid.

3. Leonard Levitt and Joe Calderone, "Contested Will: Wachtler Was Executor Despite Ethics Rules," *Newsday*, November 15, 1992, p. 47.

4. Wachtler's recollections, relayed in various conversations with the author.

5. Linda Wolfe, *Double Life: The Shattering Affair between Chief Judge Sol Wachtler and Socialite Joy Silverman* (New York: Pocket Books, 1994), p. 57.

6. Ibid., p. 61.

7. Ibid., p. 77.

8. Ibid., p. 102.

9. Lucinda Franks, "The Judge and I," *New York* magazine, November 14, 1994, p. 42.

10. Wachtler's recollection, relayed in various conversations with the author.

11. David Goldman, "Shocking, Lurid, and True!" *Biography* magazine, January 1998, p. 18.

12. Federal campaign records. Between 1987 and 1989, Joy had donated $300,000 to Bush and other Republican causes. In 1988 she held a dinner for Barbara Bush at her Southampton home, raising $235,000 from her forty-eight guests.

13. Interview with Wachtler in February 1995.

14. Ibid.

15. Joan Wachtler's undated letter to the sentencing court, approximately May 1, 1993.

16. Interview with a confidential source on September 7, 1997.

17. Report of Dr. Frank T. Miller, who examined Wachtler after his arrest. Dr. Miller's reports is part of the court record.

18. John Caher, "A Look Inside Wachtler's Psyche," Albany *Times Union*, August, 6, 1993, p. A-1.

19. Sentencing memorandum of the United States in *USA* v. *Sol Wachtler*, U.S. District Court, Trenton, N.J., 1993.

20. Ibid.

21. Ibid.

22. Sentencing memorandum.

23. Interview with Matt Crosson on August 20, 1997.

24. Interview with Wachtler in February 1995.

25. Interview with Michael Chertoff, December 1, 1997.

26. Ibid.

27. Interview with Crosson, August 20, 1997.

28. Ibid.

29. Sentencing memorandum of the United States in *USA* v. *Sol Wachtler*, U.S. District Court, Trenton, N.J., 1993.

30. Ibid.

31. Ibid.

32. Ibid.

33. Nicholas Goldberg, "Wachtler Apologizes for Disgrace," *Newsday*, November 13, 1992, p. 5.

34. Mark Litwak, *Courtroom Crusaders: American Lawyers Who Refuse to Fit the Mold* (New York: William Morrow and Co., 1989), pp. 266–67.

35. John Caher, "Wachtler Tries to Leave Kids His Good Name," Albany *Times Union*, February 19, 1995, C-1.

36. Interview with Chertoff on December 1, 1997.

37. Jack Newfield, *New York Post*, March 23, 1993.

38. Sentencing memorandum.

39. Ibid.

40. Defendant's sentencing memorandum.

41. Letter from Wachtler to the author, August 3, 1994.

CHAPTER 5

The Chief

The chief judge is often described as *primus inter pares*, or first among equals. His vote is worth no more than the others. He has no more say, theoretically anyway, in case selection than the six associate judges on the Court of Appeals. Certainly, however, the chief is in a unique position to influence the outcome of cases through his interaction with his colleagues, in the leadership role he assumes in conference, and in his public image.

A chief who is a good social leader attends to the judges' emotional needs and seeks to mold a cohesive court. A chief who is a taskmaster concentrates on the opinions. Some chiefs in the 150-year history of the Court of Appeals were intellectual leaders, coldly steering the court's juridical progress. They led sound, sober, and generally dour courts. Others were less strong on the law and better suited to attending to the judges' emotional needs. They maintained the *esprit de corps*, and in doing so fostered both cohesion and progression, but rarely greatness. Rare is a chief—like Sol Wachtler—who combined both.

Wachtler's impact lies not only in his rulings and writings, as visionary and dramatic as they could sometimes be, but also in the force of his personality. "He led, and you followed, because you thought it was the right thing to do, because he convinced you it was the right thing to do," said a former colleague.[1] Another added: "He was forceful, intelligent. He had a very quick mind, and he was *extremely* persuasive. He was a very good advocate for his side of an issue."[2]

Although Wachtler could, and would, engage in intense backroom fights, he could also be a consummate coalition builder (and he usually was). Wachtler was willing to compromise for the sake of presenting an image that the court was cohesive, even when it wasn't. He was intolerant of dissent. He wanted seven judges to speak as "a single voice." Consensus was extraordinarily important and the number of dissents dropped sharply after he took control. "You almost have to fall on your sword around here to dissent," complained one judge during the Wachtler years, after the chief had successfully convinced the jurist to join the majority.[3]

Wachtler thought dissents should only be used when there is an unavoidable and irreconcilable difference on a fundamental matter of law, never to vent the spleen—an issue that occasionally put him at odds with a sometimes vociferous dissenter and the judge who would become his closest friend on the court, Joseph W. Bellacosa. Wachtler wanted his court—unlike the fractured U.S. Supreme Court, where the multiple concurring and dissenting opinions raise far more questions than they answer and sometimes seem more aimed toward posterity than resolving the issue at hand—to speak with a firm, unified voice, as often as possible. He discouraged what is known as *dicta*, or judicial meanderings beyond what is needed to resolve the immediate problem.

"Sometimes *dictum* is important," Wachtler said. "Sometimes you can draw hypotheses. But to go out and say, 'This is something not raised and not before us, but we think it is high time it be resolved,' that is something I always felt a legislature would do. I don't think [courts] should set public policy. Sometimes they have to, if the legislature fails to act or acts irrationally, or unconstitutionally. But it should be a last resort."[4]

Once Wachtler took his seat at center court, there was never any doubt whose court it was. Through flattery, or trickery, he usually got reluctant or recalcitrant judges to capitulate or compromise. He would do it himself, settling for half a loaf so that his court could *appear* more cohesive than it really was. He agreed with his former colleague and dear friend, Judge Hugh R. Jones, who retired just before Wachtler became chief, that just "because a judge does not dissent it should not necessarily be understood that the majority opinion expresses his preferred view of the case. By failing to dissent he does represent that the opinion expresses the decision of his court, that he accepts that decision and, if he is in disagreement, that he has concluded that no sufficiently useful purpose would be served by a public disclosure of his disagreement."[5] Wachtler simply thought that a splintered vote let the public a bit too close to the court's inner sanctum, and left the law somewhat unstable.

"Wachtler's expressed emphasis on consensus in decision making harkened back to the Court of Appeals' high prestige era under [Benjamin N.] Cardozo when civility was the norm," explains scholar Luke Bierman. "As a savvy, charismatic, popular chief judge, Wachtler's objective in this regard might well have swayed the court toward agreement. Wachtler's objective for consensus is consistent with his usual votes in the majority, which could have provided leadership by example."[6]

On the other hand, he could be intimidating and manipulative. He stifled dissent through threat and swung judges, and cases, to his side by sheer, raw manipulation. Wachtler was the most masterful politician in the conference room, and he knew it. He maneuvered his court, and the judges on it, with such skill that the judges didn't always know they were being schmoozed.

"He started lavishing praise on me," one former colleague recalled, in a case where that judge was on the *opposite* side of Wachtler. "I now in retrospect know that I was being psyched out. . . . If he had his heart in one, he never ceased pressing for consensus."[7]

Wachtler would go from judge to judge, negotiating and dealing, getting one jurist to delete a paragraph here, another one there, so that a 5-2 decision would become 6-1, or better yet, 7-0. "The court was starting to break up real badly during [Chief Judge Lawrence Cooke's] tenure," Wachtler said.

There was never any real effort made to weld a consensus. My thought was when you go into new areas of law, it is important that the imprint be a strong one. The perception out there when you had a 4-3 decision is a court in a state of flux, that the decision was tentative and could be overturned in a couple of years. I thought it very, very important that in the first few years of the new court we come out as unanimously as possible, and we did that for a while. But that can last only so long and then individual judges want to start carving their own personality. And when new judges come on the court, they want to sometimes feel they can change the law overnight. I was that way. I wanted to do away with contributory negligence as a complete defense. One of the first dissents I wrote challenged that law. It was very presumptuous of me.[8]

Still, through his various devices, Wachtler was able to maintain the court's prominence as the premier common law court in the nation. If he was extraordinarily cunning, he was also extraordinarily talented.

Sol Wachtler was the twenty-first in a line of succession that included John Jay, the first chief justice of the U.S. Supreme Court; progressive civil rights activists like Stanley Fuld (1967–73) and Cooke (1979–1984); reformist Charles Breitel (1974–78); and, of course, Cardozo, the legendary jurist whose insight and razor-sharp reasoning graced dozens of Court of Appeals rulings. Cardozo was the court's, and the nation's, leading common law jurist during the early part of the century, and Wachtler wanted to assume that role in the latter part. He had inherited not only the mantle of Cardozo, his judicial hero, but even his desk, and he was in awe.

Cardozo, a New York City native, was the son of a state trial judge with a shoddy reputation.[9] Early, he surpassed his father in reputation and followed the elder Cardozo to the Supreme Court bench. Cardozo served on the trial court for only a few weeks before he was named to the Court of Appeals.[10] He became chief judge in 1927 and remained on the Court of Appeals until his appointment by President Hoover, in 1932, to the U.S. Supreme Court.

As a jurist, Cardozo had been particularly influential in applying existing law to evolving societal needs—a fact that did not go unnoticed by Wachtler. As a state judge, Cardozo had established the doctrine of implied warranty in a landmark decision. Although a Hoover appointee, Cardozo, along with liberal justices Louis Brandeis and Harlan Stone, was a critical vote for Roosevelt's New Deal social legislation. In fact, Cardozo wrote the key opinion upholding social security.

"Look," Wachtler told Joan, showing off his new chambers and desk for the first time. "It's Cardozo's desk!"[11]

"Yeah," Joan quipped, "and fifty years from now it'll still be 'Cardozo's desk.' "

Wachtler immediately began shaping his administration along the lines of Breitel, a sharp judge with a brilliant legal mind, rather than Cooke, a state constitutionalist who, in Wachtler's view, was too bogged down in the heavy duties of administering the courts. He wanted to be like Breitel, but even better. Although an effective chief, Breitel was basically an intellectual snob—abusive, demeaning, pompous*—yet Wachtler liked and respected him.

Breitel had been a close ally of governor and Republican presidential candidate Thomas E. Dewey, beginning his public service career in 1934 as a staff member of the Special Rackets Investigation headed by Dewey. He was an assistant prosecutor during Dewey's years as New York County district attorney and served as counsel to Governor Dewey for seven years before securing a judgeship. Breitel had fourteen years of appellate court experience before he was elected to the Court of Appeals in 1966, and once he became chief—by contested statewide election in 1974, the last chief to arrive by that route—he knew exactly what to do and how to do it. Wachtler was the junior judge on the court when he met Breitel in 1973.

"He took it upon himself to educate me, both because I

---

*Three sources with close connections to the Court used essentially the same words to describe Breitel. Wachtler, however, never spoke disparagingly about Breitel to me and, in fact, expressed only affection and admiration for his former colleague.

had so much to learn, and because he had so much to teach—
and he loved being a teacher," Wachtler recalled.[12] "But he
was not a gentle instructor. He labored tirelessly, demonstrating his love of the law and his devotion to the Court, and
he insisted that all the members of the Court devote the same
diligence and effort toward perfection. Although none of us
could match his energy or commitment, he was there always
to urge us on—often sternly and unrelentingly because those
were the standards he imposed on himself. Once when I
complained about his persistent methods, he said I should
not mistake his harshness for a lack of affection and regard.
He said he was guilty of no more than 'rough fondling.' "[13]

As Chief Judge, Breitel was a reformer. He modernized
and streamlined the court's procedures, reduced backlogs,
was the unrelenting force behind constitutional amendments
that did away with the elected Court of Appeals (largely
because Fuchsberg gave him an expensive run for his
money), and created the Commission on Judicial Conduct (in
part to keep tabs on judges like Fuchsberg). But Breitel could
be mean—he once had a secretary in tears, telling her she
was so fat that he didn't want to be seen with her in public—
and was perpetually and incurably out of touch with the
populace. He despised television, disdained just about every
facet of modern culture, and spoke with an odd semi-English
accent—odd because he spent his entire life in Manhattan.
Once, Wachtler took him to an Italian restaurant in Albany
and had to place his order, because Breitel, who referred to
himself as a WASH—White Anglo-Saxon Hebrew—had
never eaten Italian food before.

"I say, Sol, this is the tenderest veal I have ever eaten,"
Breitel said happily.

"Charlie," Sol responded, rolling his eyes, "it's *eggplant*."[14]

They remained close for the remainder of Breitel's life. In

the mid-1980s, after Breitel suffered a stroke, Wachtler pulled some strings, contacted John Cardinal O'Connor, and got his former colleague admitted to the Mary Manning Walsh Nursing Home in mid-Manhattan. A Catholic nursing home was an unlikely final home for an atheistic Jew, but Mary Manning Walsh was the closest to Breitel's family and Sol visited him there often.

To Wachtler, Breitel was a modern role model as both an administrator and chief, and he intended to follow in his mentor's footsteps, but with his own shoes. One of Wachtler's most effective tools was eloquence. He had a way of capturing the limelight and shining it on his court and his goals. He courted his court if not with candy and roses, then with sweet nothings and flattery. If Breitel was guilty of "rough fondling," Wachtler seduced.

Wachtler inherited a court that was ready for a charismatic leader. Courthouse veterans had found Chief Judge Cooke autocratic and his style had often undermined goals.

Manhattan District Attorney Robert Morgenthau challenged Cooke's authority to impose the system without the consent of the Court of Appeals, and brought a lawsuit that was ultimately heard in the chief's own court. The chief lost, unable to carry even his own court. "Larry was never the same after that," Wachtler recalled. "He felt he was abandoned by the court, but the court didn't abandon him at all. It was a question of *process*. All he had to do was get the permission of the court *first*, but he did it by fiat."[15]

Later, when Cooke asked his court to approve the plan, it did.

Cooke also undermined his own standing in the judiciary when, on the Friday of a holiday weekend, he invited the media to a courthouse to observe the fact that many of the judges had gone home early. The judiciary was incensed.

When Cooke took over, he found a Balkanized system of

four fiercely independent judicial departments, run with an iron fist by four presiding justices. The presiding justices wielded almost absolute power. Cooke thought the process chaotic. He cut their vacations from eight weeks to four, and told them when and where to hold court. Such reforms, while sorely needed, rarely endear the reformer to the reformed, and Cooke was unable to win over the judges with charm, as Wachtler might have, or sheer respect, as Breitel had. Cooke did, however, register significant achievements. He implemented several initiatives to relieve court congestion, fought for uniformity in sentencing, and was at the forefront of shielding rape victims from irrelevant cross-examination focusing on their sexual history. But with the administrative miscues, both his reforms of the system and decisions from the bench were overshadowed.

Wachtler, acutely aware of Cooke's mistakes, relied heavily on his chief court administrator, Joe Bellacosa, thus freeing himself to play a leadership role on the bench and allowing himself to pursue a key administrative goal, his individual assignment system of managing cases.

Wachtler had been impressed with Bellacosa's energy and innovation. "I always considered him a superb administrator. When he was chief clerk of the Court of Appeals, he literally took the court out of the pen-and-quill days. It was the most primitive of systems. Even the telephone system was antiquated. You had a half dozen instruments on your desk—one hooked to the clerk's office, one hooked to the other judges, one hooked to the outside. Joe computerized the court. He brought in a central staff. He just moved the court a light year forward."[16]

So, when Wachtler needed a chief administrator to handle the entire court system, he turned to Bellacosa, getting him named to a Court of Claims judgeship so he could claim the title of chief administrative *judge*. He became what Wachtler would describe as his "right arm and . . . left arm—administering this writhing monster we call the New York State Court System."

At his confirmation hearing, Wachtler had promised to make an immediate effort to change the way cases were assigned. "Think of it like a universe: each case is a sun and all the judges, lawyers, and administrative personnel represent planets revolving around the case in its fixed orbit . . . never getting closer. Only the seasons change. If you asked someone to devise the worst possible system imaginable, he or she might very likely propose the master calendar system which we now have. . . . To insure that it stayed the worst, I would put the judges themselves in charge of the day-to-day operation of the system. It seems to me that nothing makes less sense than putting a judge, his courtroom, and an entire administrative entourage to the task of granting adjournments on request."

Almost immediately, with Bellacosa at his side, Wachtler was able to improve the case management system and, in short order, persuade the legislature to pass the Court Facilities Act, which provided localities with fiscal incentives to improve court facilities. An ongoing, multibillion-dollar effort, the act would reap benefits well into the twenty-first century.[17]

By the spring of 1985, Wachtler was in high gear, implementing his individual assignment system, pushing for grand jury reform, speaking against plea bargaining, promoting merger of New York's byzantine court system, pushing for the power to pick and choose cases, calling for merit appointments of judges, and attempting to get child custody cases out of court and into binding arbitration—a passion, along with moderation, with Wachtler.

"In court," Wachtler later explained,

we would "force," "pressure," "hammer out" and "extort" settlements—we didn't negotiate them. Mediating or negotiating a dispute is a way of reconciling the differences between parties. "Settling" a case is getting rid of it. And I think that therein lies the difference between the resolution of disputes and the settlement of pending cases. The difference can be as graphic as two scenes from *Dances with Wolves*—one depicting the tribal leaders passing the "peace pipe" and negotiating their differences around the campfire. That's mediation. The other showing the men, women, and children being slaughtered by the merciless cavalry. That's a court-forced settlement. In both instances the dispute is resolved, but one is far more civilized than the other.[18]

In April, the Jewish Lawyers Guild gave Wachtler the Benjamin N. Cardozo Award for "compassion, knowledge and dignity." On March 27, 1985, he delivered a state of the judiciary speech to a joint session of the legislature. It was the first time a chief judge had ever done that and, in typical fashion, he mixed grace with pressure, charming his audience of lawmakers and then pushing for his agenda. "He was a good leader and his ability to lead came from his ability to have people feel easy to speak with him," said Judge Vito J. Titone.[19]

Wachtler advocated: replacing the grand jury system with judicially scrutinized affidavits provided by the district attorney's office; an "individual assignment system" where a particular case would remain with a particular judge so lawyers couldn't bring different versions of the same motion before different judges; and a judiciary chosen on merit rather than political connections, a court system unified and simplified. Wachtler wove an incredible amount of substance into what could have been a soft speech.

He used that technique again in his first Law Day address on May 1, 1985, schmoozing his audience of attorneys by singling out several by name in his opening remarks, and then impaling them with criticism of lawyers for tarnishing their own image and that of the profession with unnecessary litigation. "Litigation is expensive, time consuming, often impractical and rarely satisfying and all too often participants in civil litigation use the courts to satisfy personal animosities." He said lawyers "should think more ... [about] the processes of reconciliation, recognizing that there is often more justice in the peaceful resolution of a dispute than in obtaining a judgment." Wachtler was able to get away with such blasphemy and still maintain the respect and admiration of the bar, largely because of his personality and ability to capture an audience.

For example, shortly after his appointment as chief judge, Wachtler was interviewed by some New York *Daily News* reporters and the editorial board. Marcia Kramer, the reporter who would later get then presidential candidate Bill Clinton to admit that he smoked marijuana (but did not inhale), asked Wachtler his opinion of the system. Wachtler, pointing out that the grand jury system is secretive, excludes the defendant and his lawyer, is conducted by prosecutors asking leading questions, and relies primarily on hearsay, told her that its historical purpose had been so distorted as to render it meaningless, nothing but an easily exploited tool of the prosecution—and an unnecessary one at that.

Critics of the grand jury system, like Wachtler, say that it has reverted to its role as a device of government, largely abandoning its formal mandate as a shield against government: The prosecutor runs the show and decides what witnesses will be called, and the witnesses are not subject to cross-examination by the defense.

Investigative grand juries, in Wachtler's mind, do have a purpose, as do cases involving child molestation where there is a need for a child to testify in a nonconfrontational setting. But in most cases, he felt, it is a waste of time.

Wachtler was hardly a newcomer to grand jury reform and had been questioning their viability since at least 1974. In 1979, he wrote an opinion suggesting that the legislature "give serious consideration, as have many of our sister states, toward the eventual elimination of the grand jury as a prosecutorial tool to fashion felony indictments." As chief judge, he was able in 1985 to push harder. "Lives, careers and reputations are ruined because a grand jury indicts and the public treats a grand jury indictment as equivalent to an adjudication of criminal guilt," Wachtler said.[20] He exploited his position as chief to focus attention, with astounding effectiveness, on a pet cause. "Any prosecutor who wants to, could indict a ham sandwich," he quipped to Kramer. The issue, wrapped in a vintage Wachtlerism, exploded.

The "ham sandwich" quip made the front page of the *Daily News* and after that took on a life of its own. It found its way into several publications, including Tom Wolfe's *Bonfire of the Vanities*. A rabbi, apparently for religious reasons, changed "ham sandwich" to "bowl of Jell-O." One television script made it a bologna sandwich.

The Monroe County district attorney in Rochester called Wachtler's remarks "intemperate and unfortunate. Use of such a fatuous statement to launch a legislative drive only compounds the error."[21] The state District Attorneys Association and the Senate majority leader, Warren Anderson, also came out against Wachtler. But the American Civil Liberties Union supported him, and Mario Cuomo embraced the cause.

Wachtler, with a single one-liner, was able to attract more attention to an important, yet dry, issue than any of his predecessors.

But more essential to his role in the state's judicial history than grand jury reform—which never occurred,* although Wachtler was able to focus both political and public attention on the issue, and perhaps discourage some of the prosecutorial zeal—and Wachtler's pipe dream of gaining an appointment to the U.S. Supreme Court, was an immediate and daunting task: remaking the court in the image of Cardozo and reestablishing the panel as the preeminent common law court in the land. To do that, he needed his own court. With the court now an appointed body, both he and Cuomo realized their power to shape history.

Cuomo, a former clerk at the court who only half-jokingly suggested that he would rather be chief judge than governor, took very seriously his opportunity to appoint the members of New York's highest tribunal. Cuomo was well aware that his appointments would last longer than anything else he did, and that the decisions of his appointees would far outlive any momentary partisan concerns. "No governor in the history of this state has been afforded a greater opportunity and challenge to shape one of the state's most important institutions, the Court of Appeals," Cuomo said when he nominated Wachtler for chief.[22]

Cuomo's first pick was a shocker, but only because nobody yet knew how he would go about selecting judges. In 1983, the governor selected Richard Simons, an upstate appellate division justice, rock-solid jurist, and strict ethicist who had written the stinging dissent in the Fuchsberg scandal—and a staunch Republican.

Simons, who had grown up in Niagara Falls and competed as a national-class swimmer and diver at Colgate University, took a job as an attorney in the city of Rome, New

---

*In December 1997, Chief Judge Judith Kaye and Chief Administrative Judge Jonathan Lippman convened a panel to study grand jury reform.

York, after earning his law degree at the University of Michigan. He was only thirty-six when elected to state Supreme Court and, eight years later, became the youngest appellate justice in the state when Rockefeller put him on the Appellate Division. Simons was on that court when appointed to the Fuchsberg tribunal.

By picking Simons, Cuomo bypassed his friend Vito Titone, a close ally who, like the governor, had graduated from St. John's University School of Law. While pleased with Simons, Cuomo was annoyed, and said so, that there were no women on the list (compiled by a commission composed of appointees of the governor, chief judge, and legislature) from which he had to choose and he was, therefore, unable to fulfill a campaign promise to name the first female to the Court of Appeals.

When Fuchsberg finally quit in mid-1983, Cuomo got his chance to appoint a woman. Again, he shocked the establishment. Two women made the list, an experienced trial jurist named Betty Weinberg Ellerin, the overwhelming choice of the Women's Bar Association, and a solid judge, and Judith S. Kaye, a brilliant commercial trial lawyer with no judicial experience and no political muscle. Wachtler, who was familiar with Kaye's reputation as a trial attorney and knew her slightly since her recent appointment by the governor to the board of a group that reimburses victims of crooked counselors, recommended Kaye over Ellerin, and Cuomo selected her.

"I liked her [Ellerin] very, very much and had nothing but praise for her," Wachtler recalled. "It was very difficult to say which one I would prefer. The governor had just appointed Judith to the Lawyers Fund, Fred Miller's group, and I was familiar with her credentials from that. When the governor called me and asked what I thought of her, well, she just seemed to emerge as the very best, even though she hadn't been a judge."[23]

Until Kaye was appointed in 1983, no woman had ever served on the highest court in the state, and some skeptics pondered publicly whether the first female should be one with no judicial experience. But Wachtler wasn't concerned about Kaye's lack of time in robes. She quickly proved her merit.

Kaye was born on August 4, 1938, in Monticello, New York. Her mother and father, immigrants from Poland and Russia, respectively, operated a clothing store in Monticello. Kaye graduated from Barnard College in 1958, when she was nineteen years old. Desiring to be a newspaper reporter, she was hired as a writer for a small paper in New Jersey. Soon, she developed an interest in law and enrolled in law school at New York University. She studied law during the evening, while continuing to work for the newspaper.

Kaye graduated from law school sixth in her class of 290 and with honors in 1962. However, when she went to look for a job, Kaye found that men and women were not treated equally. She turned down the first job she was offered because the firm paid women less than men. Kaye was hired by another law firm, but was forced to leave after she and her husband conceived a child. (Mothering and lawyering were viewed as mutually exclusive vocations.) In 1969, Kaye was hired as a litigator for a large New York City law firm. She stayed with that firm—where she had been the only female partner—for nearly fifteen years, until her appointment to the Court of Appeals.

As a judge, Kaye has written many of the court's most important decisions in criminal law, human rights, free speech, and business issues. Wachtler was immediately impressed: if anyone had to replace him as chief following the downfall, his choice would have been Kaye. Indeed, Cuomo made her chief judge in 1993.

When Chief Judge Cooke and Hugh Jones, who came on

the bench with Wachtler, retired at the end of 1984, Wachtler got the chief judgeship and Cuomo appointed Fritz W. Alexander II, the first African American named to a full term (Harold Stevens had served only a few months before he was bumped off by Fuchsberg). Wachtler had known Alexander since the early 1970s, thought highly of him and happily recommended the candidate to the governor. Since the chief's position was filled from within—by Wachtler—that left another opening. The Italian community was after Cuomo to name an Italian—there hadn't been one on the court since Gabrielli retired—and only one made the list: Titone, who got the job. (The judicial nominating commission, a creature of Breitel, had a tendency for stacking its lists. For instance, when it was clear that the governor wanted an Italian American, one Italian American made the list. When an African-American judge was needed, an African-American judge— Fritz Alexander—made the list, and when he retired, another African American—George Bundy Smith—was tapped for what had become the "black seat." When a Hispanic was needed, a Hispanic jurist, Carmen Beauchamp Ciparick, made the list.* When Simons, an upstate conservative Republican, retired in January 1996, an upstate conservative Republican, Richard Wesley, made the list and won the appointment. Although Wesley came highly recommended, two other judges who were at least as qualified, but didn't fit the geographic/political bill: D. Bruce "Pete" Crew III and Thomas Mercure, both of the Appellate Division in Albany, were excluded.)

In 1985, Matthew Jasen retired and Cuomo replaced him

---

*I do not in any way mean to suggest that Alexander, Smith, and Ciparick were racial tokens or that their selection was unmerited. Rather, the point is that the committee clearly functions in a social context, not in a vacuum, and its selections reflect political and societal interests.

with Stewart F. Hancock, a progressive upstate Republican. When Bernard Meyer, a brilliant but sometimes quixotic jurist, retired at the end of 1986, Wachtler was pushing for a Buffalo Democrat, Mike Dillon. But Dillon didn't make the list, possibly because Wachtler was pushing so hard and the commission resisted his heavy-handedness, and possibly because of Dillon's rabid anti-abortion stance. Those nominated were Bellacosa, of Guilderland, Wachtler's chief administrative judge (who had not made the list for the previous appointment); state Appellate Division Justices Howard A. Levine and Richard Brown; Carolyn Gentile, associate professor at Fordham Law School; William Hogan, professor at New York University School of Law; Joseph McLaughlin, U.S. District judge from Brooklyn; and Norman Redlich, dean at New York University School of Law.

Wachtler wanted Bellacosa, a former clerk at the court who was a close friend of both the chief judge and the governor, and at the time Wachtler's top administrative judge.

Bellacosa, intelligent and intense, had clerked for Marcus Christ when Christ was presiding justice of the Appellate Division in the Second Department. Later, he was assistant dean and professor at St. John's University School of Law and then chief clerk and counsel to the Court of Appeals. Bellacosa had written the practice commentaries to the eight volumes of McKinney's Criminal Procedure Law and had operated the government law center at Albany Law School. Testy and temperamental at times, Bellacosa remained fundamentally solid.

"It is not a bloodless sport," Wachtler said of the art of jurisprudence, defending Bellacosa.[24] He would occasionally have to tone down Bellacosa's caustic dissents, but he realized from the start that Bellacosa would add a somewhat emotional element to the court. "These are not moot court cases. We are dealing here with real lives—a person's liberty, a person's fortune, a person's freedom. These *are* important matters." If Bellacosa gets worked up, well, so be it.

Bellacosa was an easy pick for Cuomo. He was once a Republican who had switched his enrollment to independent. With Bellacosa, Cuomo could legitimately say he had appointed a balanced court: three Democrats, three Republicans, and one independent. If he had appointed Levine, a tremendously competent judge, but a Republican, Cuomo would have been in the awkward position of having appointed a Republican-dominated court. Levine would have to wait until Wachtler's resignation and Kaye's elevation to take what many viewed as his rightful spot on the bench.

"I have sought to shape not just a good court but an excellent one, a court of strong and intelligent jurists who bring confidence and commitment to every case and dispense justice based on reason, logic and the accumulated experience reflected in the law," Cuomo boasted. "We now have an excellent court, the court that will fulfill the important balancing role in our governmental trinity and that will stand as a strong argument for the merit selection of judges."[25]

Wachtler had an extraordinary court to work with: Simons, rock-solid and sober; Bellacosa, articulate and scholarly, but temperamental; Kaye, brilliant on the law, persuasive and congenial, but unyielding, a steel magnolia; Alexander, devoted and sensible, but deliberative and slow; Hancock, intellectual and diligent, but stubborn and unyielding; Titone, a liberal stalwart and, occasionally, left-wing crusader. For the next five years, Wachtler's court was stable—luckily, because increasingly, the chief was not. However, he always had able administrators—first Bellacosa, then Justice Albert M. Rosenblatt, and finally Matthew T. Crosson.

Wachtler's stewardship over the court coincided with one of its most important eras, when it moved from an elected to an appointed body and grasped the power, like the U.S. Supreme Court, to largely pick and choose the cases it wished to hear. The chief was intent on distinguishing his court from all other tribunals.

For instance, in 1991 the court accepted an odd statute-of-limitations case involving an artwork that had been stolen a quarter century earlier from the Guggenheim Museum. A couple purchased the painting, having no idea that it was stolen, and displayed it in their home and exhibited it at shows. The museum, fearful of driving the artwork underground, had purposely kept quiet about its disappearance. Wachtler used the case to send a message to the U.S. Court of Appeals for the Second Circuit.

Earlier, he had reached an understanding with the federal court in which the U.S. panel would, on questions of state law, "certify" questions to the state tribunal. So, rather than interpret the state law itself or basically guess what the state court would decide, the circuit court agreed to refer those matters to Wachtler's court. That certification process was extremely important to Wachtler, as it expanded the state Court of Appeals' power beyond its constitutional limits, allowing it to review cases which were in the federal courts, but in which New York law controlled. However, the federal court reneged in a case involving a stolen artwork and whether a thief can convey good title to an unsuspecting buyer. Rather than certify the question back to Wachtler, the Second Circuit decided the matter itself, rejecting the state court's own precedents. Wachtler was furious, and in *Guggenheim Foundation* v. *Lubell*,[26] set the record straight. At oral arguments in 1991, the attorney for the people who had inadvertently purchased the stolen artwork cited the Second Circuit opinion as the decision that should guide the Wachtler court.

"We said, 'Wait a minute. We should guide the Second Circuit and, well, we've got news for you.' What we said, in essence, was the Second Circuit was wrong. . . . We had a choice to either follow the earlier line of cases [which generally se the precedent] or the art museum line of case precedents [which followed a different path]. We decided to follow the art museum cases and referred to the others as being 'anomalous.' That was a strange way of discarding precedents," Wachtler said.[27]

The decision allowed the museum to pursue its lawsuit against the buyers. The case was eventually settled.

As the court was developing, Wachtler was busy steering its jurisprudence, protecting his political and constitutional base of power and relishing the perks of his office. He was the toast of the town—and he loved it. He swore in Ed Koch as mayor of New York City and, twice, swore in Cuomo to the office he himself would later covet.

"The first time I swore in Governor Cuomo was a unique experience," Wachtler recalls in his diary. "The first family of New York State had invited me and my family to join them at the mansion on New Year's Eve. Our two families dined together and, after dinner, on the stoke of midnight, I administered the oath of office. The entire audience consisted of our wives—Joan and Matilda Cuomo—and the Cuomo and Wachtler children. That ceremony was much more memorable to me than the public inaugural which followed, although the latter was attended by thousands and accompanied by bands, choirs, and the firing of cannons."

Wachtler nurtured friendships with U.S. Supreme Court justices William Brennan, Thurgood Marshall, and Potter Stewart. (Lewis Powell sent Wachtler a copy of his biography when he was imprisoned. Harry Blackmun visited.) He worked with Warren Burger when the chief justice was chairman of the constitutional bicentennial. They had met before when they were on a panel together in Philadelphia and jointly received honorary doctoral degrees at the Claremont Colleges in California. Such memories would haunt Wachtler in prison. "The visit of the senior justice of the United States Supreme Court [Blackmun], the author of *Roe* v. *Wade*,[28] his embrace and words of praise and encouragement meant more to me than I can possibly say," Wachtler wrote in the diary. "The memory of what I once was brought me renewed hope for what I could be in the future. I also wept, thinking of what I once was but will never be again."

In 1988, he joined New York Mayor Ed Koch and Walter Cronkite as actors in a PBS documentary on New York's ratification of the U.S. Constitution. "An Empire of Reason," with Wachtler starring as John Jay, told the story of New York's ratification, by a mere three votes, of the U.S. Constitution, and Jay's role as the advocate who came up with the face-saver that allowed ratification. Marty Belsky, dean and professor of law at Tulsa, Oklahoma, was still using the documentary a decade later to instruct his law students.

Wachtler took seriously his constitutional role as the leader of a co-equal branch of government and as defender of the court system from what he thought were unjustified attacks. "Now you take a fellow who commits a misdemeanor and you negotiate a quick plea, and he's out on the street the next day; and then three days later, he's in for another misdemeanor, and the same thing happens. The third time he commits a violent felony. Then the public screams, 'Where was the idiot judge when he came before the judge twice before and was slapped on the wrist?' And the answer is: The judge was doing the very best he could, with limited resources and an overwhelming number of cases before him."[29]

He took on Senator Alfonse D'Amato, when his old nemesis described the justice system as "rotten to the core." On February 24, 1986, Wachtler and Bellacosa, then chief administrative judge, blasted Queens District Attorney John J. Santucci, essentially telling him to put up or shut up about charges that an unidentified judge stymied a probe into possible corruption of Donald R. Manes, a New York City official who committed suicide while under investigation. Wachtler was furious over Santucci's remarks and firmly believed the DA was attempting to find a scapegoat for his own inability to develop a case.

He wasn't about to let anyone intrude on his turf. But long before he fought with Cuomo, Wachtler was at perpetual odds with Manhattan District Attorney Morgenthau.

Morgenthau—whose wife, Lucinda Franks, would write scathing magazine articles about Wachtler after the arrest, without noting her relationship to the district attorney— despised the chief judge, and the feeling was mutual.[30] From Morgenthau's vantage point, there was only room for one "Super Jew" in New York, and as long as Wachtler was around it wasn't going to be him.[31] From Wachtler's viewpoint, Morgenthau was a bully who didn't show the proper respect for the chief judge.

Once, when the criminal justice system in New York City was on the verge of collapse due to a daunting caseload, Wachtler insisted on around-the-clock arraignments. All the district attorneys went along, except Morgenthau. When Wachtler spoke at the Association of the Bar of the City of New York to promote his individual assignment system, a Morgenthau assistant heckled him. Anything Wachtler wanted, Morgenthau opposed; anything Morgenthau opposed, Wachtler wanted. They viciously locked horns in a 1988 battle over an old building in Manhattan.

The building at 80 Center Street was a state-owned, eight-story court facility which the Manhattan DA had for years used for offices. Wachtler wanted Morgenthau to move, and he wouldn't. In fact, Morgenthau wanted to move in another five hundred assistants. The Center Street brouhaha, dubbed a "dance of elephants" by the press, resulted in a bizarre showdown—a power play, really—over control of the building. Wachtler admits to being "as irrational as I've ever been"[32] in the dispute over 80 Center Street.

Although the building was a court facility, Morgenthau used half of it for his offices. Wachtler wanted to take the building for the courts and move Morgenthau to more spacious facilities across the street. Since judges are supposed to be impartial arbiters, Wachtler thought it unseemly for jurists and prosecutors to share such close quarters—particularly when there was appropriate space nearby for the district attorney.

Morgenthau wouldn't go for it, so Wachtler went to Mayor Koch—in effect, the landlord—but Koch refused to get in the middle. Eventually, they agreed to let John Egan, then the state commissioner of the Office of General Services and a true statesman, broker a deal. Egan came up with a plan that was largely the same as Wachtler's and, predictably, Morgenthau refused to go along.

"It seemed that whatever I tried to do, he would try to block," Wachtler said, "but never openly or publicly. It was always done through private contacts, and that was troublesome to me."[33]

Meanwhile, Wachtler continued to fight for his administrative agenda. He lobbied for higher salaries for judges, pointing out that many were earning less than law firm associates. In 1988, he began what would become an ultimatum to lawyers: Either increase your *pro bono*—public service—

work, or be forced to donate your time to help meet the civil justice needs of the poor in matters such as evictions. The lawyers came around. Bar groups that had never had *pro bono* organizations started them. Groups that had been active became more active.

He also appointed a task force to study gender bias in the courts and devoted himself to improving the lot of women. "We could have thanked the members of the committee, promised to study the report, and then . . . implemented one piece at a time over a protracted period. Or we could do what we did—determine that the report was important, definitive and represented a remarkable opportunity to remove an intolerable impediment which confronted our justice system," Wachtler said.[34]

Two years later, the chairwoman of the committee, Kay McDonald, reported: "There has been a pervasive shift in the attitude of court system participants about the treatment of women; the problem of gender bias has been legitimized as a matter deserving of our concern. It is taken seriously now, like any other professional issue. The spirit of inquiry and evaluation informs our discussions and debates; we have fewer shouting matches of accusation and denial and we hear virtually no dismissive joking about gender."[35]

The chief addressed domestic violence a full decade before it became a hot-button topic with the trial of O. J. Simpson. "We repeatedly encounter frustration and confusion in our attempt to improve the courts' handling of this ill, because the court system is but one part of a complex web of interdependent governmental agencies charged with responsibility for addressing the problem. To do its job properly, for example, the Family Court must coordinate with the Criminal Court, the police department, the district attorneys . . . victim advocacy agencies, etc. We need to study the interrelationships of these systems, identify holes in the web they form, and propose ways to mend those holes."

Wachtler came to bat for his judges with a blistering attack on the Commission of Judicial Conduct, a group which prosecutes judges for misconduct. The commission's administrator, Gerald Stern, came under Wachtler's scrutiny when the chief thought the commission was overbudgeted and overzealous. "When the commission, through its actions, demeans the public perception of the judiciary through excessive prosecutorial zeal, then I'm bothered."[36]

In 1989, Wachtler helped derail measures that would have opened judicial disciplinary proceedings to the public. "You could not have a judge sitting on trials in the morning and then having his own hearing made public in the afternoon," Wachtler said. "And if the judge is ultimately vindicated, he or she would necessarily be under a cloud for the rest of that judge's career."[37]

He imposed new rules for sanctions against lawyers pursuing frivolous claims after the legislature failed to address the issue, and called for less secrecy in civil settlements, finding it "rather perverse" that corporations were using the public courts to resolve their business disputes and then telling the public that the resolution was none of its business.

He took on the political establishment, proposing a "merit selection" process of selecting judges. Under Wachtler's plan, he and his colleagues on the Court of Appeals would continue to be appointed by the governor. But the lower court judges would, instead of relying on political bosses for support in reelection, appear before a screening panel that would evaluate their character and qualifications. Incumbents would run on their record, unopposed in a yes-or-no retention election. If the incumbent was rejected, a regular contested election would be held.

Increasingly, too, Wachtler was battling with Cuomo annually over money, with the biggest battle occurring in 1990, during the breakdown of Wachtler's secret affair.

Cuomo blamed society's ills on the courts. Wachtler blamed the governor for having no sense of priorities, for spending too much on prison construction and not enough on prevention. At one point, Cuomo likened Wachtler to a "fish monger," asking for much and settling for whatever he could get.

The annual showdown turned particularly bitter in 1990 and by March of that year things had reached the boiling point. Cuomo wasn't returning Wachtler's calls. His top judicial adviser, Evan Davis, had banned Wachtler's top aide, Matt Crosson, from budget negotiations. Wachtler was livid. "When the governor talks about increasing the police and more tactical narcotics teams, what does he think will happen to all those arrests?" Wachtler demanded.[38]

Wachtler ended up getting much of what he wanted and limped away from the budget process with resigned, and worrisome, regret. But they made up in a private ceremony and Cuomo invited Wachtler to swear him into his third term on January 1, 1991 (Bellacosa swore in Lieutenant Governor Stan Lundine).

"Mario, he loved confrontation," Wachtler recalled. "His experience was that most of the time there was confrontation, the other side backed down. He did that with the legislature. He knew he could have trimmed this off, tucked that in and gotten his legislation through. But he wanted the legislative leaders to twist in the wind. He had a very clear sense that judges were unpopular. And he knew we could not talk back."[39]

Initially, Wachtler was characteristically diplomatic. But over the next year, he reached the breaking point in his professional, political, and personal lives—which were simultaneously growing distinct and inappropriately intertwined as the Silverman debacle took control of his life.

Meanwhile, Sol and Joan were growing ever more distant. "We were separated a great deal," Joan said. "When he was just a member of the court, he was up there [Albany] two weeks [a month] and home on weekends. When he became chief, he never really came home. He got too involved in the court and I saw a change, and the more I saw him change, the angrier I became. I went back to school and immersed myself in my career."[40]

Still, Sol remained a caring and attentive father. He would take time to visit Lauren and Marjorie at college and rarely missed one of Alison's many off-Broadway performances. His youngest child, Philip, was only ten when Wachtler joined the court, and would cry every Sunday night when "pop" would have to return to Albany. But by the time Sol was chief, Philip was a student at nearby Skidmore College, just up the road from Albany. The father and son grew close and made up for lost time.[41]

But Wachtler was growing increasing resentful of Joy's demands on his time, which took him away from his wife and children. He was losing respect for himself, and losing the respect of his colleagues.

Wachtler's clerks had always played a major, although typical, role in drafting decisions. But now they were also the chief's eyes and ears. His writing of opinions dropped way off, resulting in an increase in *per curiam* or unsigned opinions, which court observers were beginning to question. His court was beginning to slip into mediocrity as the chief was engaged—personally and professionally—in other pursuits.

The budget crisis reached its pinnacle in 1991 when Cuomo unconstitutionally tinkered with the court budget, and Wachtler sued the governor.

Under the New York State Constitution, the chief judge is a co-equal partner in government, yet he has no cards to play in budget negotiations. The chief judge, unlike the governor or legislature, has nothing to trade and no vote on the budget and is not part of the negotiating process. In New York, three men—the governor, the Senate majority leader, and the Assembly speaker—work out a budget in private. Other legislators, let alone the chief judge, are not welcome at their meetings.

The framers of New York's government recognized the inherent contradiction in having three co-equal branches of government, while keeping one branch—the judiciary—out of the loop. Consequently, the Constitution requires the chief judge to deliver his budget to the governor and mandates that the governor submit the spending plan, intact, to the legislature, with any recommendations he wants. Later, the governor has a line-item veto and is free to slash any part of the legislature-approved budget, including the judiciary budget.

In 1991, Cuomo essentially wrote his own judiciary budget ($71 million less than Wachtler's), included it in the overall state spending plan, and sent it on to the legislature. He also sent over Wachtler's proposed budget, which was dead on arrival because the governor had already accounted for the judiciary. That was the last straw.

"His [Wachtler's] anger was really directed not so much at Mario Cuomo personally, but in the manner in which he [the governor] was treating the institution, the branch of government, which in my judgment was grossly inappropriate," Crosson recalls. "It was not a personal thing with Sol. For Mario, it was personal. . . . Mario got extremely personal."[42]

Rather than do what he now says he should have done—"call the governor up and say 'This is inappropriate, let's talk' "[43]—on August 26, 1991, Wachtler and Crosson sued the governor and the legislature. They alleged that the governor violated the state constitution by submitting his own judiciary budget and that Cuomo and the legislature "failed in their obligation to provide the reasonable and necessary funding that would enable the judicial branch to fulfill its constitutional and statutory functions." He explained his reasoning with characteristic, although perhaps manic, eloquence:

> The instinct for justice is universal and it is inextricably linked to the notion of fairness. To some, justice and fairness mean conformity with the laws. To others, they mean the preservation of certain rights—to own property, to speak freely, or to receive a fair trial. Whatever their meaning, the instinct for justice and fairness dates from the dawn of civilization.
>
> The judicial process which embodies the concepts of justice and fairness arose in history alongside the emergence of family, religion and, ultimately, the state. . . . Tragically, justice in New York has been depleted by a decade of "silent encroachments." While caseloads soared during the 1980s, resources dwindled, and last year for the first time in our history, drastic budget cuts were imposed. The budget cuts further diminished an already overburdened system and depleted it to the point where justice was being denied to many New Yorkers. As Chief Judge of New York, it was my responsibility to choose between accepting this fate and fighting to maintain a meaningful system of justice for New Yorkers.[44]

Cuomo had clearly underestimated an adversary.

On July 21, 1992, Wachtler was the first to speak on a prime-time PBS special about the American judicial system with host Bill Moyers: "They say we are one of three co-equal branches of government, but I found when it comes time to negotiate our budget, some branches are more equal than others. We were like a poker player sitting around the table with no chips. The question was whether I should sit back as head of this court system and become an honorary pallbearer or whether I would do that which any other citizen aggrieved would do. That is, bring a lawsuit."

Cuomo accused Wachtler and Bellacosa of "cheap, intellectually shabby tactics." But the angrier Cuomo got, the madder—in a manic sense—Wachtler became. "The governor has claimed I should meet my budget with imaginative planning like he has done with the state budget," Wachtler said in 1992.

> I have to admit the governor has hit on a great idea. Why not privatize the judiciary? I can imagine an ad like the following:
>
> Once in a lifetime offer—now you can buy a judge—legally!
>
> What nicer present for Christmas for your loved one who has everything than his or her very own Court of Appeals Judge for only $300,000? (Prices may vary slightly from judge to judge. For instance, Judge Bellacosa costs a bit more because he also does windows.)
>
> If you are charitably minded, you can participate in our Adopt-A-Judge Program. Only dollars a day can help feed some of our starving judges. With each adoption, we send you a picture of your judge, along with some biographical data describing your judge's customs, what he or she likes to eat, and a little bit about the judge's brothers and sisters. Each Christmas you will also receive a handwritten note by the judge with a "So Entered" stamp across the top.[45]

On June 6 at the annual Legislative Correspondents Association (LCA) show—an annual spoof of state government by reporters who cover the Capitol—at the Empire State Plaza, Wachtler brought down the house: "You know, the governor got pretty rough on me during the court-funding disagreement. 'Court-funding disagreement.' That's a good euphemism," he said sarcastically.

"One of the governor's spokespersons said, 'Wachtler is political and arrogant. He has no knowledge of the law and even less understanding of people.'"

After a dramatic pause, he quipped: "Well, I say, `Picky, picky, picky.'"

Wachtler continued:

> Speaking of the lawsuit . . . were we speaking of the lawsuit? Anyway, you might recall the exchanges going on between me and the governor. He said, "Wachtler wants ermine robes!"
>
> I do. I like ermine robes.
>
> He also said—this is a direct quote—I "obviously want to take money away from sick children and hospitals." That's true, too. I didn't say I *had* to get the money from hospitals. I said I would *prefer* if the money came from sick children in hospitals. I would have accepted money from AIDS patients, the destitute, the homeless, schoolchildren. I would have accepted money from them. But I wouldn't have accepted one red cent from the $160,000 used to pay the salary of state Health Commissioner Mark Chassin.

After years of debating lesser minds in the legislature, Cuomo, like a bully who has met his match, panicked when Wachtler sued, and seemed to come unhinged as the chief judge playfully poked fun at the governor, even while his court upheld the governor's agenda by a two-to-one margin that almost always included the chief.

Wachtler was well beyond the pale, but seemingly only Cuomo realized it. (On *Larry King Live* in April 1997, Wachtler told a national audience that the first thing Cuomo said to him after his arrest was, "I knew you were crazy when you sued me.") Everyone else seemed amused, energized by the chief's ramblings.

After Wachtler sued the governor in state court, Cuomo claimed he couldn't get a fair shake in the state court system run by such a chief judge, even though Wachtler was a frequent target, and frequent loser, of various cases involving his official administrative capacity. Cuomo retaliated: he filed a federal civil rights lawsuit in Brooklyn against Wachtler, alleging that his liberties were somehow violated when he was sued; he sought to have Wachtler's state court case removed to Albany; he asked to consolidate both cases in the federal court in Brooklyn; he withdrew the suit in Brooklyn; he filed the same suit in Albany; and he attempted to withdraw his federal suit and still retain the right to refile the action. At that point, U.S. District Judge Thomas J. McAvoy, an astute and exceptionally diligent federal jurist who doesn't like his time wasted by politicians, was so irritated that he threw out Cuomo's suit with prejudice—meaning it could not be refiled—and ordered the governor to pay Wachtler's legal fees. Wachtler waived his right to collect fees and the governor essentially provided much of the money the chief judge sought. But the relationship between the two New York titans would never be the same.

Shortly after taking office in 1985, Wachtler told the *State Bar News*: "No political consideration could make me leave office before my term expires. I'm here for the next fourteen years, until 1999."[46] One of his predecessors as chief judge, Alton Parker, left the court in an unsuccessful run against Teddy Roosevelt for president.* Parker was the first (and

---

*Parker, a tough conservative who had been a school teacher before attending Albany Law School (graduating in 1873), had always been politically active. However, he mounted a "lifeless, colorless campaign.

only) chief judge who quit to do so. Would Wachtler be the first to leave to challenge a sitting governor?

By 1992, with the lingering bitterness he felt toward Cuomo, Wachtler was ready to enter the gubernatorial sweepstakes of 1994—and would have had it not been for the Silverman scandal. Increasingly, his private behavior was bizarre, and his public conduct beginning to raise questions as well.

"It seemed perverse that after having had some 1,200 opinions and over one hundred articles published that my epitaph and legacy would somehow relate to a ham sandwich," Wachtler wrote in his diary a year after the arrest. "On the other hand, considering how the events of this last year will be reflected when I am remembered by history, I would have been better off."

Immediately after Wachtler's resignation, Simons, as the senior associate, took over as acting chief and calmly and expertly kept the court on course and appropriately distanced from the growing circus-like atmosphere of the scandal. However, when it came time to appoint a new chief, Cuomo bypassed Simons (Titone also applied, but wasn't among those found qualified by Jones's committee) and selected Kaye. In short order, Kaye was able to pick up on Wachtler's unfinished projects. She showed surprising political acumen for a woman who had never been involved in politics, and grasped the opportunities for reform that Wachtler had let slip by.

He was ponderous and heavy and uninspiring,"[47] and was destroyed by Roosevelt. Parker returned to private practice, but two years later was elected president of the American Bar Association.

Notes

1. Interview with a confidential source on September 5, 1997.
2. Interview with another confidential source on September 5, 1997.
3. Interview with a confidential source in 1990.
4. Interview with Wachtler, August 20, 1997.
5. Hugh R. Jones, *Cogitations on Appellate Decision-Making*, 34 Rec. Association of the Bar of the City of New York, 1979.
6. Luke Bierman, "Institutional Identity and the Limits of Institutional Reform: The New York Court of Appeals in the Judicial Process," unpublished doctoral dissertation, 1994.
7. Interview with a confidential source on September 5, 1997.
8. Interview with Wachtler on May 5, 1997.
9. "Benjamin Cardozo," *Compton's Living Encyclopedia* (Compton's Learning Co., 1996). (Internet)
10. Ibid.
11. Wachtler has told this story on numerous occasions.
12. Interview with Wachtler on September 7, 1997.
13. Ibid.
14. Interview with Wachtler on May 5, 1997.
15. Ibid.
16. Ibid.
17. Frederick Miller, "New York State's Judicial Article: A Work in Progress," *Decision 1997: Constitutional Change in New York*, Gerald Benjamin and Henrik N. Dullea, eds. (Albany: The Rockefeller Institute Press, 1997), p. 140.
18. Interview with Wachtler in August 1997.
19. John Caher, "Wachtler Leaves a Mixed Legacy after 20 Years," Albany *Times Union*, January 31, 1993, A-1.
20. Shirley Armstrong, "Grand Jury System under Indictment by Its Critics," Albany *Times Union*, February 10, 1985, p. 1.
21. Howard R. Relin, "Would a Grand Jury Indict a Ham Sandwich?" Rochester *Democrat and Chronicle*, February 10, 1985, p. 23A.

22. Jeannie H. Cross, "Republican Gets Chief Judgeship," Albany *Times Union*, January 3, 1985, p. 1.

23. Interview with Wachtler on August 15, 1997.

24. Interview with Wachtler on August 20, 1997.

25. E. R. Ship, "New York's High Court Is a Cuomo Production," *New York Times*, January 18, 1987, p. 35.

26. *Guggenheim Foundation* v. *Lubell*, 77 NY2d 311 (1991), 569 NE2d 426.

27. Interview with Wachtler on August 15, 1997.

28. *Roe* v. *Wade*, 410 U.S. 113 (1973).

29. Duncan Christy, "Law, Order and the Judge," *M*, July 1985, p. 79.

30. Interview with a confidential source close to both Wachtler and Morgenthau, May 1995.

31. Ibid.

32. Interview with Wachtler in February 1997.

33. Ibid.

34. Interview with Wachtler on May 5, 1997.

35. Report of the Committee on Gender Bias.

36. John Caher, "Conduct Panel Criticized," Albany *Times Union*, October 9, 1988, p. A-1.

37. Gary Spencer, "Bill on Judicial Conduct Panel Stalled," *New York Law Journal*, May 25, 1989, p. 1.

38. Frank Lynn, "Cuomo's Fiscal Battle with Judge Pits Dollars and Judicial Dignity," *New York Times*, March 19, 1990, B-3.

39. Interview with Wachtler on May 5, 1997.

40. Interview with Joan Wachtler on September 26, 1997.

41. Separate interviews with Lauren, Alison, Marjorie, and Philip Wachtler in October 1997.

42. Interview with Matthew Crosson on August 20, 1997.

43. Interview with Wachtler on May 15, 1997.

44. Press release distributed on behalf of Wachtler, August 26, 1991.

45. Wachtler's archives.

46. "Wachtler Sets His Sights on Court Reform," *New York State Bar Association Bar News*, March 1985, p. 1.

47. Frank R. Kent, *The Democratic Party*, 1924, p. 361.

PART II

The Mind

CHAPTER 6

The Court of Appeals

M oments before 2 P.M. during the eight two-week sessions in which the Court of Appeals meets annually,
the chief judge pushes a button in his chambers, setting off a
gong in the offices of the panel's six associate judges. It is
their signal to head down to the robing room in daily preparation for their most public of duties, hearing arguments in
the courtroom. At precisely 2 P.M. (except on Friday, when the
session starts and ends an hour earlier), with the judges suit-
ably attired in their black robes, the chief knocks twice on the
door behind the bench and the crier announces the arrival of
the jurists. "The Judges of the Court," he announces. Everyone rises as the judges enter the courtroom in order of
seniority.

The ornate courtroom is decorated with oak trim, a hand-
carved oak bench, and a Mexican onyx fireplace. The court-

house rotunda, adorned in Ionian and Doric columns, is capped by the interior of the dome, on which is painted the state's seal. A life-sized bronze statue of Robert R. Livingston, the first "chancellor" of the state, faces the judges, staring toward the bench in perpetuity. Portraits of past judges line the walls, with the chiefs perched on the top row and the former associates below.

"Hear Ye, Hear Ye, Hear Ye. All persons having any business before this Court of Appeals, held in and for the State of New York, may now draw near, give their attendance, and they will be heard," declares the crier.

The chief then calls the first case. The lawyer for the party bringing the case, the "appellant," goes first, sometimes reserving a few minutes for rebuttal.

At the end of the session, the crier adjourns the court. "All Please Rise: Hear Ye, Hear Ye, Hear Ye. All persons having any further business before this Court of Appeals, held in and for the State of New York, may depart hence and appear here tomorrow afternoon at two o'clock, to which time this Court now stands adjourned."

The court is comprised of seven judges, six associates and a chief. At least five hear every case, and four votes are required for a decision. The chief sits in the center and controls switches that operate two tiny bulbs on the lawyers' lectern. When the white bulb is illuminated, the attorney may speak. When red is on, the court has heard all it intends to hear and the lawyer is silenced. No exceptions. No extra seconds.

As often as not, an attorney will approach the court, begin a well-rehearsed address—and get cut off at the knees by probing questions from some of the top legal minds in the nation. For three hours or so, the judges will torment attorneys with a game of cat and mouse, allowing a total of thirty minutes or so to a case and hearing four to six matters in an afternoon. An observer can never tell for sure how the court or even a particular judge is leaning during oral arguments. Oftentimes, the judges indulge in some intellectual fun at the expense of a poor suffering lawyer, and sometimes at the expense of each other.[1] The court can be an intimidating place, for even the most seasoned of lawyers.

"I'm scared to go to the Court of Appeals," admitted Albany attorney Terence L. Kindlon in 1988, three years after Wachtler's ascension to chief.[2] He has argued several cases before New York's top court. "You prepare to open your mouth and they start hitting you with questions. Wachtler is just penetrating, incredibly astute and knowledgeable."

Court insiders love to tell the story of Michael J. Connolly, an appellate expert in Albany, who was nervously pitching his argument, talking a mile a minute, when Judge Bellacosa cut him off in mid-monologue. "Take a step back, Mr. Connolly," the judge demanded. Bellacosa simply wanted Connolly to revisit a point he had raced by in his argument. Connolly turned white as a sheet, fearing he had unwittingly stepped over an invisible line on the floor that he was not allowed to cross and quickly obeyed Bellacosa—literally: He took a step backward. Bellacosa almost fell off his chair.

Another time, a nervous advocate approached the lectern and immediately launched his argument, neglecting to begin with the traditional greeting: "May it please the court." Judge Fuld, the perfect gentleman, politely cut him off and insisted that he properly introduce himself to the judges. The flustered advocate obeyed, literally: he walked up to each judge, shook his hand, and introduced himself.

On another occasion, a blustering sycophant of a lawyer was attempting to schmooze Judge Gabrielli. "Oh, judge, what a brilliant, brilliant question," the attorney said in response to a question from Gabrielli. Gabrielli asked another question. " Judge, that question is even more brilliant than the previous," the attorney responded.

One big problem: The lawyer kept calling Judge *Gabrielli* "Judge *Garibaldi.*" After several minutes, Wachtler leaned forward and said softly, "Counselor, I'm sorry to interrupt you, but it's GABRIELLI!" Flustered and horribly embarrassed, the attorney said: "Oh my God, I'm so humiliated. Thank you. Thank you, Judge *Wachtel.*"

After the opposing lawyers finish their arguments—or, more accurately, after the judges have finished with the lawyers—the jurists retire to the privacy of their "tea" room, where index cards bearing the name of each case is laid face down on a table. In order of seniority, the judges draw cards to determine which case they will summarize in the next morning's conference.[3] Then they will have dinner together —the location at the sole discretion of the chief judge—before returning to the courthouse and working until midnight with their clerks.

The random case assignment system was implemented by Chief Judge Charles Breitel. The court had long operated as a "cold bench," or one in which the judges knew next to nothing about the case being argued. Since judges were assigned cases in advance, only one—the judge assigned— really paid attention during oral arguments, and lawyers could easily figure out who had their case and, consequently, whom they had to sway. In 1974, Breitel did away with that system and created a "hot bench." Now, judges don't learn until after arguments which case is theirs, so they need to be prepared for them all.

There are some insiders, judges among them, however, who have occasionally thought the process wasn't as random as it was supposed to be. At one point, someone in the court drew a caricature of Breitel as as river boat gambler, stacking the deck. At another, the other judges were so skeptical of Wachtler's tendency to draw the juicy case that they accused him of marking the cards. Wachtler denies it. "I was always the last one to draw, so how could I fix it?" Wachtler insisted.[4]

The morning after oral arguments—after working a sixteen- or eighteen-hour day that stretches late into the night— the judges return to the court house around 7:30 A.M. and pick up where they left off the previous evening. For two or three hours, the judges and their clerks* continue preparing summaries of the case they drew and await the chief's summons, when they will wheel briefs into the conference room to begin deliberations.

The discussion begins with the reporting judge, the one who drew the card for whatever case they are considering, stating his or her opinion and explaining his or her reasoning. From there, the judges, in reverse seniority order, offer their impressions.

Cases are primarily decided in conference, but the decisions are not finalized until draft opinions have circulated. Typically, if the reporting judge holds a majority, he or she will write for the court. Otherwise, the junior judge in the majority will write the main opinion. If a dissent must be written, usually the first one to raise an objection—frequently a more junior jurist since the case is conferenced in reverse order of seniority—gets the chore. When all the judges are satisfied, the final opinions are conferenced for final approval. Typically, the decision is announced publicly in four to six weeks, but what goes on in that conference room—where virtually every issue of significance to society

---

*The associate judges each have two, the chief three. Law clerks at the Court of Appeals are typically cream-of-the-crop recent law school graduates who use the clerkship as a stepping stone to a Wall Street law firm.

eventually arrives—is a closely guarded secret, and has remained so for 150 years, an illustration of the court's aloofness and majesty.

The justice system, and by extension the Court of Appeals, traces its roots back three thousand years, when the Sumerians became the first civilization to recognize the "state" as an entity separate from its ruling authority—a precursor to the "nation of laws, not of men" concept. Five centuries before Hammurabi of Babylon there were laws to protect the weak and the poor. New York's judiciary, dating to 1691 when the Assembly of the New York Colony directed that a court system be "duely and constantly kept," has been at the forefront of that tradition. Free speech rights were ensured in New York fifty years before the Bill of Rights was written. The Fifth Amendment guarantee of due process of law was taken directly from a New York statute.

The Court of Appeals was a creature of the 1846 constitutional convention, and a public lobbying campaign capped by journalist Horace Greeley. Greeley had declared New York courts to be in a "deplorable state" and roused public sentiment in a topic that previously had interested only governors and isolated pockets of lawyers, nonlawyers, and citizens who happened to have first-hand experience of a dysfunctional judicial system.

In the early 1800s, governors DeWitt Clinton, William Marcy, and William H. Seward pressed to reform the cumbersome Court for the Trial of Impeachments and Correction of Errors. But their efforts were largely in vain. Greeley, in a *New York Tribune* editorial of January 20, 1845, brought his influential newspaper behind a movement for court reform: "A great primary impulse of this movement has been the confessedly deplorable state of our higher courts of justice, choked with litigation which lingers from year to year and ruins clients by its enormous expensiveness without bringing their suits to a conclusion."[5]

Greeley continued to push the point, and on Election Day of 1845 the citizens of New York voted overwhelmingly to call a constitutional convention. With the elected leaders unable or unwilling to take on court reform themselves, the electorate forced the issue. Critical to what emerged was the makeup of the convention delegates: Among the delegates were forty-eight lawyers, the largest professional representation.[6] Chief among them was Charles J. Ruggles, who became convention chairman. When all was said and done, the New York Constitution had a new provision, Article VI, section 2, which declared: "There shall be a Court of Appeals." The new court would be comprised of eight judges, chosen not by the governor, but by popular election. It would be limited to lawyers (its predecessor, the Court for the Trial of Impeachments and Correction of Errors had included nonlawyer state senators). And it afforded New Yorkers an opportunity, at least every twenty years, to rewrite their constitution, to rework their government.

The new court took the bench for the first time on September 7, 1847, and, a mere two days later, Chief Judge Freeborn G. Jewett announced the panel's first decision—a case titled *Pierce* v. *Delamater*—in which the jurists found nothing improper about a Court of Appeals judge, Greene Bronson, reviewing his own lower court decisions.[7] Wachtler made light of the case frequently in speeches over the years.

"Let me set the scene," he began in one typical opening to the Greene Bronson matter.

Not only does the Court hold that Bronson can sit on the case, but the Court holds that, far from being wrong, this is the best method of conducting business. Let me quote: "There is nothing in the nature of the thing which makes it improper for a judge to sit in review upon his own judgments. If he is what a judge ought to be—wise enough to know that he is fallible, and therefore ever ready to learn; great and honest enough to discard all mere pride of opinion, and follow truth wherever it may lead; and courageous enough to acknowledge his errors"—and here's the kicker—"he is then the very best man to sit in review upon his own judgments. He will have the benefit of a double discussion. If right at first, he will be confirmed in his opinion; and if wrong, he will be quite as likely to find it out as anyone else."

Incidentally, guess who wrote the opinion? You got it, good old Justice Bronson. And I might add he affirmed the court below. If he didn't, he probably wouldn't have been able to live with himself.

Now can you see poor Mr. Pierce [the man appealing the case decided by Judge Bronson when he was on a lower court] paying all that money for an appeal and he walks into the Court of Appeals, and there's good old Justice Bronson—"Hi-ya fella!" I hear Pierce was going to try for cert [*certiorari*] but was afraid it might provoke Bronson's appointment to the Supreme Court.[8]

Over the next quarter century, the court continued to evolve into its present configuration of a chief judge and six associates, all serving fourteen-year terms and all required to retire at the age of seventy.

Shortly after its establishment, the Court of Appeals began carving its reputation as one of the finest and most progressive common law courts in the land, and one that was not afraid to snub the highest court in the land and find protections for New Yorkers beyond those available in the federal constitution. The court's zealous protection of criminal rights, particularly in the right to counsel and search-and-seizure areas, is exceeded only by its historical respect for individual liberties. For example, in 1857, the U.S. Supreme Court ruled in the *Dred Scott* case that a Congress had no authority to limit slavery in the territories. Three justices went so far as to find that a black man descended from slaves had no rights as an American citizen. But in New York, the Court of Appeals decided a similar case in 1860, *Lemmon* v. *The People*,[9] securing freedom for a Virginia slave who passed through the state en route to Texas, where she was to join her owner's other household property.

Over the next century and a half, it overturned laws that barred consensual sodomy and forced stores to close on Sundays. It ruled that topless dancing is protected free speech, but child pornography is not. It upheld restrictions on working hours in 1901, supported zoning in 1920, and backed rent controls in 1921. Through Cardozo's famous writing in *Palsgraf* v. *Long Island Railroad Co.*[10] in 1928, the court rewrote the law of negligence for the industrial age. Particularly through Cardozo, it established a national scheme for the law of negligence in the Industrial Age.

Palsgraf was a case that started when railroad guards attempted to assist a passenger attempting to board a moving train. During the maneuver, the passenger dropped an unmarked package containing fireworks. The fireworks exploded, causing a scale at the other end of the platform to topple onto the plaintiff. Was the railroad liable? Cardozo, writing for a split court, denied liability, in a typically eloquent statement: "The risk reasonably to be perceived defines the duty to be obeyed, and the risk imports relation; it is a risk to another or to others within the range of apprehension. . . . Negligence, like risk, is thus a term of relation. Negligence in the abstract, apart from things related, is surely not a tort, if, indeed, it is understandable at all."[11]

From that background, eleven New Yorkers, plus Thurgood Marshall, a Baltimore native who served on a federal appeals court in Manhattan, have worn the robes of U.S. Supreme Court justice.

John Jay, New York's first chief judge and the the U.S. Supreme Court's first chief justice, served from 1789 to 1795 following his appointment by Washington and was later elected governor of New York. Henry Brockholst Livingston of New York City was appointed by Jefferson and served from 1807 to 1823. Smith Thompson, a Monroe appointee from Westchester County, sat on the high court from 1823 to 1843. Samuel Nelson of Hebron served from 1845 to 1872 following his nomination by Tyler.

Ward Hunt of Utica was appointed by Grant and served from 1873 to 1882. Hunt had served on the Court of Appeals.

Joseph P. Bradley of Albany, another Grant appointee, was on the high court from 1870 to 1892. Samuel Blatchford of New York City was appointed by Arthur and served from 1882 to 1893. Rufus Wheeler Peckham Sr. of Altamont served from 1895 to 1909 following his appointment by Cleveland. Peckham had served on the Court of Appeals. Cleveland also nominated his brother, Wheeler Hazard Peckham, who, however, failed to win Senate confirmation. Rufus's son, Rufus Jr., later served on the Court of Appeals.

Charles Evans Hughes of Glens Falls served as an associate Supreme Court justice from 1910 to 1916 and as chief justice from 1930 to 1941. Hughes was appointed by Taft in 1910, quit to run for president against Wilson in 1916, and, after losing that race and serving stints as secretary of state under Harding and Coolidge, was nominated for chief justice by Hoover in 1930.

The last native New Yorker to make the ascent was the famous Cardozo, a Hoover nominee who left the Court of

Appeals to spend six years in Washington, from 1932 to 1938. However, Robert H. Jackson, a Franklin Roosevelt appointee, served from 1941 to 1954. Although a native of Pennsylvania, Jackson grew up in the Jamestown area of Western New York.

With its historical posture as one of the nation's top legal tribunals, New York's Court of Appeals is watched closely by other state and federal courts and its decisions have intellectual and jurisprudential impact beyond the state's borders.[12] Yet, the court is more than a legal phenomenon. It is also a cultural one.

"Appellate Courts today are speaking to matters as diverse as the fate of the homeless and who will win the America's Cup," Wachtler said. "The judges are no longer writing only for lawyers and other judges and law review articles, they are now writing for the public."[13]

The Court of Appeals operates like the Supreme Court, with selective jurisdiction, meaning it largely chooses its cases. But it has historically cherished its independence and power to find more rights under the state constitution than the Supreme Court holds are required under the federal constitution. Hence, free speech enjoys greater protections in New York than virtually anywhere else in the country. Likewise, citizens have a far more powerful shield against police intrusiveness.

The court had been seeking more power to select its cases since at least 1967, when Chief Judge Fuld's plan to end automatic appeals was opposed by the New York State Bar Association. It finally obtained that power in 1985, shortly after Wachtler became chief. When Governor Cuomo signed the bill giving the court *certiorari* power, the court—and often Wachtler—could largely pick and choose the cases it wanted to consider, just as the U.S. Supreme Court did.

Under chief judges Cooke and Breitel, the court greatly

expanded criminal rights, particularly in the right-to-counsel arena. But by 1981, when Wachtler's influence was growing, the court began taking a more pragmatic approach to crime and punishment. Wachtler was furious when a Legal Aid Society report suggested he was drifting right. "I don't think I can be predicted in terms of liberalism or conservatism," Wachtler replied angrily. "Any judge who responds to public clamor or newspaper editorials is doing himself and his position a great disservice. I hope that I'm judged only in terms of justice and reasonableness."[14]

If the court was drifting right in the early 1980s—and that is debatable—Wachtler was clearly aware of its historical independence and clearly wanted his court to be nationally distinctive. He frequently took on the critics of so-called judicial activism, including President Reagan's attorney general, Edwin Meese, and left little doubt that under his reign, the court would do as it pleased.

"There is a place for judicial restraint," Wachtler said. "But the protection of such things as individual and privacy freedoms is a uniquely judicial obligation and responsibility. Judicial restraint should not be confused with judicial abdication."

But that put Wachtler in a politically tenuous position. He was acutely aware that his outspoken activism could jeopardize any chance of garnering a U.S. Supreme Court seat. On the other hand, Wachtler's brand of conservatism was still far too liberal for the Reagan administration.

On the first day back in session after Wachtler's arrest, the judges wrestled with the question of the center seat. Should it remain vacant? In the end, a dour Dick Simons, the senior associate and acting chief, took the center, and the court quietly settled down to business, oddly to consider two sexual misconduct cases: the privacy rights of a girl who had been molested and a $4 million-plus award to a *Penthouse* magazine centerfold who said she was forced to perform sexual favors for the magazine's founder, Robert Guccione. The judges made no comment, but issued a memorandum to court personnel: "We will not presume to know your feelings, but for those of us who worked closely with the chief judge, we return to our work this week with a profound sadness mixed with the hope that the circumstances will be resolved quickly and justly without further pain to any of the parties involved. . . . No transition is painless, and we undertake ours at a time when the emotional strain of the past days is still fresh and the public scrutiny unusually intense."

Years after Wachtler's resignation and several years into his redemption, one portrait has remained conspicuously absent from those of the chiefs and associate judges that line the courtroom walls. Some day, when the scandal has been forgotten or its details lost in the haze of time, Wachtler will take his place among the chiefs.

Notes

1. Luke Bierman, "Institutional Identity and the Limits of Institutional Reform: The New York Court of Appeals in the Judicial Process," unpublished doctoral dissertation, 1994.

2. John Caher, "N.Y.'s Chief Judge Brings Vigor, Leadership to Job," Albany *Knickerbocker News*, January 28, 1988, p. 1A.

3. Judith S. Kaye, "The Importance of State Courts: A Snapshot of the New York Court of Appeals," *Annual Survey of American Law*, New York University School of Law, 1994.

4. Interview with Wachtler on August 15, 1997.

5. Francis Bergan, *The History of the New York Court of Appeals 1847–1932* (New York: Columbia University Press, 1985), p. 3.

6. Ibid., 15.

7. *Pierce v. Delamater*, 1 NY 3 (1847).

8. Wachtler's archives.

9. *Lemmon v. The People*, 20 Nr 562 (1860).

10. *Palsgraf v. Long Island R. Co.*, 162 NE 99 (1928).

11. Ibid.

12. Vincent Bonventre, "State Constitutionalism in New York: A Non-Reactive Tradition," *Emerging Issues in State Constitutional Law* 31 (1989): 31–32.

13. John Caher, "When Lawyers Talk, Few Understand," Albany *Sunday Times Union*, April 15, 1990, p. A1.

14. David Margolick, "New York's Court of Appeals Faces Vast Changes as a New Era Begins," *The New York Times*, November 7, 1982.

CHAPTER 7

Crime

L ouis DeBour was walking along a Brooklyn street, seemingly minding his own business, when he attracted the attention of police on foot patrol. It was after dark in a high crime area and DeBour nervously crossed the street when he saw police officers approaching. The officers thought DeBour looked suspicious, and the closer they got to the man, the more the bulge in his jacket resembled a gun. Did the police have the right to frisk?

In the absence of any concrete indication of criminality, the state and federal courts have devised only a hazy line between permissible and impermissible police-citizen encounters. They have found that police can briefly detain a citizen on something less than the "probable cause" required for an arrest, but that something must be more than curiosity or a hunch.

The U.S. Supreme Court split 8 to 1 and yielded a decision with four separate written opinions when it tried to define that something in the 1967 case of *Terry* v. *Ohio*. "Police officers must be able to point to specific and articulable facts, which, taken together with rational inferences from the facts, reasonably warrant that intrusion," Chief Justice Earl Warren wrote for the Court.[1]

But Justice William O. Douglas, dissenting, expressed grave concern: "If the individual is no longer to be sovereign, if the police can pick him up whenever they do not like the cut of his jib, if they can 'seize' and 'search' him in their discretion, we enter a new regime." The Supreme Court defines that something as an "articulable suspicion."[2]

Terry v. *Ohio* arose out of an incident in downtown Cleveland when a veteran detective spotted two strangers who seemed to be casing out a store. The men alternately walked back and forth, pausing to stare in the same store window. Each circuit—about twenty-four trips in total—was followed by a conference on the street corner. At one point, they were joined by a third man.

The detective approached the men, identified himself, and asked for identification. One of the men mumbled something and the detective spun him around, patted him down, and found a pistol. He similarly searched the other two suspects, and found that one of them was also packing a weapon. The question for the Supreme Court, following their conviction on weapons charges, was whether the officer had any right to conduct the search.

The Court went well beyond the limits of this particular case and established a benchmark for future search-and-seizure cases. What the Court said was: the Fourth Amendment shield against unreasonable searches applies as much on the street as it does in the home; whenever a police officer restrains an individual, he has "seized" that person within the context of the Fourth Amendment; a police officer who reasonably fears for his or her safety or the public's can search for weapons, even absent "probable cause" to arrest; such a search must be evaluated in the context of the exigencies of the unique situation at hand.

"We conclude," the Court said,

> that the revolver seized from Terry was properly admitted in evidence against him. At the time he seized petitioner and searched him for weapons, Officer McFadden had reasonable grounds to believe that petitioner was armed and dangerous, and it was necessary for the protection of himself and others to take swift measures to discover the true facts and neutralize the threat of harm if it materialized. The policeman carefully restricted his search to what was appropriate to the discovery of the particular items which he sought. Each case of this sort will, of course, have to be decided on its own facts. We merely hold today that, where a police officer observes unusual conduct which leads him reasonably to conclude in light of his experience that criminal activity may be afoot and that the persons with whom he is dealing may be armed and presently dangerous, where, in the course of investigating this behavior, he identifies himself as a policeman and makes reasonable inquiries, and where nothing in the initial stages of the encounter serves to dispel his reasonable fear for his own or others' safety, he is entitled for the protection of himself and others in the area to conduct a carefully limited search of the outer clothing of such persons in an attempt to discover weapons which might be used to assault him. Such a search is a reasonable search under the Fourth Amendment, and any weapons seized may properly be introduced in evidence against the person from whom they were taken.[3]

People v. *DeBour*[4] is New York's *Terry* v. *Ohio*, and the seminal case on search and seizure. Sol Wachtler, who seemed to have a knack for drawing search-and-seizure cases, drew *DeBour* and crafted it into a landmark.

"The basic purpose of the constitutional protections against unlawful searches and seizures is to safeguard the privacy of each and every person against all arbitrary intrusions by government," Wachtler wrote for the 5-2 court when he was an associate judge in 1976. "Therefore, any time an intrusion on the security and privacy of the individual is undertaken with intent to harass or is based upon mere whim, caprice or idle curiosity, the spirit of the Constitution has been violated."

On that standard, Louis DeBour's conviction for weapon possession was upheld. The Court of Appeals held that police were justified in talking with the suspect, and then frisking him when it appeared he had a gun. In a later case, however, where police frisked a suspect based only on an anonymous tip, Wachtler wrote the opinion overturning the conviction and finding that the rights of citizens would be "severely eroded" if authorities were allowed to conduct searches on such flimsy evidence.

What Wachtler did through *DeBour* and its progeny was to establish an extraordinary four-tiered shield that protects the citizenry from overzealous police, and seeks to provide police at the same time with a formula for peeling away those levels of protection. At the first level, an officer needs nothing more than some "objective credible belief" before approaching a person and requesting information. At the second level, police may stop, but not seize, a person when there is a "founded suspicion that criminal activity is afoot." A brief detention and frisk requires a "reasonable and articulable suspicion" of criminal activity, or something more than the "founded suspicion" required at level two. Finally, an arrest requires "probable cause" to believe that a crime has been committed and that the suspect committed it.[5]

The Court of Appeals was usually at the vanguard of criminal rights, more often proactive than reactive. Wachtler, despite his political entreaties to the conservative wing of the party, generally respected that tradition. But he became more pragmatic—legally and politically—in his later years when, as chief judge, he was more acutely aware of the crime problem and, in the eyes of skeptics, resurrecting the crime-fighting image he invented in his successful run for the Court of Appeals in 1972. The same judge who, as a candidate, had himself filmed slamming a prison door shut, said at his confirmation hearing for chief judge:

> It might be bureaucratically comforting to say that if the courts did their job, the war on crime would be won. But to do so is misleading. The courts do not cause crime and the courts do not prevent it. And even if the courts were to function at maximum efficiency, it would still make only a small impact on crime prevention because the courts are simply at the wrong end of the criminal cycle. The courts' principal job is not to stop crime, but rather to administer justice. It cannot be repeated too often or too loudly that the courts and the judges are not quiet implementers or expeditors of the prosecutor's office. They are the guardians of justice in our society.

Whether attributed to internal turmoil or political opportunism, Wachtler's record on criminal law was seemingly inconsistent and increasingly influenced by pragmatism. Four years after *DeBour*, for instance, Wachtler led the court in reinstating the conviction of a man found, during a questionable search, with an illegal weapon.

"It would, indeed, be absurd to suggest that a police officer has to await the glint of steel before he can act to preserve his safety," Wachtler wrote for the court.[6]

In a 1981 address, he said:

When law and order breaks down, civilization itself threatens to break down. And that is precisely what is happening in many areas of America today. Law and order is breaking down and unless we win the war against crime, our civilization will also break down. That is a broad and harsh statement, but I believe it is an accurate one. The crime statistics we have heard . . . are testimony to the nightmare which is paralyzing our society, a nightmare which causes our citizens to live fearful and distorted lives behind triple-locked doors—a caricature of a citizen in a nation that prides itself on freedom and civil liberties.[7]

Even then, however, Wachtler was supportive of fundamental constitutional rights, and fearful that politicians pandering to public fear would dilute those rights.

"As repugnant as it may seem to some," Wachtler reminded his audience,

every one of our citizens comes into our criminal justice system presumed to be innocent. He has a right not to be forced into confession. He has a right to counsel. If evidence was unlawfully obtained, that evidence may not be used to convict him. These rights we deem constitutionally guaranteed—they represent a commitment which we have with our Founding Fathers and which I believe are essential to our fundamental sense of fairness and our belief in freedom.

But as sacrosanct and immutable as our Constitution may seem, it was not etched by lightning on tablets of stone. The freedoms declared by the Constitution are granted by the people and those same people can revoke them. This was observed by Alexander Hamilton when the Constitution was being adopted. He noted that however fine an instrument it might be, its survival would depend on "public opinion and the general spirit of the people."[8]

Other times, he was a classic liberal, viewing crime in terms of social injustice. Mainly, however, he tended to give the police a long leash, with which they could—and sometimes did—hang themselves.

"If you were to measure the 'toughness' of judges by the jail population, you would find that, excluding the political prisoners in Russia and South Africa, the United States has the highest rate of imprisonment in the world," Wachtler said in an early 1980s speech.

And we in New York State are doing our part . . . we have put so many people in our state prisons that we have run out of space. But the public still says that we have to put more people in jail while at the same time it refuses to provide the funds for more prisons. . . . The public should know of the inefficiency and confusion caused by our antiquated multi-layered court structure. It should be told that jail is a precious correctional commodity to be used sparingly and only for serious crimes. It should be informed of the fact that the principal job of the courts is not to stop crime, but rather to administer justice.[9]

Wachtler wrote to uphold the right of police officers to draw their weapons and pat down suspects in some instances and to affirm the attempted murder and weapons possession conviction of a Black Liberation Army militant who gunned down two cops. In that 1977 case, he ruled that Richard Moore[10] received a fair trial, despite adverse pretrial publicity and despite evidence introduced at trial to show that the defendant was anti-police.*

In 1980, the court, in a decision written by Wachtler, reversed a lower court and upheld a pat-down-search that yielded a weapon. The case involved a New York City cop who found a weapon while frisking a suspect. A lower court threw out the charge, finding the frisk illegal. Wachtler, writing for the unanimous court, said: "It would, indeed, be absurd to suggest that a police officer has to await the glint of steel before he can act to preserve his safety."

He was infuriated by the *Bartolomeo* case of 1981 and, when he was chief judge ten years later, voted to overturn it.

Peter Bartolomeo was a 23-year-old Deer Park, Long Island, man who shot and killed a man during a late-night burglary on April 15, 1978. The Court of Appeals threw out Bartolomeo's confession and conviction. By a 4 to 3 vote, the court ruled that when police want to interrogate someone, they have to ask him if he already has a lawyer in the previous matter. If so, the suspect can't be questioned without the lawyer's permission and can't even waive that right outside the presence of the lawyer.

The *Bartolomeo* decision added a duty to inquire, which Wachtler thought absurd. He wrote the dissent, joined by colleagues "Mike" Gabrielli and Matthew Jasen, saying the new rule provided "what is in effect a dispensation for the persistent offender" and "an obstacle to law enforcement" that carried the "right to counsel to unheard-of extremes." A decade later, when Wachtler was chief, the court overruled its own precedent and reversed *Bartolomeo*.

"I thought it was a terrible decision," Wachtler later said of *Bartolomeo*.[11] Wachtler also dissented, with judges Hugh

---

*See chapter 8, "Pornography and Free Speech," for additional details on the *Moore* case.

Jones and Gabrielli, from a 1982 decision in which the court ordered a new trial for a man who admitted three different times to the sex-slaying of a college student, a minister's daughter. The majority said police misbehaved when they used a close friend of the suspect to snitch.

Wachtler despised *Bartolomeo*, which said that a suspect represented by counsel on one charge—say trespassing— could not be questioned on an unrelated charge—say, intentional murder—even after waiving his or her right to an attorney, and dissented when the court announced the rule in 1981. In 1990, in the case of *People* v. *Bing*,[12] the court overruled *Bartolomeo*, prompting a Kaye-led minority to criticize the majority for breaking with the panel's tradition.

"We time and again restated . . . our view that the right to counsel is a jealously guarded, cherished principle, so fundamental that the highest degree of vigilance would be exercised in its defense," Kaye wrote in a dissent joined by Alexander and Titone. Kaye had urged an exceptionally expansive reading of *Bartolomeo*. The majority, however, held that if Kaye's interpretation of *Bartolomeo* was accurate, then *Bartolomeo* was fundamentally flawed and had to be reversed. Wachtler was thrilled, Kaye disgusted.

"Today," Kaye complained, "the Court breaks with its proud tradition. . . . Not often in our history have we explicitly overruled a recent precedent, and rarely *if ever* have we done so by a closely divided Court."[13]

In 1983, Wachtler authored the unanimous opinion that overturned a rape conviction because the victim recalled her assailant only through hypnosis. "It has not been generally accepted in the scientific community as a reliable method of restoring memory."[14] The decision said hypnosis is an unreliable tool for refreshing memories and that testimony induced by hypnotism should not be allowed.

Wachtler put the 911 emergency call system in jeopardy in 1983 by upholding a $1 million award to a Kenmore murder victim. The court found that Erie County and Buffalo had erroneously dispatched police to the wrong place.

Other times, in his more liberal mode, Wachtler blamed crime on poverty and unemployment, drugs and other social factors, and sided with the underdog. He always opposed the death penalty, calling it the "chicken soup of politics" and arguing that capital punishment has no place in a civilized society. "It is an old folk remedy. . . . Nobody knows if it truly does what its proponents claim, but as any fancier of old fashioned remedies can tell you, like chicken soup, 'it can't hurt.' "[15]

In the early 1980s Wachtler predicted: "If we see a return of the death penalty, the initial enthusiasm will be great. The public may even swarm to watch the first executions on cable TV. But after a few months, we'll be back to watching reruns of *Gilligan's Island* and complaining that it still isn't safe to go to the corner drug store without an armed escort. It's all chicken soup. At its best it does no harm unless the public starts to believe that enacting the death penalty will cure the cancer of crime."[16]

The Supreme Court has wrestled, and will likely continue to wrestle, with the death penalty, with regard both to its constitutionality and its application.

In 1972, the U.S. Supreme Court held in *Furman* v. *Georgia*[17] that the death penalty, as then administered, was unconstitutional. The problem, the court found in that case, was that there were insufficient guidelines for who would die and who would not. "These death sentences are cruel and unusual in the same way that being struck by lightning is cruel and unusual," Justice Potter Stewart wrote.[18] The Court decided that the Eighth Amendment "cannot tolerate the infliction of a sentence of death that permits this unique penalty to be so wantonly and freakishly applied."[19]

Stewart, however, found nothing wrong with utilizing the death penalty as a tool for social retribution. "The instinct for retribution is part of the nature of man, and channeling that instinct in the administration of criminal justice serves an important purpose in promoting the stability of a society governed by law," Stewart wrote. "When people begin to believe that organized society is unwilling or unable to impose upon criminal offenders the punishment they 'deserve,' then there are sown the seeds of anarchy—self-help, vigilante justice, and lynch law."

Four years later, the Court revisited the issue in *Gregg* v. *Georgia*,[20] sidestepping the question of whether the death penalty was *per se* a violation of the Eighth Amendment. Put otherwise, convicts can be put to death, if appropriate procedures and safeguards are followed. That decision opened the floodgates.

The death penalty had long been part of New York's law and tradition by the time the state adopted its first constitution in 1777. In fact, the original constitution failed to even address cruel and unusual punishment.[21] Executions were mandated for first offenses of any of thirteen crimes, ranging from theft from a church to murder and rape. Hangings apparently fulfilled a role as public entertainment.

However, over the next two centuries, New York generally restricted its imposition of the ultimate penalty. Governors Alfred E. Smith and Herbert H. Lehman habitually commuted death sentences to life in prison in those cases where the Court of Appeals affirmed a conviction by a split vote. New York abolished the death penalty in 1965 in all cases except those involving the murder of a prison employee or police officer, or when the killer was already serving a life sentence for another crime. In those cases, the death penalty was mandatory. Governors Hugh Carey and Mario Cuomo repeatedly vetoed legislation to restore the death penalty after it was shot down on constitutional grounds.

Notwithstanding the fact that the Supreme Court had shot down the death penalty in 1972 because it was too arbitrary (and reinstated it four years later in *Gregg*), the Court of Appeals, shortly before Wachtler's ascension to center seat, rejected New York's capital punishment statute as too inflexible.

There was a 1984 case involving multiple killer Lemuel Smith, a Schenectady man already serving double 25-years-to-life terms for two Albany murders when he killed rookie prison guard Donna Payant at Green Haven Correctional Facility in Dutchess County. Under the existing statute, the penalty for that crime was death—no ifs, ands, or buts, and no room for judicial discretion. Justice Albert Rosenblatt—the same fine jurist who would shortly serve as Wachtler's chief administrator—sentenced Smith to the electric chair, as was required under the law. The court, with Wachtler playing only a limited role, shot down the law.

Judge Kaye, then the freshman jurist on the court, had been a member of the panel for only a year when she drew *People* v. *Lemuel Smith*.[22] Through Kaye, in an opinion joined by Wachtler, the court found the mandatory capital punishment statute unconstitutional. "A mandatory death statute simply cannot be reconciled with the scrupulous care the legal system demands to insure that the death penalty fits the individual and the crime," she wrote.[23]

When New York reinstated the death penalty in 1995, it specifically attempted to circumvent the Lemuel Smith problem and tried to head off other potential challenges. Two years later, the issue was still winding its way toward the Court of Appeals.

Wachtler, meanwhile, spent many of his years at the helm stumping for criminal justice issues. In a March 19, 1981, article for *Newsday,* Wachtler took on Chief Justice Warren Burger, who had just told the American Bar Association that criminal safeguards were too strict. Burger, sounding the conservative cry for victims' rights, asked: "Is a society redeemed if it provides massive safeguards for accused persons and yet fails to provide elementary protection for its decent law-abiding citizens?"

Wachtler responded:

The choice is not—and never has been—between safeguarding the accused and protecting the law-abiding. The two are not incompatible. We can have both, or we can have neither, but the lesson of history is that we cannot have one without the other. . . . Crime is born and lives in the slums, amid squalor and poverty. It grows in ignorance and it thrives on hopelessness. It stems from the collapse of respect and encouragement for high moral values, which society and government have a responsibility to nurture. What we do not know is what to do about it or, to be more precise, whether we are willing to devote the resources to try.[24]

In March 1985, Wachtler said the courts have a limited impact on crime, no matter how many judges are appointed or prisons built. "We are the janitors who clean up society's debris. We can't stem the flow of crime until we can get to the origins."[25]

And what are those origins? He claims ignorance, in contrast to previous statements on poverty. "Since we do not know the causes of crime we do not know very much about the rehabilitation of criminals," Wachtler said in an oft-repeated law-and-order speech.

We have found that you cannot tell much about how a man will behave free by studying how he behaves in a cage.

And we do know that prisons do not rehabilitate—they are more likely to be hotbeds of advanced criminal technology and homosexuality. That is not to say, of course, that society can afford to give up and abandon its responsibility. We must do a better job and continue to be as creative as possible in educating and training the inmates in our local and state facilities as much for their benefit as for ours.[26]

Wachtler had always been an enemy of the grand jury system, and getting indicted himself did nothing to endear him to a stacked process.

A grand jury is usually made up of twenty-three people, often the first twenty-three whose names are picked, not a carefully selected group like a trial jury. Their job is to determine if there is enough evidence to believe that a crime has been committed, and that the person arrested committed the crime. A simple majority vote sends the suspect to trial.

"Consider how today's grand jury functions," Wachtler offers.

Information comes to a district attorney concerning the commission of a crime. Witnesses are interviewed and evidence is gathered. The prosecutor concludes that sufficient proof exists to charge an individual with a crime. Now, with mind made up, the district attorney goes to the grand jury to obtain an indictment. The stamp of approval will be sought. The same witnesses, already interviewed, and the same evidence, already gathered, will now be presented to the grand jury. The legal adviser to the grand jury will be the same district attorney. The prosecutor alone will decide what they will hear. The defense has no right to present its case, or cross-examine, or have counsel present. It is, by design, a one-sided affair.[27]

Consequently, Wachtler said in the early 1980s, long before he was indicted on several charges, including extortion, that the government could never prove that "lives, careers and reputations are ruined because a grand jury indicts and the public treats the grand jury indictment as equivalent to an adjudication in criminal court. . . . We assume that where there's smoke there must be fire."

Wachtler lobbied tirelessly, and fruitlessly, to do away with grand juries. "Why not permit a felony prosecution upon a judicial determination that the available evidence—submitted by affidavits of the same persons we now require to appear before the grand jury—constitutes probable cause to believe that the felony charged has been committed by the defendant?" he asked repeatedly. "That determination, like the issuance of a search warrant, will be subject to judicial review and will be open, unlike grand jury proceedings, to public scrutiny and we will have saved the enormous expenditure of time, money, and personnel now required to submit every felony charge to a grand jury. Police officers, who must now spend untold hours waiting to testify before grand juries, can put their time to better use deterring crime on the streets."[28]

Wachtler, however, was in favor of maintaining one aspect of the grand jury system: the investigative aspect. Grand juries have proven useful in investigating organized crime and municipal corruption, and Wachtler had no intention of denying the citizenry that degree of control.

Judicially, the court under Wachtler addressed grand juries in several cases. It dismissed an indictment in a matter where the prosecutor's instructions were so confusing that the grand jury couldn't have carried out its proper function,[29] but upheld a conviction in a case where the prosecutor's questioning of the suspect was extremely aggressive, because the defendant, before being questioned, had been permitted to address the grand jury and to give an uninterrupted statement.[30]

During Wachtler's time as chief judge, the proliferation of drugs reached epidemic proportions and caused massive case management problems. Initially a supporter of the harsh "Rockefeller drug laws" that mandated tough sentences for narcotics violations, over time Wachtler saw the futility of that approach. His decisions began to evince some doubt as to the effectiveness and fairness of the drug laws. And, after experiencing prison and meeting scores of prisoners whose main crime was addiction, Wachtler regretted not taking a firmer stance against the Rockefeller laws.

"I wrote a dissent in a case where I attacked the Rockefeller drug laws," Wachtler told an audience of criminal defense attorneys in 1977. "I would have attacked it more vigorously, used more leadership and would have been more of an activist in doing away with them. . . . I must tell you that when Nelson Rockefeller first spoke to me about those drug laws, I thought they were fantastic. I thought they would be a wonderful deterrent. And how wrong I was. And how wrong are those people who believe that harsh penalties resolve crime."[31]

When Wachtler became chief, there was about 35,000 people in the state prisons. When he resigned, there were about 60,000. In between, New Yorkers paid $5.5 billion to build twenty-seven new prisons. As chief judge, and potential governor, Wachtler could not help but be influenced by the raw statistics.

He became an outspoken critic of the way the drug problem was being addressed by the federal and state governments, believing that education and rehabilitation—not lengthy incarceration—were the keys. He delivered lectures from Portland, Oregon, to Portland, Maine. He was on the drug committee of the Conference of Chief Justices and delivered the keynote address at the National Drug Conference held in Washington, D.C., in 1991. The irony struck him: While carrying on a crusade against illicit drugs, he was destroying his life taking a potpourri of prescribed medications.

Wachtler also altered his view of plea bargains, which he first called a "tacit form of blackmail" and later endorsed, to at least some extent. "There is nothing intrinsically unfair about a plea bargain," Wachtler said after becoming chief.

> Indeed, the plea bargain is heavily relied on by defense and prosecution alike precisely because both sides "lose" a little and both sides "gain" something and, therefore, the logic is that the plea agreement is "fair" to both sides. But a system that depends on plea bargaining to the extent that our present system does becomes, over time, less fair not only to defendants and victims, but to the people of New York.[32]

In *Wilkinson* v. *Skinner*,[33] Wachtler upheld an inmate's right to a trial on a claim that he was unjustifiably placed in solitary confinement for five days. In *People* v. *Bernhard Goetz*[34] in 1986, Wachtler clarified the law of self-defense, writing that a person is justified in using deadly force only if the individual "reasonably"—as opposed to irrationally or arbitrarily—believes such conduct is necessary. The decision sent Bernhard Goetz to trial, and eventually prison, for shooting youths he believed were going to rob him in a New York subway.

"We cannot lightly impute to the legislature an intent to fundamentally alter the principles of justification to allow the perpetrator of a serious crime to go free simply because that person believed his actions were reasonable and necessary to prevent some perceived harm," Wachtler wrote for the court. "To completely exonerate such an individual, no matter how aberrational or bizarre his thought patterns, would allow citizens to set their own standards for the permissible use of force. It would also allow a legally competent defendant suffering from delusions to kill or perform acts of violence with impunity, contrary to fundamental principles of justice and criminal law."[35]

He wrote the 1990 opinion in *People* v. *Manfred Ohrenstein*[36] that let the Senate minority leader off the hook for putting staff members to work on political campaigns. The Wachtler-led court concluded that since there was no law making it illegal for Manfred Ohrenstein to do what he did, the politician could not be prosecuted. Judge Simons was amazed. "I would have thought the use of public funds to finance the election campaigns of the candidates of one party and defeat the candidates of the oppositions was so clearly unlawful that it was not worth discussion," Simons wrote in dissent. "Any other view devalues the democratic process by leaving incumbent legislators free to perpetuate themselves in office at government expense."[37]

Wachtler, and his majority, however, were willing to give Ohrenstein an out.

Wachtler's perceived flip-flops on criminal justice matters are actually more typical than atypical and reflect, in part, the differing standards employed under the state and federal constitutions.

What confused the situation, according to Wachtler, was in his later years when the liberal Warren Court gave way to the Burger and Rehnquist courts. The variations and evolutions show the essential flexibility of the Constitution. "Instead of requiring strict prerequisite standards before a search warrant could be issued, the Supreme Court changed the rule to require the issuing court to look only to 'the totality of circumstances,'" Wachtler said.

The question arose as to whether the more flexible approach was consistent with the perceived aims of the State Constitution. In cases where the old rule announced by the Supreme Court has been well settled and provided workable guidelines for those who must employ it, New York has generally adhered to the settled precedent as a matter of state constitutional law, particularly when confusion generated by the new rule might jeopardize individual rights.[38]

In a similar vein, under the U.S. Constitution a person in custody does not have the right to have an attorney present at a lineup until formal charges are lodged. But in New York, the suspect does have such a right.

"The State Constitution contained no equivalent of the Fourth Amendment until 1938," Wachtler notes.

The amendment adopted that year is worded in terms identical to the federal counterpart. For many years, the Court of Appeals followed a policy of conforming the state constitution to the federal constitution, not only because of the identical wording, but also because of the desirability of having a single, clearly stated rule to guide police officers in the often rapidly unfolding situations they encounter on the streets. Through this process of adopting the federal rule, a consistent body of case law was developed under the state constitution.[39]

Both the New York and federal constitutions, for example, guarantee the assistance of counsel to someone charged with a crime. That seems simple enough. But figuring out when that right "attaches" or becomes relevant has bedeviled the courts for years. Obviously enough, the right to counsel is pertinent when a defendant is formally charged. But what if he is simply taken into custody?

The Supreme Court had ruled as early as 1932 on a somewhat vague right to counsel, waiting until 1938 to recognize a right to representation in a federal felony prosecution. Twenty-five years later, in *Gideon* v. *Wainwright*,[40] the justices finally declared that the Sixth Amendment right to counsel is such a basic, fundamental liberty that it must be respected by the states as well as the federal government. *Miranda* v. *Arizona*[41] was a broad—very broad—extension of that philosophy by an activist court on June 13, 1966.

Ernesto Miranda had been confronted by police on March 13, 1963, at his Phoenix, Arizona, home and accused of kidnapping and rape. Miranda was taken to the police station and interrogated by police officers who did not tell him of his right to have an attorney present. Two hours later, he signed a written confession. Miranda was convicted of kidnapping and rape. The Supreme Court, however, in a 5-4 vote, overturned the conviction and held for the first time that a suspect in custody must be apprised of her or his rights. While many state courts reluctantly adhered to the *Miranda* provisions, New York actually extended them.

"There's a school of thought," Wachtler said, "which tells us not to suppress evidence but, instead, to allow the evidence to be introduced while at the same time discouraging police misbehavior by permitting the defendant to sue the police officer for a constitutional violation. Can you picture a jury awarding damages to a convicted felon because the police officer didn't read him his *Miranda* warnings prior to his confession that he mugged and raped an elderly citizen?"

The Court of Appeals has added additional restrictions to. Once a defendant in New York is represented by an attorney, authorities cannot interrogate the suspect without the lawyer present, and the suspect cannot even waive his or her right to representation without the presence of an

Sol Wachtler in high school, 1947. (Wachtler's archives)

ELECT
Sol
WACHTLER

REPUBLICAN

REPUBLICAN

TOWN COUNCILMAN
TOWN OF NORTH HEMPSTEAD

"Elect Sol Wachtler" campaign card from his 1963 race for North Hempstead town council. (Wachtler's archives)

Top: The Wachtler family, 1965. From left to right are: Marjorie, Joan, Philip, Lauren, Sol, and Alison. (Wachtler's archives)

Bottom: Sol, second from left, in the town hall day care center he opened in North Hempstead, so that women with children could attend town hall meetings. (Wachtler's archives)

Wachtler and New York Governor Nelson Rockefeller during the 1967 race for Nassau County executive. (Wachtler's archives)

Sol and Joan on election night, 1967. Sol lost a close race for county executive to Eugene Nickerson, but won an important ally in Nelson Rockefeller. (Wachtler's archives)

Top: Wachtler's swearing in as a Court of Appeals judge in 1973 in the New York State Capitol. From left to right are: Judge Hugh Jones, Wachtler, Governor Rockefeller, Chief Judge Stanley Fuld, and Lieutenant Governor Malcolm Wilson. (Wachtler's archives)

Bottom: Wachtler's court, 1991. From left to right are : Stewart F. Hancock, Fritz W. Alexander, Richard D. Simons, Chief Judge Sol Wachtler, Judith S. Kaye, Vito J. Titone, and Joseph W. Bellacosa. (Photo courtesy of *Albany Times Union*)

Top: Governor Mario Cuomo signing a bill, late 1980s. From left to right are: Judges Titone, Simons, Alexander, Governor Cuomo, Chief Judge Wachtler, and Bellacosa. (Wachtler's archives)

Bottom: Wachtler giving a speech in Albany to mark the city's tricentennial year, 1986. (Photo courtesy of *Albany Times Union*)

Sol's 60th birthday party. From left to right are: Wachtler; his mother, Faye, then 90; and his brother, Morty. (Wachtler's archives)

Joy Silverman in 1989. (AP/Wide World photo)

Top: Immediately after Wachtler's arrest in 1992 (note the empty center chair), the court was shorthanded because the chief had resigned and two other judges had to recuse themselves from a case. Pinch hitting, at the far right, is Appellate Division Justice Leonard A. Weiss. (Photo courtesy of *Albany Times Union*)

Bottom: Wachtler shown with Barbara Walters during a break in an interview for *20/20* in August 1993. (AP/Wide World photo)

Top: Wachtler joins his former court at the annual Albany Bar Association dinner in February 1995 after his release from prison. From left to right are : Judge George Bundy Smith, Judge Joseph Bellacosa, and Wachtler. (Photo courtesy of *Albany Times Union*)

Bottom: Senator Alfonse D'Amato and Michael Chertoff, the prosecutor who brought Wachtler down, during Senate Whitewater hearings on December 15, 1995. (AP/Wide World photo)

attorney. This "indelible" right to counsel rule is, by most standards, the strictest in the nation, and it often plays out in an extremely controversial manner.

Consider the case of Bernard Harris, a man who brutally murdered and nearly decapitated his girlfriend in 1984 because, in his opinion, she was a bad mother. Even though police had time to obtain an arrest warrant, they had not bothered. Harris confessed to the crime at least three times, but only after police effected an illegal, warrantless search. The U.S. Supreme Court upheld Harris's conviction for murder, by a 5-4 vote. But the Court of Appeals in 1991 overturned the conviction.

"We conclude that the Supreme Court's rule does not adequately protect the search-and-seizure rights of the citizens of New York," Judge Simons—one of the court's more *conservative* members wrote—for the 5-2 majority.[42]

Despite the fact that the Fourth Amendment to the U.S. Constitution and its counterpart in the New York Constitution, Article 1, Section 12, are worded identically, the state court gleaned a different meaning. In *People* v. *Bernard Harris*,[43] the court reasoned: In New York, police cannot obtain an arrest warrant until criminal proceedings have begun, and once those proceedings begin, the suspect cannot be questioned without an attorney present. In the Harris case, police did not have a warrant, and even if they had had one, they wouldn't have been able to interrogate the suspect in the absence of his lawyer.

"Because the language of the Fourth Amendment of the United States Constitution and section 12 of article 1 of the New York State Constitution prohibiting unreasonable searches and seizures is identical, it may be assumed, as a general proposition, that the two provisions confer similar right," Simons wrote for the court. "Such consistency is desirable because it facilitates implementation of search-and-seizure rules. Nonetheless, the two documents do not present a monolithic legal code. Our federalist system of government necessarily provides a double source of protection and state courts, when asked to do so, are bound to apply their own constitutions notwithstanding the holdings of the United States Supreme Court."[44]

Wachtler, however, dissented along with Bellacosa and, in the view of some observers, had come full circle: During the early years, he followed conservatives like Gabrielli and Jones. In his middle years, he was more liberal. At the end, he seemingly followed the law-and-order path of his close friend, Bellacosa.

"When a judge first comes onto the court who has been in the civil practice, you don't have great familiarity with the criminal law," Wachtler said. "You are tentative at first and later become knowledgeable and firmer in your convictions. Judge Bellacosa came on the court with great knowledge of the criminal law. Others, who came out of the district attorney's office, had the same advantage. But, by and large, the others—like Hugh Jones, like Judith Kaye, like Sol Wachtler—would have come without any great practical experience with the criminal law."[45]

In his dissent in the Bernard Harris case, Bellacosa found "no reason to stretch precedent and twist logic in order to rescue this defendant from a United States Supreme Court decision against him. . . . [Police] had . . . cause to believe that the defendant had committed a heinous murder and they did what society expects its law enforcement officials to do: They set out to locate and apprehend the suspected murderer." Wachtler signed off on the dissent, and found himself in a 5-2 minority.

It was an important loss for Wachtler at a time when, studies show, he was leading the court on a more conservative path.

In 1991, in *People* v. *Erick Jackson,*[47] Wachtler led a bitterly divided court as it further weakened New York's right-to-counsel rule. At the heart of the ruling was a rule requiring that any prior statement of a prosecution witness must be turned over to the defense before trial. Until *Erick Jackson,* any failure to do so was grounds for an automatic reversal. But in 1991, Wachtler wrote an opinion diluting that protection, holding that reversal was required only when the case was actually prejudiced by the violation.

Toward the end of his career, eyeing the governor's mansion and having seen the problems of crime and punishment from the perspective of a man in charge of the judicial system, Wachtler became more willing to follow and less willing to lead in the arena of criminal rights. Perhaps the evolution of his criminal law position was simply following the track described by Sir Winston Churchill: "Any man who is under thirty, and is not a liberal, has not a heart; and any man who is over thirty, and is not a conservative, has no brains."

Regardless, *Bing* and *Erick Jackson* were watershed events in the conservative retrenchment of the Court of Appeals, a retrenchment generally attributed to Wachtler. Court scholar Vincent Bonventre of Albany Law School lamented that the Wachtler court was abandoning its traditional posture as a protector of individual rights and becoming "a Rehnquist court on the Hudson."[48]

A little firsthand experience at the wrong end of government power, however, brought Wachtler back to the fold. In his prison diary, the judge's tone on criminal justice mirrors his middle, more liberal, years on the Court of Appeals, not the beginning and the final years. Hindsight, as they say, is 20-20, particularly when it is your own hind in sight.

"Frankie, my executive assistant, and Neil, my security officer, used to tell me that . . . I never knew the pain of indifference—the rudeness of the clerk behind the counter or motor vehicle window," Wachtler wrote in his prison diary. "During my incarceration these past months, I have known what it is to be ignored and the subject of incredible rudeness. Worse yet, I have been treated by persons in authority as a nonperson, worthy not of respect, but only contempt, and not because of what I did to get here, but solely because I am here."

Just a few years earlier, perhaps, he would have seen little wrong with that.

But there is the legitimate question of whether Wachtler was truly growing more conservative on criminal rights, or just so distracted by his infidelity that he was failing to pay much attention and generally following Bellacosa. The 1992 cases of *People* v. *Scott* and *People* v. *Keta*[49] suggest the latter.

These cases,* decided together, dealt with critical matters of search and seizure, exactly the type of issues that had intrigued Wachtler for twenty or more years. Yet the chief judge was nowhere to be found in over forty pages of decision and—more importantly—his court was uncharacteristically fractured. Wachtler, who abhorred that type of judicial sniping, and looked down on the U.S. Supreme Court for tolerating such public cattiness, was virtually AWOL. Yet no one realized that the chief was coming unglued, and Wachtler himself, to the extent that he thought about the divisiveness of the *Scott* and *Keta* cases at all, more or less figured that his judges, by this time veterans, were simply testing their authority. It wasn't until later—when it was too late—that he recognized how distracted and disturbed he had been during that period.

---

*See chapter 11, "Errant Knights and Activism," for a more thorough examination.

Notes

1. *Terry* v. *Ohio,* 392 U.S. 1, 24–25 (1967).
2. Ibid.
3. Ibid.
4. *People* v. *DeBour,* 40 NY2d 210 (1976), p. 217 352 NE 2d 375.
5. Ibid.
6. *People* v. *Benjamin,* 51 NY2d 257 (1980).
7. Wachtler's archives.
8. Ibid.
9. Ibid.
10. *People* v. *Moore,* 42 NY2d 421 (1977), 366 NE 2d 1330.
11. Interview with Wachtler on August 21, 1997.
12. *People* v. *Bing,* 76 NY2d 333 (1990), p. 351, 558 NE 2d 1011.
13. Ibid.
14. *People* v. *Hughes,* 59 NY2d 523 (1983), 453 NE 2d 484.
15. Wachtler's archives.
16. Ibid.
17. *Furman* v. *Georgia,* 408 U.S. 238 (1972).
18. Ibid.
19. Ibid.
20. *Gregg* v. *Georgia,* 428 U.S. 153 (1976).
21. James Acker, "New York's Proposed Death Penalty Legislation: Constitutional and Policy Perspectives," *Albany Law Review* 54 (1990): 551.
22. *People* v. *Lemuel Smith* 63 Nf 2d 41 (1984), p. 78, 468 NE 2d 879.
23. Ibid.
24. Comments on the NBC-TV program "Today" in New York, March 10, 1985.
25. Wachtler's archives.
26. Ibid.
27. Ibid.
28. Ibid.

29. *People* v. *Caracciola,* 78 NY2d 1021 (1991), 581 NE 2d 1329.

30. *People* v. *Karp,* 76 NY2d 1006 (1990), 566 NE 2d 1156.

31. "Preparing to Win: Strategic Trial Preparation," National Association of Criminal Defense Lawyers. Boston, spring seminar, 1997.

32. Wachtler's archives.

33. *Wilkinson* v. *Skinner,* 34 NY2d 53 (1974), 312 NE 2d 158.

34. *People* v. *Bernhard Goetz,* 68 NY2d 96 (1986), 497 NE 2d 41.

35. Ibid., p. 111.

36. *People* v. *Manfred Ohrenstein,* 77 NY2d 238 (1990), 565 NE 2d 493.

37. Ibid.

38. Wachtler's archives.

39. Ibid.

40. *Gideon* v. *Wainwright,* 466 U.S. 648 (1964).

41. *Miranda* v. *Arizona,* 384 U.S. 436 (1966).

42. *People* v. *Bernard Harris,* 77 NY2d 434 (1991), 570 NE 2d 1051.

43. Ibid.

44. Ibid.

45. Interview with Wachtler on August 21, 1997.

46. *People* v. *Bernard Harris.*

47. *People* v. *Erick Jackson,* 78 NY2d 638 (1991), 585 NE 2d 795.

48. John Caher, "Taking a Conservative Swing?" Albany *Times Union,* February 17, 1992, p. A-1.

49. *People* v. *Scott* and *People* v. *Keta,* 79 NY2d 474 (1992), 593 NE 2d 1328.

CHAPTER 8

Pornography and Free Speech

An undercover investigator with the Erie County sheriff's department made several secret visits in 1982 to Village Book and News, an adult bookstore just north of Buffalo and a reputed den of prostitution. He observed sexual activity by the other patrons, and was himself solicited for sex, before reporting to Erie County District Attorney Richard Arcara. Arcara vowed to shut down the store as a public nuisance, but Sol Wachtler stood in his way.

Wachtler had just become chief judge when Arcara's case came to his court the first time, and he unhesitatingly found that closing the bookstore violated the free speech provision of the U.S. Constitution. But the Supreme Court reversed,[1] ruling that under the federal constitution a state can shut down a bookstore because the customers are doing something illegal—in this case, promoting prostitution—even though the owner is completely innocent.

Encouraged, Arcara returned to the Court of Appeals, but in a line-in-the-sand ruling, the young Wachtler court stood its ground, snubbed its nose at the highest court in the land, and found a safeguard in its own constitution. Holding that under New York's free expression clause, it's not who is aimed at, but who is hit,[2] the state must show that no other measures, such as prosecuting the patrons, will eliminate the nuisance before the store can be closed. The court found that prosecutors could use the law to halt sexual activity, but that closing the store was too drastic a solution to the problem and an unnecessary limit on free expression.

By basing its decision on the state constitution, the Wachtler court issued a ruling beyond the scope of the U.S. Supreme Court, an announcement to the state and nation that the independent tradition of the New York Court of Appeals was safe with Sol Wachtler at center seat. Wachtler and his court sent the same message in a pair of decisions written by Judge Simons, both resulting from an incident in Erie County that involved, again, District Attorney Arcara. In the two *People* v. *P.J. Video* cases,[3] the court relied on the state constitution to shield a video store that would not have been protected under federal law.

P.J. Video had been charged with various obscenity counts after a judge approved a search warrant based on a somewhat vague description by a police officer of what were apparently obscene materials. In the first case, in 1985, the court voided the warrants because the police affidavits were not sufficiently detailed. Arcara took the case to the U.S. Supreme Court, which found nothing wrong with the affidavits and remanded the matter to the Court of Appeals. On remand, the court affirmed its previous ruling. But far more importantly, it declared its independence from the justices in Washington, announcing that even though the search-and-seizure provisions of the state constitution are identical to those in the federal document, New York can, and at times will, construe greater protections.

Simons noted:

We, of course, are bound by Supreme Court decisions defining and limiting federal constitutional rights but "in determining the scope and effect of the guarantees of fundamental rights of the individual in the Constitution of the State of New York, this court is bound to exercise its judgment and is not bound by a decision of the Supreme Court of the United States limiting the scope of similar guarantees in the Constitution of the United States." (citations omitted)[4]

The *Cloud Books* and *P.J. Video* decisions were important early statements from the Wachtler court, which would, to some extent, set the tone for years to come.

Generally, obscenity falls outside the purview of the First Amendment and although the U.S. Supreme Court has declared unconstitutional bans on publications, it has also permitted government to regulate the sale and distribution of obscene works. The federal court has consistently required narrowly drawn regulations, based on the rather vague notion of "community standards." As Justice Potter Stewart once said, he could not define obscenity, but would know it when he saw it.

The Supreme Court made its first attempt to define obscenity in the 1957 case of *Roth* v. *United States.*[5] Justice William Brennan, writing for the majority, said that a work was obscene and outside the protections of the First Amendment if it appealed primarily to prurient interests. With *Roth*, the average person and the community set the standard.

"Under a national Constitution, the fundamental First Amendment limitation on the powers of the state do not vary from community to community, but this does not mean that there are, or should or can be, fixed uniform national standards of precisely what appeals to the 'prurient interest' or what is 'patently offensive,' " the Court said in *Roth*.

> These are essential questions of fact, and our nation is simply too big and too diverse for the court to reasonably expect that such standards could be articulated in all [fifty] states in a single formulation, even assuming prerequisite consensus exists. When triers of fact are asked to decide whether "the average person, applying contemporary community standards," would consider certain materials "prurient," it would be unrealistic to require the answer be based on some abstract formulation. The adversary system, with lay jurors as the ultimate fact finders in criminal prosecution, has historically permitted triers of fact to draw on the standards of their community, guided always by limiting instructions on the law. To require a state to structure obscenity laws around evidence of a national "community standard" would be an exercise in futility.[6]

But by 1973, Brennan himself concluded that the definition was unworkable. "I am forced to conclude," he said, "that the concept of 'obscenity' cannot be defined with sufficient specificity and clarity to provide fair notice to persons who create and distribute sexually oriented materials, to prevent substantial erosion of protected speech as a byproduct of the attempt to suppress unprotected speech, and to avoid very costly institutional harm."[7]

The Supreme Court, in the 1973 case of *Miller* v. *Cali-*

fornia,[8] established a test for determining if material is or is not obscene. Under the test, a work is obscene if it: appeals to the prurient interests of the average person, whoever that may be; describes sexual conduct in a "way that is patently offensive; and lacks "serious literary, artistic, political or scientific value" when taken as a whole. The following year, the high court clarified its ruling when it overturned a Georgia court's finding that Mike Nichols's *Carnal Knowledge*—a film starring Jack Nicholson, Ann-Margret, Art Garfunkel, and Candice Bergen—was obscene.

"It would be a serious misreading of *Miller* to conclude that juries have unbridled discretion to determine what is 'patently offensive,'" Justice William Rehnquist wrote for the court.[9] In a concurring opinion, justices William O. Douglas, William Brennan, and Thurgood Marshall—all of whom had dissented from *Miller*—reasserted their argument that the *Miller* standard was impractical as it effectively relegated to the Supreme Court the final word on what is and what is not obscene.

Pornography remains constitutionally protected free speech, until and unless it falls afoul of the definition—whatever that may be at the moment—of "obscenity." That leaves the state courts to decide, within the confines of their own constitutions, where to draw the line. As the Supreme Court said explicitly in *Miller*: "We emphasize that it is not our function to propose regulatory schemes for the states." That, the justices said, "is the role of the state legislatures and courts."[10]

The Court of Appeals has long flexed its muscle of independence in free-speech cases. For instance, it is far harder to obtain a warrant to seize allegedly obscene films in New York than in other states.

After *Miller*, the Court of Appeals heard a series of obscenity cases, some of them quite shocking to the moral conservatives on the bench. Once, an attorney approached the court and, just as he was beginning his presentation, was interrupted by Judge Adrian Burke, who demanded: "You're not defending one of those disgusting magazines, like *Playboy*, are you?" Actually, he was trying to convince the court, and Burke, that a photograph of a man having sex with his child—the kind of thing *Playboy* would never run—did not qualify as obscene. The judges, who were somewhat shocked by mainstream adult magazines, disagreed. Another time, the court was called on to examine the artistic merit of a porn film classic, *Debbie Does Dallas*.

The film was described at some length in the brief, but Wachtler's clerk, Michael Trainor, had seen it and thought the description inaccurate. Trainor went on and on about the alleged mischaracterizations, and Wachtler decided to have some fun with him. One day, Judge Kaye—prim, proper, and reserved and far more likely to have seen the latest opera than a porn film—came into Wachtler's chambers and, with Trainor in earshot, said, "You know Sol, that's not how I remember *Debbie Does Dallas* at all." Trainor cut in, "Yeah, remember that scene where . . ." and went on for several minutes before Kaye and Wachtler collapsed in side-splitting laughter, and Trainor realized he'd been had. Kaye, of course, had not seen the film.[11]

Generally, all but the most offensive speech—pornography included—was safe in Court of Appeals Hall. However, the New York court has not *always* been at the vanguard of free speech and, on rare occasions, has been ruled too restrictive by the Supreme Court. Take for example, the "Son of Sam Law" (named for the killer David Berkowitz, who called himself the "Son of Sam"), which was designed to prevent criminals from profiting from their crime by writing books. After the Court of Appeals, including Wachtler, upheld the constitutionality of the law, it was stricken by the U.S.

Supreme Court in *Simon & Schuster* v. *New York Crime Victims Board.*[12]

"Our feeling was if there was a profit made by virtue of a crime being committed, that the perpetrator of the crime shouldn't benefit from it," Wachtler explained.[13] "There just seemed to be something wrong with someone who commits a heinous crime and then makes money. It almost seemed against public policy because it could be an inducement to commit a crime."

After the Supreme Court struck down the New York law —the one Wachtler voted to uphold—the state enacted a weaker version. (Ironically, after Wachtler published his own book, *After the Madness: A Judge's Own Prison Memoir,* in the spring of 1997, the New York attorney general threatened to go after the proceeds, invoking the "Son of Sam" statute.)

Also, in 1959, the Supreme Court overturned a New York law requiring movie producers to get a license before distributing films.[14] Kinglsey Pictures Corp. had produced a film version of *Lady Chatterley's Lover* by D. H. Lawrence and the state Board of Regents denied it a license, finding three scenes immoral. The Supreme Court shot down the board's ruling. "What New York has done," the court said, "therefore, is to prevent the exhibition of a motion picture because that picture advocates an idea—that adultery under certain circumstances may be proper behavior. Yet the First Amendment's basic guarantee is of freedom to advocate ideas. The state, quite simply, has struck at the very heart of constitutionally protected liberty."[15]

Within that framework and context, and determined not to make the mistakes of the past, Wachtler constructed the state court's opinion in *Cloud Books.* "New York has a long history and tradition of fostering freedom of expression, often tolerating and supporting works which in other states would be found offensive to the community," Wachtler wrote for the court in the *Cloud Books* case.[16] "Thus, the minimal national standard established by the Supreme Court for First Amendment rights cannot be considered dispositive in determining the scope of this state's constitutional guarantee of freedom of expression."

Wachtler's opinion in *Cloud Books* was not a given, however, since his views on free speech—as in other areas of the law—were tempered, with firm conviction often giving way to pragmatism. A case in point is the 1979 matter of *Curle* v. *Ward.*[17]

Joseph Curle was a prison guard at Elmira Correctional Facility. Benjamin Ward, the commissioner of the Department of Correctional Services, forbid guards from becoming members of the Ku Klux Klan. Curle, suspected of Klan membership, was fired when he refused to respond to questions about his alleged affiliation with the racist group. He challenged the disciplinary action on free-speech grounds, and the Court of Appeals stood by his side—with Wachtler dissenting. "It has long been recognized that the constitutional guarantees of freedom of speech and assembly necessarily imply like protections for the freedom of association," Wachtler wrote. "On the other hand, it is true . . . that our commitment to liberty must sometimes yield to the exigencies of maintaining an orderly society."[18]

Wachtler pointed out that the prison population was, at the time, more than 70 percent African American and Hispanic, and that the Klan openly professed its hatred for those groups. He said that the mere presence of a guard subscribing to Klan doctrine could "infest the prison environment with the taint of racism" and "paralyze the rehabilitative process," adding: "Even if the prisoner does not know that a guard is a Klansman, his attitude may nonetheless be conveyed. The perception by inmates of their attitudes may breed frustration, hatred and disruption. Hence, grave and immediate harm may be caused by the communication of racist attitudes regardless of the absence of illegal specific intent or [readily] demonstrable racist behavior."

Wachtler was willing to sidestep the free-speech concerns of the guard in order to head off *potential* troubles in the prison system. "If the threat to the prison system is shown to be grave and immediate, it would be irresponsible and indeed indefensible to await catastrophe as a necessary antecedent to preventative action. The First Amendment does not require such a result, and the conscience will not allow it."[19]

Wachtler's views on pornography were similar, although he generally thought consenting adults should be able to do whatever they wished, so long as they weren't violating the rights of others.

"Sexual acts between consenting adults should not be criminal offenses, unless they violate the rights of others to be in a public place without fear or solicitation or embarrassment," Wachtler told a January 1979 audience at Hofstra University. He did not, however, necessarily extend that protection to pornography: "The seeds of blight are sown by those who use the public streets and residential neighborhood as a marketplace to peddle vice. This is not to be confused with victimless crime."[20]

On the other hand, two years later Wachtler took a public thrashing when he wrote a decision striking down part of a kiddie porn law. The decision was widely misunderstood and damned by everyone from Terence Cardinal Cooke on down. The court struck down just one provision, but left intact the provisions regulating the use of children in sexual performance and the sale or distribution of kiddie porn.

Wachtler viewed free speech and free expression as the

core of political power in a democracy—absolutely essential to self-government, crucial to any search for truth, and the foundation of self-fulfillment. He was, therefore, reluctant to restrain the free press even of pornographers, although willing to do both under certain circumstances.

In Wachtler's view, a necessary condition of democracy is the presumption that opinions—valid or not—are worthy of protection, and that the best arbiter of truth is the marketplace of ideas. Free speech, in his mind, is a means, not an end, a process and not a result. Wachtler embraced strongly the free-speech philosophy of Justice Oliver Wendell Holmes.* "When men have realized that time has upset many fighting faiths, they may come to believe even more than they believe the very foundations of their own conduct that the ultimate good desired is better reached by free trade in ideas—that the best test of truth is the power of thought to get itself accepted in the competition of the market and that truth is the only ground upon which their wishes safely can be carried out," Justice Holmes wrote in a 1919 dissent.[21]

Wachtler's statement echoes Holmes's: "It is intolerable to think of any branch or agency of government being given the power to curb, moderate, or interfere with the communication of the free thoughts of a free people," Wachtler said. "Any attack on press freedom which is subversive of First Amendment guarantees must be resisted—not only in the interest of the press—but also in the public interest."[22]

Wachtler dissented when the Court of Appeals declined to recognize a right to hand out leaflets in a private shopping mall. The handbill case, People v. Remeny,[23] involved a man named Ronald Remeny who was arrested in 1974 for distrib-

---

*Some legal scholars suggest that Holmes's First Amendment views were not sufficiently capacious *until* he was influenced by a famous federal court jurist from New York: Leonard Hand.

uting handbills in violation of a New York City ordinance. Remeny had been distributing advertisements for jazz concerts on the sidewalk in front of Madison Square Garden when he was arrested. He was convicted and fined ten dollars.

Three decades earlier, the U.S. Supreme Court had upheld the constitutionality of the New York ordinance.[24] The state court shot it down with Wachtler's decision.

"The city of course has a legitimate interest in seeing that the exercise of the right does not contribute to the litter on the streets or otherwise violate the law," Wachtler wrote for the court. "Thus they may enact reasonable regulations governing the time, place and circumstances of distribution. But in our view they cannot enact an ordinance absolutely prohibiting all distribution of commercial handbills on city streets and call it a reasonable regulation of the activity. Although we sympathize with the city's desire to eliminate litter from the streets, we have concluded that the ordinance, as presently worded, is unconstitutional."[25]

In *Remeny*, Wachtler won a split decision, but he lost a tougher one a few years later in the shopping mall case.

Smith Haven Mall was a suburban shopping center on Long Island owned by the Prudential Insurance Co. The owners prohibited all types of political gatherings and leafletting inside the mall. In the summer of 1980, groups opposing nuclear energy, the "Shad Alliance," went to the mall and started handing out leaflets. A security officer ordered them to stop, and the groups sued.

It is important to note that New York's free-speech guarantee is considerably broader than that contained within the First Amendment to the U.S. Constitution, which states merely: "Congress shall make no law . . . abridging the freedom of speech." Article 1, Section 8 of the New York State Constitution reads: "Every citizen may freely speak, write and publish sentiments on all subjects, being responsible for the abuse of that right; and no law shall be passed to restrain or abridge the liberty of the press." Instead of just declaring what the government may *not* do, which is what the First Amendment does, the state counterpart affirmatively bestows a right upon the citizens of New York; it establishes, in context, what citizens *can* do. Additionally, since the clause was added to the state constitution in 1821, well after the First Amendment was adopted, it seems clear that the framers made a clear and conscious decision to extend the boundaries of the federal Bill of Rights.

Within that framework, the Court of Appeals wrestled with the thorny case of *Shad* v. *Smith Haven Mall.*[26] A tenuous majority, led by Judge Titone, won out over a dissent written by the chief. Titone and his followers—Jasen, Simons, Kaye, and Alexander—found Wachtler's position untenable and result-oriented. They refused to find a free-speech right to distribute leaflets in a private shopping mall, deferring instead to property rights: "A disciplined perception of the proper role of the judiciary, and, more specifically, discernment of the reach of the mandates of our State Constitution, precludes us from casting aside so fundamental a concept as State action in an effort to achieve what the dissent perceives as a more socially desirable result."[27]

Wachtler argued forcefully, and manipulatively, working on Titone over and over. The chief told Titone—who wears his liberalism like a badge of honor—that he wouldn't be worthy of his liberal credentials unless he signed on. But Titone grew even more stubborn, began politicking on his own, and succeeded in winning over Jasen and ensuring that his side would win a majority. It marked one of the few early occasions when Wachtler truly, really wanted a particular result and could not persuade his court to take the law where he wanted it to go.

He pointed out that the mall was frequently used for charity auctions, presentations by the Boy Scouts and Girl Scouts, voter registration drives, and the like. He further noted that the mall conceded that the political activities of the Shad alliance did not in any way disrupt the mall's operation.

"There can be little doubt, of course, that the right of free expression is one of our most cherished liberties and is essential for the functioning of a democracy," Wachtler wrote in a dissent joined by Judge Bernard Meyer.

> The question thus becomes whether protecting the peaceful and orderly exercise of free speech in a large shopping mall is required to uphold the fundamental values enshrined [in the state constitution]. . . . Our State Constitution is an innovative document. It was intended to ensure that rights and privileges granted in the past would be preserved in the future under changing conditions. In the past, those who had ideas they wished to communicate to the public had the unquestioned right to disseminate those ideas in the open marketplace. Now that the marketplace has a roof over it, and is called a mall, we should not abridge that right.[28]

Wachtler was well aware that some states had construed their constitutional free-speech provisions to apply to *private* property—typically malls and universities—and was eager to have New York join them. He generally adhered, in free-speech cases, to the philosophy of Justice Louis D. Brandeis, who wrote in 1927:

> Those who won our independence believed that the final end of the state was to make men free to develop their faculties; and that in its government the deliberative forces should prevail over the arbitrary. They valued liberty both

as an end and as a means. The believed liberty to be the secret of happiness and courage to be the secret of liberty. They believed that freedom to think as you will and to speak as you think are means indispensable to the discovery and spread of political truth; that without free speech and assembly discussion would be futile; that with them, discussion affords ordinarily adequate protection against the dissemination of a noxious doctrine; that the greatest menace to freedom is an inert people; that public discussion is a political duty; that this should be a fundamental principle of the American government.[29]

The Founding Fathers had enacted the First Amendment largely because of the so-called seditious libel doctrine, under which a person could be criminally convicted of crime for publishing an unflattering, albeit true, account of a public official. The genesis was the 1734 prosecution of John Peter Zenger, a publisher who was jailed for accurate articles which he printed in his New York *Weekly Journal*. Although Zenger was clearly guilty under the law—he *did* publish the articles, and they *were* offensive to the rulers—Andrew Hamilton secured his acquittal by convincing the jury that the law was unjust. One of the drafters of the Constitution, Gouverneur Morris, called the Zenger trial "the germ of American freedom—the morning star of that liberty which subsequently revolutionized America."[30]

That basic American appreciation for free speech evolved, and continues to evolve, with the help of the courts. And, for the most part, the New York Court of Appeals has been at the vanguard, for a simple reason: The U.S. Constitution prohibited *Congress*, not the states, from abridging the freedom of speech. It wasn't until 1925 that the Supreme Court, taking the hint from a state court ruling, held that free speech was among the fundamental liberties protected, through the Fourteenth Amendment's due process clause, at all levels of government.

Over the ensuing decades, the federal courts and the Court of Appeals dealt repeatedly with myriad intermingled free speech issues. One of the crucial ones focuses on an apparent conflict between the First Amendment right of free speech and the Sixth Amendment guarantee of a fair trial. At what point can the right to speak or print be abridged to ensure that a citizen's right to a fair trial is preserved?

"First Amendment absolutists are just as bad as Sixth Amendment absolutists," Wachtler scoffs. "Both feed at the extreme ends of reality and reason. For a prisoner awaiting trial who faces the loss of his freedom and indeed of his life, the promise of a fair trial is not an abstraction. For a nation which prides itself on freedom, the need for a free press is no abstraction—both are real—both are essential—both must be preserved—both must co-exist."[31]

With that concept in mind, Wachtler wrote a controversial opinion for the court in 1977. In *Gannett v. DePasquale*,[32] a Seneca County Judge, Daniel A. DePasquale, had closed to the public evidentiary hearings in a highly publicized murder case. Wachtler wrote that the press could be excluded, in the name of a fair trial, from some pretrial proceedings in a sensational case.

Wayne Clapp, a former town police officer who had lived in his Seneca County community for all of his forty-two years, was reported missing on July 19, 1976. Rochester newspapers and television stations were all over the story, reporting that Clapp had last been seen leaving a marina and that his truck and .357 magnum revolver were missing. On July 22, 1976, the media announced that police in Michigan had captured a sixteen-year-old Texas boy, Kyle Greathouse, and his 21-year-old friend, David Jones. The press reported that the suspects had confessed.

At a pretrial hearing, the defense attorneys asked the judge to exclude the public and the press, arguing that additional publicity would further erode their clients' right to a fair trial. The judge granted the request, and Gannett Co., which operated two newspapers in nearby Rochester, went to court to obtain transcripts of what had occurred behind closed doors. An appellate court ordered that the transcripts be provided; eventually, the suspects pleaded guilty. Normally, that would have been the end of it, but Wachtler felt it necessary to address the issues raised in the case.

"This is far from an ordinary appeal," Wachtler remarked in the decision. "It crystallizes a recurring and delicate issue of . . . significance both to the courts and the news media. And in its broadest implications, it presents a challenge to a fundamental precept of judicial administration—the courts' inherit power to control their own process. For these reasons, combined with the fact that matters of this character typically evade review, we have retained jurisdiction to entertain this appeal."[33]

What concerned Wachtler at the time was ensuring that courts retained the authority to close courtrooms when necessary, while trying to balance the First Amendment right of free speech with the Sixth Amendment guarantee of a fair trial. Stopping far short of adopting any kind of hard and fast rule, the judges declared that courts can close courtrooms to "safeguard the integrity of the process" and urged jurists to distinguish between legitimate matters of public interest, where there can be little justification for closing a courtroom, and mere curiosity. The court said, essentially suggesting a policy:

Here the public's concern was not focused on prosecutorial or judicial accountability; irregularities, if any, had occurred out of State. The interest of the public was chiefly one of active curiosity with respect to a notorious local happening. While the defendants were still in jeopardy (of prosecution), any true public interest could be fully satisfied, consonant with constitutional free press guarantees, by affording the media access to transcripts redacted to exclude matters ruled inadmissible during the closed suppression hearings.[34]

It was a fairly Solomonic compromise: The press would get all relevant materials, just not as quickly as it might prefer, and the defendants' rights to a fair trial would be secured. He had addressed, in a case that received far less attention, the same issue earlier that year.

Richard Moore had been charged with a shooting on May 19, 1971, in Manhattan. Two police officers, sitting in a marked car outside the home of then New York County District Attorney Frank Hogan, observed a car going the wrong way on a one-way street. They pursued the car, stopped it, and were met with a barrage of machine gun bullets. Both officers were seriously hurt, but survived the attack. Neither could identify the assailants.

Two days later, a young black woman left a package at a Harlem radio station, WLIB, and a black man deposited a similar parcel, folded inside a copy of the *New York Times.* Each package contained a New York license plate, a .45 caliber cartridge (the same type used in the assault), and a letter discussing the "shooting of two N.Y.P.D. pigs on Malcolm's birthday," a reference to the May 19 birthday of Malcolm X. Richard Moore's fingerprints were found on the newspaper. At an apartment where Moore sometimes lived, authorities found black militant literature—and Moore's fingerprints. They had the makings of a circumstantial case.

During jury selection, two more New York City police officers were attacked by black militants armed with automatic weapons. The media reported the similarities to Moore's case and, following his conviction, a key question in *People* v. *Moore*[35] was whether media coverage of similar crimes had effectively deprived the defendant of a fair trial.

In that case, Wachtler dissected the free trial-fair press arguments and set out three circumstances in which the courts should be concerned about publicity: (1) when the media actually state, pretrial, that the defendant is guilty; (2) when the media describe prior crimes of the defendant; and (3) when the media report on similar crimes by individuals or groups associated with the defendant. Citing Supreme Court precedents, Wachtler noted that there is no right to be tried by a jury totally ignorant of the facts, but there is a right to a trial that has not been prejudiced by adverse publicity.

"The major question on this appeal is whether publicity of this nature could affect the defendant's right to a fair trial," Wachtler wrote for the unanimous court.

> Taken as a general proposition, and carried to its logical extreme, it would mean, for instance, that no one accused of robbery could receive a fair trial as long as the media continued to report the numerous robberies committed daily—unless the courts, as a matter of course, employed extraordinary measures to shield the jury from unending publicity. Of course, attacks on police officers are less common than robberies and "assassinations" by militants are rarer still. But if there is a right to be shielded from publicity of similar crimes, it cannot depend on the novelty of the offense. The right to a fair trial applies to all and not just those accused of unusual crimes.[36]

It would have been sufficient for the court simply to affirm Moore's conviction. Yet Wachtler felt compelled to go beyond the four corners of that particular case and suggest ways for courts to deal with similar situations in the future. He said judges could order a continuance, or grant a change of venue request, to protect both the rights of the accused and interests of the press.

Regardless of the conciliatory tone in both the *Moore* and *Gannett* cases, and despite efforts to strike a balance between the rights of the accused and the interests of the press, Wachtler took a beating in the media. "Whenever a decision is written by the courts which suggests in a particular instance that a defendant's Sixth Amendment right to a fair trial is more important than the public's right to know, I am amazed not so much by the instantaneous criticism, sometimes warranted, but by the often grossly inaccurate assault by the press on the court or on the particular judge whose misfortune it was to dare author that opinion," Wachtler observed. "These attacks may serve as a journalistic catharsis but they do not inform the public, and only add to the erosion of the public's confidence in the courts."[37]

Wachtler and the court revisited *Gannett* only two years later in the context of a Westchester County rape case. The case stemmed from a series of rapes and sexual assaults that occurred during the summer and fall of 1976. In November of that year, police arrested a suspect named Alexander Verrone. Verrone's attorney filed notice of an insanity defense and the court ordered a mental competency hearing to determine if the defendant was fit to stand trial.

Over the strenuous objections of the press, the judge closed the hearing and refused to say why, merely commenting that to explain his decision to lock the courtroom "would be self defeating." A mid-level appellate court upheld the ruling.

"The case, once again, imposes upon the courts the obligation of reconciling the competing rights of the accused to a fair trial free of damaging pretrial publicity, with the right of the public to be informed, particularly by the press, of what takes place in the courts," Wachtler wrote in *Westchester Rockland Newspapers* v. *Leggett*.[38]

As a beginning proposition, the court articulated a strong preference for open courts—to further not only the ends of justice, but the perception that justice was being done. Wachtler wrote:

> The public, of course, is not only concerned with seeing that the accused is fairly treated. The public also has an interest in seeing that there is justice for the accuser—the police and prosecutors who must enforce the law, and the victims of crime who suffer when the law is not enforced with vigor and impartiality. And when justice has been done, public awareness "serves to instill a sense of public trust in our judicial process" (*People* v. *Hinton*, 31 NY2d 73, 1972) assuring the innocent and impressing the guilty with the power of the rule of law. Justice must not only be done; it must be perceived as being done.[39]

At the same time, the court recognized that publicity does not always ensure the defendant a fair trial, and may have the opposite effect: "The right of the public and the press to attend court proceedings is not absolute. All court proceedings are presumptively open to the public, but when they would jeopardize the right of the accused to a fair trial, the competing interests must be balanced and reconciled as far as possible."[40]

And how should a judge weigh those competing interests? Other than a broad suggestion that courts should be closed only as a last resort, and that criminal suspects must be shielded from a lynch mentality, Wachtler and his colleagues offered little specific guidance.

"Thus recognition of a public right of access to court proceedings does not mean that the defendant's right to a fair trial assumes a secondary role," Wachtler observed. "Even if the public's right were founded in the First Amendment, it could not serve to diminish the rights of the accused, for the primary purpose of the Bill of Rights and the corresponding provisions of the State Constitution is to insure the individual, particularly the unpopular individual, a measure of protection against oppression by a majority."[41]

Wachtler was almost always sympathetic to the concept of a free press, and was a strong proponent of "shield laws," which protect reporters from having to disclose the identity of confidential sources. He was still more than a year away from becoming chief when he wrote a strong concurring opinion in a shield law case, arguing that in New York reporters should enjoy not just a *statutory* shield—which can be taken away by the legislature at its whim—but a *constitutional* protection.

Dick Beach was a reporter for a Schenectady television station, WRGB, who had been contacted by a secret source and informed that a grand jury had secretly recommended that the Rensselaer County sheriff be removed from office. The special prosecutor in the case, Donald J. Shanley of Troy, subpoenaed Beach, demanding to know the identity of his source. In a landmark opinion, Chief Judge Cooke wrote an opinion overturning a mid-level court and finding that the shield law protects reporters, even in a case where revealing information to a reporter is a crime (it is illegal to disclose what went on in the secrecy of a grand jury proceeding). The attorneys for the reporter, Peter Danziger and Salvatore D. Ferlazzo—once a clerk at the high court—could not persuade the majority to find a constitutional right. They did, however, win an important, and later useful, ally in Wachtler.

Although Wachtler generally disapproved of concurrences and the sometimes extraneous dicta that judges like to add to decisions, in *Beach* v. *Shanley*,[42] he went out of his way to suggest the court's future course. "This State has long provided one of the most hospitable climates for the free exchange of ideas," Wachtler noted:

> The tradition existed in colonial times, as is exemplified by the acquittal in 1735 of John Peter Zenger who, interestingly, was prosecuted for publishing articles critical of the New York colonial governor after he refused to disclose his source. In the nineteenth century, a large portion of the publishing industry was established in New York and the State began to serve as a cultural center for the Nation. It still enjoys that status.
>
> It is consistent with that tradition for New York to provide broad protections, often broader than those provided elsewhere, to those engaged in publishing and particularly to those performing the sensitive role of gathering and disseminating news of public events. The ability of the press to gather information is deterred if the press can be compelled to disclose their sources to the government. Similarly, publishers and reporters will be reluctant to publish what they have learned if they can be jailed, fined, or otherwise held in contempt for refusing to disclose the source of their information to state investigators.
>
> In my view, therefore, protection from contempt for refusal to disclose a source is not merely a privilege granted to the press by the legislature, but is essential to the type of freedom of expression traditionally expected in this State and should be recognized by the State Constitution.[43]

Two years later, the court addressed the same issue, when Wachtler was chief, and in one of the cases Danziger played into the chief's hands.

In 1987, the court specifically—and somewhat shockingly —interpreted narrowly the shield law. A few months later, with Danziger and his appellate expert, Barbara G. Billet, playing off Wachtler's concurrence in *Beach,* the court found the constitutional right that the chief was looking for.

The first shield law case in 1987, *Knight-Ridder* v. *Greenberg,*[44] resulted from a murder investigation in Albany. In February 1986, television station WTEN broadcast an interview with a man named Donald Bent, who tearfully described how his wife was missing and how badly he wanted her to return. Only about one minute of a lengthy interview with reporter John McLoughlin was aired.

After Mrs. Bent was found dead in the trunk of a car, Assistant Albany County District Attorney Daniel S. Dwyer subpoenaed the unaired portions of McLoughlin's interview with the husband, at that point the prime suspect. McLoughlin's employer invoked the shield law. But the court found that the Shield Law protected only sources who provided information on promise of confidentiality. Since Bent had not secured such a promise from McLoughlin, the "outtakes"—unaired portions—were fair game for the prosecution. The media were horrified. "So why didn't Channel 10 cooperate with the legally constituted authority simply trying to do its job 'on behalf of the public welfare and safety?' " asked Harry Rosenfeld, editor of the Albany *Times Union.* "The answer that the news industry would give is that to do so would impair its ability in the first place to gather news, and, in the second place, it would impair its credibility with its public, and therefore its ability to perform its proper and ordained function in society."[45]

Bent was convicted of second-degree murder and sentenced to a 25-year-to-life prison term. The jury that returned the guilty verdict asked, within hours of beginning delibera- tions, to replay the videotape of the McLoughlin interview, in which Bent spoke of his wife as if he knew she was never coming back.[46] Shortly after the *Knight-Ridder* case, Danziger argued a related matter, *O'Neill v. Oakgrove Construction.*[47] In that case, a State Supreme Court justice in Rochester, Eugene Bergin, had ordered Gannett Rochester Newspapers to turn over nineteen photographs of an accident scene, most of which were not published. The photographs were sought by the plaintiff in a civil action. Danziger argued under both the shield law *and* the state constitution—making essentially the argument that Wachtler proffered in *Beach*—and came away with a stunning victory. The court arrived at the *constitutional* right that the chief had been searching for nearly four years earlier: "This decision substantially fills the policy gap cre- ated by the holding [in the *Knight-Ridder* case] and does so on a higher order of law—the State Constitution," wrote an elated Judge Bellacosa in concurrence. Bellacosa had dis- sented sharply in *Knight-Ridder v. Greenberg.*[48]

On libel issues, Wachtler was extraordinarily protective of the press.

In the 1975 case of *Chapadeau v. Utica Observer-Dispatch,*[49] Wachtler led the court in declaring that a private figure cannot sustain a libel claim on a matter of legitimate public concern without demonstrating gross responsibility. *Chapa- deau* essentially made it harder for all citizens to successfully sue for libel when the press is pursuing a public issue. The case involved a public school teacher who had been arrested on drug charges. Unlike most states, New York does not nor- mally consider a public school teacher a public person.

Joseph L. Chapadeau was a public school teacher who was arrested in Utica on June 10, 1971, and charged with possessing heroin and drug paraphernalia. The following day, the *Utica Observer-Dispatch* reported that Chapadeau and two other men were "part of a group at a party in Brookwood Park where they were arrested. Drugs and beer were found at the party." The Court of Appeals, through Wachtler, held that although the article was partly inaccurate—apparently, Chapadeau had no connection to the other two men—the issue was of such significance and the error so relatively trivial that the lawsuit should be dismissed.

The *Chapadeau* decision was an extension—a state court extension—of a benchmark established by the U.S. Supreme Court in 1964. In *New York Times* v. *Sullivan*,[50] the Court held that debate on public issues "should be uninhibited, robust, and wide open."

New York Times v. *Sullivan* stemmed from a libel suit brought by the police commissioner in Montgomery, Alabama, against various defendants, including the *New York Times*. The *Times* had published an advertisement on March 29, 1960, by a civil rights organization. Although the commissioner, L. B. Sullivan, was not named in the advertisement, he alleged he was defamed by a partly inaccurate statement regarding police conduct in Montgomery.

The Court might have overturned the verdict against the *Times* on any number of existing grounds, but it chose to make a new law, holding for the first time that libel is within the protective shield of the First Amendment. "The constitutional guarantees require, we think, a federal rule that prohibits a public official from recovering damages for a defamatory falsehood relating to his official conduct unless he proves that the statement was made with 'actual malice'—that is, with knowledge that it was false or with reckless disregard for whether it was false or not," Justice Brennan wrote for the Court[51] in a decision that made him a darling of the press.

From that point on, public officials and, later, public figures were required to prove "actual malice" in order to sustain a libel action. What that meant is that a police chief or star athlete could not be awarded damages for defamation, even if the article was inaccurate, without proving that the reporter knew the information was false or recklessly disregarded the facts. *New York Times* v. *Sullivan* is the practical impact of the philosophies of Louis Brandeis and Oliver Wendell Holmes carried to their logical extreme.*

Chapadeau expanded on that decision, holding that where the plaintiff is a private individual involved in matters of public concern, he must establish, by a preponderance of the evidence, that publication of erroneous and defamatory information resulted from grossly irresponsible reporting, evincing a disregard for standard and reasonable newsgathering techniques.

"Our court extended the constitutional privilege to publishers of libelous statements concerning private individuals who were involved in matters of public interest," Wachtler noted. "We now hold that . . . where the content of the article is arguably within the sphere of legitimate public concern, which is reasonably related to matters warranting public exposition, the party defamed may recover; however to warrant such recovery he must establish, by a preponderance of the evidence, that the publisher acted in a grossly irresponsible manner without due consideration for the standards of information gathering and dissemination ordinarily followed by responsible parties."[52]

In the case of Joseph Chapadeau, Wachtler looked first to the nature of the offending communication: It concerned the

---

*The decision affords journalists so much leeway that they can write almost anything about a public official with little fear of legal consequences.

arrest of a public school teacher on a felony drug charge. "Thus stated it becomes abundantly clear that the challenged communication falls within the sphere of legitimate public concern. Chapadeau's occupation, one highly influential with the youth of the community, coupled with the oft-cited menace of heroin addiction makes further expatiation unnecessary."[53]

As *Chapadeau* shows, Wachtler was willing to give the press a great deal of leeway, but called upon the media to respond to that power responsibly. "I believe that the institutionalized press would place itself in a better position to fight the real enemy if it acknowledged, more readily than it is now likely to do, that 'the enemy is us'—that whenever the press destroys a person's reputation or invades a person's privacy in order to satisfy public curiosity, the act causes some degree of public ill will," Wachtler said in a 1984 address at a libel litigation symposium. "The public might be curious about certain facts, but it can also consider the medium which brings them the story as being arrogant, intrusive, and too eager to violate a person's right to privacy or to humiliate that person. . . . I believe that this animosity finds its way into the jury room and is expressed in boxcar verdicts."[54]

The media have been extremely successful in getting judges, Wachtler included, to throw out libel suits on various grounds; about three of every four libel cases is dismissed before ever going before a jury. However, those that do get to a jury tend to go against the press, and in a big way. Some media pundits call for legislative reforms that would, for instance, limit the amount of damages in libel cases. Wachtler's solution, however, is a greater concern for professional discipline.

After writing an opinion that sought to distinguish between prurient curiosity and legitimate public interest, Wachtler was criticized by members of the press, who asked:

Who is to draw the distinction. His answer: The press must draw the distinction. And if it is drawn properly, the press will have its greatest defense against a negative public perception. If the press can't see the difference—if it thinks it can demean or ignore any person's rights to privacy simply to satisfy the public's curiosity they're wrong. Even if they win the lawsuit—they're still wrong and they can't afford to be wrong. The press is no longer thought of as the always-to-be-trusted local neighborhood newspaper. It is now perceived of as an impersonal corporate conglomerate, and everyone knows that corporate conglomerates are ruthless, not entirely trustworthy, and seldom seen as symbols of integrity.[55]

Notes

1. *Arcara* v. *Cloud Books*, 478 US 697 (1985).

2. *People ex rel Arcara* v. *Cloud Books*, 68 NY2d 553 (1986), 503 NE2d 492.

3. *People* v. *P.J. Video*, 65 NY2d 566, 483 (1985), NE2d 1120; *People* v. *P.J. Video*, 68 NY2d 296 (1986), 501 NE2d 296.

4. *People* v. *P.J. Video*, 68 NY2d 296 (1986), 501 NE 2d 296.

5. *Roth* v. *United States*, 354 U.S. 476 (1957).

6. Ibid.

7. *Paris Adult Theatre* v. *Slaton*, 413 U.S. 49 (1973).

8. *Miller* v. *California*, 413 U.S. 15 (1973).

9. *Jenkins* v. *Georgia*, 418 U.S. 153 (1974), p. 160.

10. *Miller.*

11. Interview with Michael Trainor on September 7, 1997.

12. *Simon & Schuster* v. *New York Crime Victims Board*, 502 U.S. 105 (1991).

13. Interview with Wachtler on August 15, 1997.

14. *Kinglsey International Pictures Corp.* v. *Regents*, 360 U.S. 684 (1959).

15. Ibid.

16. *Cloud Books.*

17. *Curle* v. *Ward*, 40 NY2d 1049 (1979), 46 NY2d 1049 (1979), 389 NE2d 1070.

18. Ibid.

19. Ibid.

20. Wachtler's archives.

21. *Abrams* v. *United States*, 250 U.S. 616 (1919).

22. Wachtler's archives.

23. *People* v. *Remeny*, 40 NY2d 527 (1976), 355 NE2d 379.

24. *Valentine* v. *Chrestensen*, 316 US 52 (1942).

25. *Remeny*, 530.

26. *Shad* v. *Smith Haven Mall*, 66 NY2d 496 (1985), 488 NE2d 1211.

27. Ibid., p. 505.

28. Ibid., p. 512.

29. *Whitney* v. *California*, 274 U.S. 357, 375 (1927).

30. Frank B. Latham, "The Trial of John Peter Zenger, August 1735," 1979, Franklin Watts, p. 61.

31. Wachtler's archives.

32. *Gannett* v. *DePasquale*, 43 NY2d 370 (1977), 372 NE2d 544.

33. Ibid., p. 376.

34. Ibid.

35. *People* v. *Moore*, 42 NY2d 421 (1977), 366 NE2d 1330.

36. Ibid., p. 433.

37. Wachtler's archives.

38. *Westchester Rockland Newspapers* v. *Leggett*, 48 NY2d 430, 437 (1979), 399 NE2d 518.

39. Ibid., p. 436.

40. Ibid.

41. Ibid., p. 444.

42. *Beach* v. *Shanley*, 62 NY2d 241 (1984), 465 NE2d 304.

43. Ibid., p. 255.

44. *Knight-Ridder* v. *Greenberg*, 70 NY2d 151 (1987), 511 NE2d 1116.

45. Harry Rosenfeld, "Shield Law Ruling Impairs Ability of Press to Do Its Job," Albany *Times Union*, July 12, 1987, p. A2.

46. Carol DeMare, "Jury Sees Videotapes of Bent Mourning Missing Wife," Albany *Times Union*, April 14, 1988, p. B9.

47. *O'Neill* v. *Oakgrove Construction*, 71 NY2d 521 (1988), 523 NE2d 277.

48. Ibid.

49. *Chapadeau* v. *Utica Observer-Dispatch*, 38 NY2d 196 (1975), 341 NE2d 569.

50. *New York Times* v. *Sullivan*, 376 U.S. 254 (1964).

51. Ibid., p. 250.

52. *Chapadeau.*

53. Ibid.

54. Wachtler's archives.

55. Ibid.

CHAPTER 9

Human Rights

"**A**n unjust law is a manmade code that squares with the moral law or the law of God. To put it in terms of St. Thomas Aquinas, an unjust law is a human law that is not rooted in eternal and natural law. Any law that uplifts the human personality is just. Any law that degrades human personality is unjust."[1]

The words belong to Dr. Martin Luther King Jr., penned in April 1963 from the Birmingham City Jail, but they echo Sol Wachtler's sentiments on human rights, from his earliest days on the bench, when he tried to assist black teenagers, to his days on the Court of Appeals, when he was responsible for a series of rights-expanding rulings. Wachtler's decisions opened doors for the handicapped, minorities, and women (oddly, and sadly, many feminists promptly shunned Wachtler, forgetting his long record, because of the scandal). His decisions literally opened the closed doors of exclusive men's clubs; put teeth behind the determinations of the state Division of Human Rights; and helped broaden the definition of a handicap, thus legally shielding more people from the indignity of discrimination. There is perhaps no other area of the law where he was so consistent, so sure of himself.

As an administrator, Wachtler did even more, actively working to improve the lot of women and minorities in the criminal and civil justice systems; lobbying for a more diversified Court of Appeals; and appointing blue-ribbon commissions to identify, and help rectify, both flagrant and insidious bias. He forced a large newspaper chain to stop running separate employment ads for men and women, wrote the first opinion in the nation that said a person could not be denied a job because of obesity, and forced the Moose Lodge to pay damages for discrimination.

Despite portraying himself as a tough lock-'em-up-and-throw-away-the-key conservative in the 1972 race for the Court of Appeals, Wachtler was offered—and accepted—the endorsement of Gay Alliance of Brooklyn when homosexual rights were at least fifteen years away from entering the realm of the politically correct.

Wachtler had been on the bench only a year when he drew the case of the *National Organization for Women* v. *State Division of Human Rights*.[2] The case involved the Gannett newspaper chain which, like many other publishers, maintained separate columns in its advertising section for jobs seeking men and jobs seeking women. For instance, construction jobs were routinely listed in the "men's" category, secretarial jobs in the "women's category."

NOW accused Gannett of violating antidiscrimination laws, but the state Division of Human Rights found no wrongdoing. The Court of Appeals, through Wachtler, overturned the human rights division's finding. Although Gannett had not directly discriminated against anyone, it had, according to Wachtler's analysis, "aided and abetted" sexual discrimination.[3] "An analysis of this issue must start with the recognition that unlawful discrimination against women is widespread and cannot be tolerated," Wachtler wrote in 1974. "To designate separate ad column listings as 'Help Wanted-Male' and/or 'Help Wanted-Female' reinforces the very discriminatory practices which the federal and state antidiscrimination laws were meant to eliminate."[4]

By the time the decision came down, Gannett had already voluntarily stopped designating separate male and female job advertisements, so the issue in that particular case was basically moot, but Wachtler thought the court should comment anyhow.

"It may well be that more women are interested in secretarial jobs than are men," Wachtler, then the junior member, wrote for the unanimous court. "Or that more men are interested in accounting jobs than women. However, it is often the case that a person or organization acting in a manner which genuinely intends to be descriptive becomes in effect prescriptive. A policy purporting to reflect a statistical phenomenon actually becomes a self-fulfilling prophecy which helps to generate the very presumptive foundation for its existence."[5]

That same year, Wachtler led the court in *Batavia Lodge* v. *State Division of Human Rights.*[6] In that case, the Moose Lodge invited black people to attend a fashion show and then refused to serve them at the private bar. The human rights division awarded each of the victims $250, but the Appellate Division struck the award as punitive. The Court of Appeals, through Wachtler, reinstated the award. "The unlawful discrimination in this case was blatant and intolerable," Wachtler wrote for the unanimous court. "It is evident that such conduct perpetrated in a place used as a public accommodation cannot be tolerated."[7]

While the Gannett and Moose Lodge cases were fairly easy victories for Wachtler—all his colleagues agreed with his reasoning—another bias case in 1980 was a much tougher fight. Wachtler carried the 4-3 court, prevailing on the majority to order a restaurant owner to apologize to a waitress and pay her two years' back wages, plus $500, for making a racist remark.

Eleanor F. Rose, a mother of three, was attending graduate school and working weekends in the Imperial Diner. On October 24, 1976, she was assigned to work behind the counter—a less desirable assignment than waiting tables. The next day, after drawing the same duty, Rose complained to her boss. Later, when the head waitress reassigned her to tables, Rose, thinking the boss had been responsible for the reassignment, went over to thank him. She was greeted with anti-semitic remarks suggesting that she thought she was special, "just like all those other fucking Jewish broads around here."[8] Rose insisted on an apology and, when the boss again insulted her, she left the job.

The Division of Human Rights ordered an apology and $500 damages but again, as in the *Moose Lodge* case, the Appellate Division reversed. In the Rose matter, the mid-level court found no pattern of systematic discrimination and noted that Rose not only had not been fired, but had been told she could remain on the job.

Wachtler, displaying the pragmatic streak that would run throughout his judicial career, said there was no need to "find that this was a regular practice," and no need to "wait for it to become one."[9] Writing for the majority, he said:

As in other areas of discrimination, it is unrealistic to hold that an employee can only be said to have been the victim of a discriminatory discharge when the employer has expressly fired him on the basis of race or creed or some other discriminatory ground. It is also possible, and perhaps more likely, that an employer who believes certain individuals are undesirable employees because of some discriminatory factor will engage in conduct which encourages the employee to quit. . . . Thus, in this case, although the employer did not in so many words fire [Rose], and in fact told her she could return to work, the commissioner [of the Division of Human Rights] could attach greater significance to the fact that the employer had never apologized for his remarks and, indeed, adamantly refused to do so even several days after the incident. He never withdrew the reprimand or stated any change in his attitude that her efforts to improve her working conditions were viewed, by him, as an undesirable trait associated with her religion. He simply let the remark stand and offered her continued employment, on a take-it-or-leave-it basis, presumably in the same intolerable atmosphere.[10]

The issue of employment discrimination arose again in 1985, shortly after Wachtler became chief judge, in the case of Catherine McDermott, a computer programmer seeking a job in 1974 with Xerox.[11] She was offered a job on the condition that she pass a physical. However, when McDermott, 5 feet 6 inches tall, tipped the scales at 249 pounds, Xerox refused to hire her, citing "obesity" as the reason.

McDermott filed a complaint, alleging she had been the victim of discrimination and claiming that her obesity was a disability. The commissioner of the Division of Human Rights agreed that obesity was a handicap, but the human rights board did not. The Appellate Division argued that it was, and the matter landed before Wachtler and the high court.

Xerox argued that it had not denied McDermott the job because of a present impairment, but because of the statistical likelihood that her obese condition would affect her health and working ability in the future. Wachtler didn't buy the argument and neither did his court. "The statute covers a range of conditions varying in degree from those involving the loss of bodily functions to those which are merely diagnosable medical anomalies which impair bodily integrity and thus may lead to a more serious condition in the future," Wachtler wrote for the court.

> Disabilities, especially those resulting from disease, often develop gradually and, under the statutory definition, an employer cannot deny employment simply because the condition has been detected before it has actually begun to produce deleterious effects. . . . The statute protects all persons with disabilities and not just those with hopeless conditions. . . . We have found nothing in the statute or its legislative history indicating a legislative intent to permit employers to refuse to hire persons who are able to do the job simply because they have a possibly treatable condition of excessive weight.[12]

The same year that the Wachtler-led court gave the human rights board more authority than it thought it had, it told the mayor of New York City that he had less clout than he thought in an effort to shield gays and lesbians from job discrimination. In 1985, Wachtler led the court in refusing to implement Ed Koch's plan to end job discrimination against homosexuals by contractors doing business with the city. Wachtler found the effort "commendable," but said the court declined to impose its will on the city. Two years later, the Court of Appeals addressed the question of whether private clubs could be barred from denying membership to women and minorities. The result was, predictably, unanimous for a court that had, seven years earlier, stopped dining at an exclusive men's club in Albany.

The decision in *New York State Club Association* v. *City of New York*[13] stemmed from a 1984 local law in New York City which said that a club could not deny membership on the basis of race, sex, color, creed, or national origin if it had more than four hundred members; served meals regularly; or was reimbursed for member-incurred expenses by a nonmember, such as an employer.

The New York State Club Association, a consortium of about 125 private clubs, challenged the law on constitutional grounds. It argued that the law violated the members' "freedom of expressive association." But Wachtler, writing for the court, found that "compelling governmental interests, unrelated to the suppression of ideas—here the city's strong public policy to eliminate discrimination against women and minorities—manifestly justify some infringement" on the right to free association.[14]

Wachtler's reasoning centered around the fact that much business is conducted in those clubs. He thought it fundamentally unfair, and legally improper, to exclude women and minorities from those business contacts. But the judge also had an axe to grind.

Years earlier, Wachtler had resigned form the Harmonie Club in New York City after learning he could not enroll his three daughters, because of their gender. "We are a product of our history," Wachtler said. "I can remember those thoughts [of the Harmonie Club] being in my mind when this case [*New York State Club Association* v. *City of New York*] came along, how outrageous it was."[15]

The Harmonie Club eventually changed its bylaws to admit women, and Wachtler rejoined. But the issue would come up again, in a personal way, in 1987, only a month after the *New York Club* decision. Wachtler had accepted an invitation to speak at the annual Friendly Sons of St. Patrick Dinner in Albany, not realizing it was a male-only event. Under criticism from the National Organization for Women and Mary O. Donohue, a conservative female attorney who would later serve as Rensselaer County district attorney and as a Supreme Court justice, Wachtler pulled out.

Wachtler displayed a sensitivity to women's issues from his first days on the bench, when judicial support was hardly a given. Long before he became chief, a women's rights case came before the court in which the female attorney for the cause was taking a beating from Judge Breitel (whose daughter, Eleanor Breitel Alter, became an attorney and, ironically, represented Joy Silverman when her husband sued for divorce, alleging infidelity with Wachtler). Wachtler cut in and thanked the attorney for her presentation, which he remarked sarcastically to Breitel, had been "very good for a woman."

The "women's rights" ruling that may well be Wachtler's most important emerged in the context of a 1984 criminal case, *People* v. *Liberta*.[16] In that case, the court, led by then Associate Judge Wachtler, ruled for the first time that a man could be convicted of sexually assaulting his wife—a fairly revolutionary concept.

Mario Liberta of Buffalo had raped and sodomized his wife in the presence of their two-and-a-half-year-old son, and claimed there wasn't a thing society could do about it. Wachtler and his court had other ideas.

Records show that Mario and Denise Liberta were married in 1978. Shortly after their son was born in October of that year, Mario began to beat Denise. About eighteen months later, Denise obtained an order of protection requiring Mario to move out of their home and stay away from his wife. He was afforded visitation with his son each weekend.

Mario did not visit his son the weekend of March 21, 1981; on the following Tuesday he called Denise and asked her if he could come over and see the boy that day. Denise refused to allow him to come to her home, but did agree to bring the child to the motel where Mario was living after receiving assurances that a friend of his would be there at all times. However, as soon as Denise arrived, the friend left—and the attack began.

Mario attacked his wife, threatened to kill her, forced her to perform fellatio, and raped her while the child, under his orders, watched. Mario was indicted for first-degree rape and first-degree sodomy. Attempting to evade prosecution, Mario cited state penal law and claimed there was a "marital exemption" to the criminal statutes—and there was, in effect. The rape statute defined the offense as forced sexual intercourse with a "female person who is not married to the actor" and the sodomy statute defined the act as deviate sexual conduct "between persons not married to each other." The trial court dismissed the indictment and, on the law, the judge was right. Both law and tradition supported the premise that marital rape is an oxymoron.

British jurist Sir Matthew Hale wrote in the seventeenth century that a husband could not be guilty of raping his wife because, in accepting him as her spouse, she had "given herself in this kind unto her husband."[17] In 1922, a court in New York had upheld the marital exemption, finding that it existed "on account of the matrimonial consent which [the wife] has given, and which she cannot retract."[18] But Wachtler said the law was wrong. "Rape is not simply a sexual act to which one party does not consent," he observed. "Rather, it is a degrading, violent act which violates the bodily integrity of the victim and frequently causes severe, long-lasting physical and psychic harm. To ever imply consent to such an act is irrational and absurd. . . . Certainly, then, a marriage license should not be viewed as a license for a husband to forcibly rape his wife with impunity."[19]

The court found the law unconstitutional, rejecting, through Wachtler, the arguments that marital rape is too hard to prove, that eliminating the exemption would lead to fabricated claims by vindictive wives, and that spousal rape is not as serious an offense as other rapes. Wachtler continued:

> Justice Holmes wrote: "It is revolting to have no better reason for a rule of law than that it was laid down in the time of Henry IV. It is still more revolting if the grounds upon which it was laid down have vanished long since, and the rule simply persists from blind imitation of the past [Oliver Wendell Holmes, "The Path of the Law," *Harvard Law Review* 10: 457, 469]." This statement is an apt characterization of the marital exemption; it lacks a rational basis, and therefore violates the equal protection clauses of both the Federal and State Constitutions.[20]

It's essential to understand the context in which *Liberta* was decided. At the time, a handful of determined advocates were pushing states to abolish the marital exemption to rape statutes. However, they were getting nowhere: conservatives were reluctant to arm women with a sword that could potentially be used maliciously; liberals were reluctant to embrace anything that appeared pro-prosecution. Consequently, the legislatures were basically ignoring the problem. Wachtler's decision gave courts around the nation the insight, and in some cases the impetus, to declare judicially what the lawmakers would not do legislatively or politically.

There are several critical elements to *Liberta*. The court declared that: rape is not part of the marital contract; although sex is understood to be a part of marriage, there is nothing about the covenant that gives the husband a right to intercourse on demand; marital privacy statutes and considerations cannot be used as a shield for violence; just because marital rape may be difficult to prosecute does not make it any less of a crime than other sexual assaults; and there is no basis for the argument that marital rape laws would encourage false reporting by vindictive wives. It was the right decision, at the right time, and helped turn the tide nationally.

Liberta was one of Wachtler's many pro-woman decisions that many feminists seemingly forgot about following his downfall. One who did not, however, is Laura "X,"* spokesperson for the National Clearinghouse on Marital & Date Rape in Berkeley, California. In a moving 1993 letter to U.S. District Judge Anne Thompson, who sentenced Wachtler, Laura "X" wrote eloquently of the impact of *Liberta*, and of Wachtler himself:

> . . . His extraordinary, yet basically humane and decent, *Liberta* decision made it unnecessary for the campaign to continue there because he struck down the marital exemption as [an] unconstitutional denial of equal protection for wives versus nonwives. . . .
>
> The *Liberta* decision has been our beacon and anchor for the past nine years. . . . Courts in Alabama and Illinois have simply copied it and it has been our strongest argument before legislatures. . . .
>
> Although virtually unthinkable and earth-shaking at the time, the key statement in the *Liberta* decision that there is "no rational basis for any distinction" is an eminently fair statement. . . .
>
> Here was a court of men voting unanimously for us and being led by a very great person. Women's experiences

*Laura "X" adopted the name in protest against antiquated laws that denied women an identity.

were simply not understood or taken seriously by people in power in the country and in their daily lives. . . .

This is not Senator Kennedy or Senator Packwood. For twenty years, Senator Packwood was warned by many people that he would come to a bad end if he did not cease his harassment. The women's rights groups were and often are put in the position to look the other way about these politicians' "personal" behavior because they "voted right." . . .[21]

Later, "X" credited *Liberta* with providing the impetus for a resolution signed by every country on earth at the Beijing Women's Conference in 1995. Even the Vatican signed on to a declaration that a woman has a right to say no—anytime, anywhere, even in marriage.

"It was astonishing that that could happen," "X" said. "And there was a direct line from Sol's opinion. He gave us leverage. He gave us a place to stand, and we had never had that before. It was more important than the legislative victories because it was constitutional. It wasn't just a matter where somebody wanted votes from women. It is a very strong decision on equal protection grounds, on bodily integrity and, especially, on privacy. It is better on privacy than *Roe* v. *Wade*. This is about *sovereignty*."[22]

Laura "X" notwithstanding, many feminists generally condemned Wachtler after his arrest,* ignoring, or perhaps just ignorant of, decisions like *Liberta* and another that put teeth in a law that protected the so-called DES daughters.

DES—diethylstilbestrol—was a synthetic estrogen-like substance marketed between 1947 and 1971 by some three hundred manufacturers. Prescribed to prevent miscarriages,

---

*During a publicity tour for his book, Wachtler's appearance on national television shows, such as *Oprah* and *Larry King Live*, were protested by women's and victims' groups.

it was banned in 1971 after studies linked *in utero* exposure to vaginal and cervical cancer. In other words, the daughters of women who had taken DES were at risk of cancer. By the time the federal Food and Drug Administration reversed its 1951 statement that DES was safe, roughly two million pregnant women had taken the drug.[23]

During the 1980s, victims of DES were beginning to emerge, but the courthouse doors were often shut because of the statute of limitations. In 1986, Governor Cuomo pushed for passage of a toxic torts act, which opened a three-year window for victims to file lawsuits after discovering their injury. But getting into court was only half the battle; the other half was proving which of the dozens of companies had produced the particular brand of DES that had been ingested by the plaintiff's mother. In most cases, they had no idea. Wachtler and his court remedied the problem.

In a decision of national significance, Wachtler cleverly wrote a landmark decision that established a "market share" liability standard. That meant that the producers of DES would all be on the hook for damages, based on their market share, caused by the drug. So, if a company produced 10 percent of the DES sold in the time that it was taken by the victim's mother, the company would be liable for 10 percent of the judgment.

"It would be inconsistent with the reasonable expectations of a modern society to say to these plaintiffs that because of the insidious nature of an injury that long remains dormant, and because so many manufacturers, each behind a curtain, contributed to the devastation, the cost of injury should be borne by the innocent and not the wrongdoers," Wachtler wrote.[24]

Once again, the DES case demonstrates Wachtler's application of theory to law. The legislature had enacted a law with a gaping hole. Wachtler and the court built a bridge over that gap.

"If the legislature saw fit to open the window of liability
... then we had to assess the reason for that," he explains.
"The reason was to be sure that people who suffered by virtue
of this drug had some avenue of recompense. If we said, 'In
order to get recompense you have to identify the specific drug
manufacturer,' we would have been undoing what the legislature did. What we said was if you made 50 percent of the
market share, you were 50 percent liable. It was as close as we
could come. We were dealing with hypotheticals."[25]

Just two years later, Wachtler and his court revisited DES
in a novel case that asked the judges to extend liability to the
granddaughters of those affected. The case involved a
woman, Patricia Enright, who blamed her mother's use of
DES in the 1950s for her own in utero injuries, her four spon-
taneous abortions, and the premature birth of her daughter
in 1981.[26] That, however, was too much of a stretch for the
court and the chief. "For all we know, the rippling effects of
DES exposure may extend for generations," Wachtler wrote.
"It is our duty to confine liability within manageable limits.
Limiting liability to those who ingested the drug or were
exposed to it *in utero* serves this purpose."[27]

Once again, Wachtler tempered principle with pragmatism, an approach that generally served him well—as it had
in 1976 *In the Matter of Denise R.*[28]

Denise R. was a 42-year-old genetic male who had considered himself a woman trapped in a man's body since he
was ten years old. Nearly two decades earlier, he had abandoned his male identity and was living as a woman. He became a salesperson in a women's dress shop. Denise sought
public funding for a sex-change operation, claiming eligi-
bility for Medicaid under a provision in Social Services Law
that promises medical assistance for qualified people when
such assistance is "necessary to prevent, diagnose, or cure

conditions in the person that cause acute suffering, endanger life, result in illness or infirmity, interfere with his capacity for normal activity, or threaten some significant handicap."[29] The court, through Wachtler, rejected the claim, deciding that the judiciary should not create a benefit that the legislature has not provided. "The court cannot assume the role of either social agency or legislative body," Wachtler wrote.[30]

The chief's most enduring human rights decision may well be one involving mandatory drug testing of probationary teachers. A Long Island school district, Patchogue-Medford, required its probationary teachers to undergo a complete physical one year into the job and just before being granted tenure. At at time when the Reagan administration—and, in particular, U.S. Attorney General Edwin Meese—was pushing hard for mandatory drug testing of public employees,[31] Wachtler wrote a first-in-the-nation decision that repudiated the administration's position, and unquestionable undermined any chances the chief had of securing a Supreme Court nomination.

Probationary teachers were asked to provide a urine sample, which would be tested for the presence of illegal drugs. Those who refused were fired, as were those who failed. The teachers' union challenged the rule as an impermissible search and seizure.

At the outset, there was a legal issue of whether providing a urine sample under threat of ouster is a "search" or "seizure" at all under the Constitution. The school district argued that it was not because the person's body was not being invaded, as it would be, for example, if a blood sample were sought. The court, through Wachtler, quickly dismissed that argument. "Ordering a person to empty his or her bladder and produce their urine in a container for inspection and analysis by public officials is no less offensive to personal dignity than requiring an individual to empty his pockets and produce a report containing the results of a urinalysis examination," he wrote.[32]

Beyond that, however, are profound questions of public policy as well as constitutional analysis—questions that directly confronted Wachtler's long history in both search and seizure and human rights.

On the one hand, there is the question of the Fourth Amendment and the limits it places on the government— and a public school run by public officials is undeniably the government. But what makes the scenario in a school so much different from that on a street corner is the fact that the school/government, by essentially taking into custody classrooms full of students for six or more hours a day, has assumed a responsibility to protect these children. A police officer cannot be held liable if someone wanders onto a busy street corner with an illegal gun and starts firing, but a school district may well be responsible for any harm that comes to a child within its walls. So the state has both an interest and an obligation to ensure a safe environment in school.

"The state has a legitimate interest in seeing that its employees are physically fit and that their performance is not impaired by illegal drug usage," Wachtler wrote for the court in *Patchogue*.[33] Yet he argued that the state's interest in maintaining drug-free schools cannot outweigh the rights of teachers when there is no reason to believe they are suing illegal drugs.

The court was in unanimous agreement that the urinalysis mandate simply violated the teachers' employment contract. However, Wachtler took the court beyond that issue and insisted that the question be framed, and addressed, as a fundamental constitution question. In drafting the opinion, the first in the nation on the issue, Wachtler relied equally on the federal and state constitutions, assuring that the privacy rights the court recognized for teachers would not be undercut by the Supreme Court or the Reagan administration.

Judge Simons, agreeing with the bottom-line result, wrote a separate concurrence to voice his displeasure with the methodology, a topic that would bother him throughout his career. Specifically, Simons was uncomfortable with finding a state constitutional protection—as it did in *Patchogue*—from that point on. "I do not question that we may invoke the safeguards of the state constitution and guarantee our citizens even greater protection than the Fourth Amendment provides under appropriate circumstances," Simons wrote in concurrence. "If the issue had been raised, we would be justified in adopting a higher state standard to maintain a body of coherent and stable law—as we sometimes, but not necessarily, do in the face of changes in Supreme Court rulings—or because of important considerations involving the legal institutions and environment in the state."[34]

Regardless, Wachtler, as usual—particularly at this stage of his career on issues of human rights—prevailed with his expansive view. He was well aware that teachers were being tested for drug use without a shred of evidence that they had done anything wrong, and profoundly concerned about the privacy violations. A urine test for drugs can also determine who has asthma, which employees are pregnant, and whether a worker is being treated for a mental condition or a heart problem.

"By restricting the government to reasonable searches, the state and federal constitutions recognize that there comes a point at which seizures intended to serve the public interest, however effective, may undermine the public's interest in maintaining the privacy, dignity and security of its members," Wachtler wrote for the court. "Thus random searches conducted by the state without reasonable suspicion are closely scrutinized, and generally only permitted when the privacy interests implicated are minimal, the government's interest is substantial, and safeguards are provided to ensure that the individual's reasonable expectation of privacy is not subjected to unregulated discretion. In this case those requirements have not been met."[35]

In his own case, some years later, those requirements were met, and the man who wrote *Patchogue* was forced to regularly submit to urine tests and to suffer the degradations from which he had shielded others.

Notes

1. Martin Luther King Jr., letter from Birmingham Jail, April 16, 1963.

2. *National Organization for Women* v. *State Division of Human Rights*, 314 NY2d 416 (1974); 314 NE2d 867.

3. Ibid., p. 421.

4. Ibid., p. 420.

5. Ibid., p. 421.

6. *Batavia Lodge* v. *State Division of Human Rights*, 35 NY2d 143 (1974), 316 NE2d 318.

7. Ibid., p. 145.

8. *Imperial Diner* v. *State Division of Human Rights*, 52 NY2d 72 (1980), 417 NE2d 525.

9. Ibid., p. 78.

10. Ibid.

11. *McDermott* v. *Xerox*, 65 NY2d 213 (1985), 480 NE2d 695.

12. Ibid., p. 219.

13. *New York State Club Association* v. *City of New York*, 69 NY2d 211 (1987), 505 NE2d 915.

14. Ibid.

15. Interview with Wachtler on August 20, 1997.

16. *People* v. *Liberta,* 64 NY2d 152 (1984), 474 NE2d 567.

17. *Stopping Sexual Assault in Marriage,* Center for Constitutional Rights Report, 1990.

18. *People* v. *Meli,* 193 NYS 365 (1922).

19. *Liberta,* p. 164.

20. Ibid., p. 167.

21. Portions of Laura "X"'s letter are reprinted here with her permission.

22. Interview with Laura "X" on August 20, 1997.

23. Henry Gilgoff, "The DES Daughters Get Day in Court," *Newsday,* May 1, 1989, business page 1.

24. *Hymowitz* v. *Lilly & Co.,* 55 NY2d 571 (1989).

25. Interview with Wachtler on August 15, 1997.

26. *Enright* v. *Lilly & Co.,* 77 NY2d 377 (1991), 570 NE2d 198.

27. Ibid., p. 382.

28. *In the Matter of Denise R.* v. *Lavine,* 39 NY2d 279 (1976), 347 NE2d 893.

29. Social Services Law, section 365-a, subdivision 2.

30. *Denise R.,* 39 NY2d 283.

31. Adam Z. Horvath and Ina Navazelskis, "High Court Bars Teacher Drug Tests without Suspicion," *Newsday,* June 10, 1987, p. 3.

32. *Patchogue-Medford* v. *Board of Education,* 70 NY2d 57, 68 (1987), 510 NE2d 325.

33. Ibid.

34. Ibid.

35. Ibid., p. 70.

CHAPTER 10

The Last Right

Faye Wachtler, the judge's elderly mother, lay near death, tethered to life support. She pulled her son close and whispered, "Let me die." Wachtler refused to pull the plug; his mother survived the illness, recovered completely, and was forever grateful that her son wouldn't give up her life even when she herself was willing to do so. Years later, the incident would continue to haunt Wachtler as he, more than any other judge, was responsible for erecting in New York the nation's most stringent right-to-die standard. He would, from that point onward, refer to the right to die as "the last right."

"The fact is," he said in various speeches,

> that in this area medical technology has outdistanced law and poses a challenge to our traditional, ethical, and legal

standards. People who are terminally ill rarely die at home because of the success of medicine which has shifted the place of dying to health care institutions. This has the effect of transferring control over treatment away from the patient and his family to the provider of health care. In most instances there is an accommodation with respect to treatment. But what of the case where a terminally ill patient wishes to forego treatment for any number of reasons such as pain and suffering, financial concerns or religious beliefs? Does the public have a right to interfere? Whose life is it anyway?[1]

Although modern medicine brought a renewed interest to the debate, questions of law and public policy have been enmeshed with both the spirituality and politics of death since at least the Middle Ages. Many medieval woodcuts depict death scenes with a doctor, a priest—and a lawyer.

"Today, in many cases that picture would have to include a judge," Wachtler said in various speeches.

The judge would be there to determine whether too much or too little is being done to prolong the life of a patient who, because of illness or general mental incompetence, is unable to personally determine the course of treatment.

Many consider the court's presence in these matters offensive. But this is not a role which the judiciary has assumed for itself. It has been thrust upon the courts by advances in medical treatment which can extend the lives of the terminally ill beyond medical and legal precedent. As a result, family members and doctors called upon to provide for a person who is both terminally ill and incompetent frequently come to court to determine in advance whether a decision to administer, withhold, or discontinue a particular medical treatment may subject them to civil or criminal liability.[2]

It was an issue that pursued Wachtler throughout his judicial life and death, and seemingly one from which he could not escape. (The patient in one of his most important right-to-die decisions, Mary O'Connor, would become the imaginary figure "Theresa O'Connor" in his crazed scheme against Joy). He wrote almost all of the most important cases on the topic and, before authoring the landmark opinions but after the incident with his mother, was tormented by a thorny case involving the alleged "wrongful life" of a child with Down's Syndrome.

The parents of the child, Dolores and Arnold Becker, had accused their doctor of negligence for failing to explain to them the risks of pregnancy (when Dolores was thirty-seven years old) and for neglecting to perform an amniocentesis test, which would have shown that the fetus was afflicted. If they had known, they argued, they would have aborted the child. The Beckers sued their doctor for the costs of raising a child they said should never have been born.

Wachtler was hedging, not quite sure which way he wanted to go, when he happened to meet a Down's child. Limited to be sure, but happy, joyous and, in her own way, beautiful. Wachtler fell in love with the little girl.

When the court conferenced *Becker* v. *Schwartz*[3] in 1978, Wachtler feared that if the court imposed on the doctor the cost of raising a handicapped child, such children would be routinely aborted. He began to think of the wonderful, albeit handicapped, child he had met, and he began to weep. The child, he realized, would never become a doctor or a judge. She would never amount to anything—except, perhaps, a happy human being. And that was too precious to squander.

"She was probably the sweetest, gentlest child I had ever spoken to, loving and cuddly," Wachtler said. "In *Becker* v. *Schwartz*, they were saying the amniocentesis would have detected the defective fetus and permitted the mother to have an abortion. I said to hold the doctor liable would be to presume the mother would have an abortion, which is to presume the mother should have an abortion, which is to presume the mother wouldn't want the child. It struck me as terribly wrong to speculate in that fashion. I became very emotional remembering the child."[4]

His dissenting vote was cast.

"A doctor exposed to liability of this magnitude will undoubtedly, in marginal cases, be inclined to practice 'defensive medicine' by advising abortion rather than run the risk of having to pay for the lifetime care of the child if it is born with a handicap," Wachtler wrote.

> Thus the majority's decision will involve human costs as well, in those cases where otherwise healthy children will be unnecessarily aborted as the only alternative to the threat of pecuniary liability. In sum, by holding the doctor responsible for the birth of a genetically handicapped child, and thus obligated to pay most, if not all, of the costs of a lifetime of care and support, the court has created a kind of medical paternity suit. It is a tort without precedence, and at variance with existing precedent both old and new.[5]

Since at least 1914, the Court of Appeals had recognized the right of a competent adult to refuse medical treatment. In *Schloendorff* v. *Society of New York Hospital*,[6] Judge Cardozo wrote: "Every human being of adult years and sound mind has the right to determine what shall be done with his own body, and a surgeon who performs an operation without his patient's consent commits an assault, for which he is liable in damages." But the court continued to struggle with those cases in which a patient is unable to express his or her wishes, particularly as medical science reached a level where it could sustain almost perpetually a vegetative life. Judges were torn and without clear direction. After all, whose life was it? Solely the individual's, or did the family have a say? What about society's interest, and God's? Who could make decisions for a patient unable to make his or own? Wachtler, in some of his most difficult and controversial decisions, provided that direction: Err on the side of life.

The implications of that philosophy were, and are, profound. "At first there was a great howl from the medical community which said that the courts should not be dealing with this problem—as if we spent our time walking the hospital corridors looking for the business," Wachtler recalls. "And now many people who originally criticized the courts for making these unwarranted intrusions into the sickroom are critical of the courts for not going far enough to settle the law, or predict the outcome, in cases that have not yet reached the courts."[7]

He said the first cases to reach the court came "like a surprise attack," for which the judges had no contingency plan. "Our precedents, drawn from the venerable traditions of the common law, where a life-or-death decision usually meant a criminal execution, did not anticipate and could not anticipate the legal consequences of discontinuing a respirator for a person in a persistent vegetative state."[8]

At the crux of the issue is the individual's right of privacy and the state's interest in preserving life. As early as 1891, the U.S. Supreme Court recognized the right of competent adults to make their own health care determinations. "No right is held more sacred, or is more carefully guarded, by the common law, than the right of every individual to the possession and control of his own person free from all restraint or interferences of others, unless by clear and unquestionable authority of law," the high court said in *Union Pacific Railway Co. v. Botsford.*[9] But the Supreme Court was generally silent on the issue for most of the next century.

The right-to-die issue first attracted widespread public attention in 1976, when a New Jersey Supreme Court decided that a comatose young woman named Karen Ann Quinlan could be removed from a respirator upon the wishes of her father. But the U.S. Supreme Court really didn't address the issue until the Nancy Cruzan case in 1990, and even then the High Court essentially handed it off to the states.

The *Cruzan* case involved a thirty-year-old woman who, as a result of a car wreck, had been in a vegetative state for five years. After she lost her gag reflex and a feeding tube was inserted, her parents sought a court order to remove the apparatus. A lower court said the tube should be removed. But the Missouri Supreme Court, voting 4 to 3, reversed. It held that life-sustaining treatment could be withdrawn only upon the "informed consent" of the patient, and that the patient could only give that consent on the death bed. "It is definitionally impossible for a person to make an informed decision—either to consent or to refuse—under hypothetical circumstances [because] neither the benefits nor the risks of treatment can be properly weighed or fully appreciated."[10] In 1990, the U.S. Supreme Court said in the *Cruzan* case that states could erect standards as high as Missouri's, or lower, and that the panel in Washington wasn't inclined to get into the fray absent an issue specifically keyed to the U.S. Constitution.

Meanwhile, the New York Court of Appeals, and primarily Wachtler, was struggling with the issue. Initially, the internal debate centered on Wachtler and Hugh Jones—with Jones arguing to liberalize the law. Later, Judge Simons, who had watched a relative die a slow, painful death, carried Jones's baton.

"Those were very, very respectable positions," Wachtler

said, referring to the arguments of Jones and Simons. "Those were very, very difficult decisions. You realize that you are setting a pattern that affects life and death. The big argument was whether we, as a court, should sanction 'substituted judgment,' and whether that should not better be done by the legislature."[11]

Part of the difficulty was in defining death. Years earlier, Judge Cooke had somewhat boxed the court in with a decision that defined death as a flat brain wave.[12] In that case, a person, the victim of an assault, was virtually dead and his organs were harvested for donation. The defendant, charged with murder, argued that not he but the doctors killed the patient by removing the organs. The Court of Appeals was not about to let the assailant off, and Cooke and his court came up with the flat brain wave definition. Later, however, a state panel charged with investigating issues surrounding the right to die simply sidestepped the definition question, leaving the matter muddled. Wachtler, haunted by the incident with his mother, and profoundly reluctant to bestow on government the power to determine whose life was of value and whose was not, continued to explore the issue in his decisions, extrajudicial writings, and speeches.

"Is the next of kin an appropriate person to make a life or death determination for an unconscious or incompetent patient?" Wachtler asked.

Could not emotional trauma or upset and even selfish motives impede the next of kin's ability to make sensitive and reasoned judgments? What distinguishes "extraordinary" from "ordinary" means of treatment? Is there a difference between withholding or withdrawing 'extraordinary' means when the patient does not face imminent death but rather a gradual demise without hope of recovery? Although physicians may not be compelled to attempt heroic measures in hopeless cases—how do we define "heroic" and who determines hopelessness?[13]

Many of those issues arose in New York eight years before Cruzan in two cases entitled *Matter of Eichner* and *Matter of Storar*,[14] both decided in opinions by Wachtler in 1981, and both very difficult cases for the court to resolve.

Matter of Eichner—the Brother Fox case—involved an 83-year-old member of the Society of Mary. Brother Fox was in a permanent vegetative state and being maintained on a respirator when the director of the society applied, as the friar's court-appointed guardian, to have the machine removed. The guardian maintained that the artificial life support was contrary to the wishes Brother Fox had expressed before lapsing into a coma. In *Storar*, a state hospital sought a court order to administer blood transfusions to a profoundly retarded 52-year-old man with terminal bladder cancer. John Storar's mother refused to sign a consent, arguing that a transfusion would only prolong her son's suffering and would be against his wishes if he were competent.

Brother Fox was allowed to die, but only because the friar had, while competent, made his wishes clearly known. "The district attorney . . . urged that whatever right the patient may have is entirely personal and may not be exercised by any third party once the patient becomes incompetent," Wachtler told an audience at Stetson University College of Law on November 11, 1983.

His argument was founded on the principle that a right to decline lifesaving treatment conflicts with a patient's fundamental and constitutionally guaranteed right to life and to permit a third party to choose between the two means; in effect, that the right to life is lost once the patient becomes incompetent. We decided in favor of the guardian—

but we did so because Brother Fox made the decision for himself before he became incompetent. We did not answer the district attorney's argument as to whether in the case of unconsciousness or incompetency, a decision to discontinue the life-sustaining mechanism may be made by someone other than the patient.[15]

Storar was never competent and, therefore, Wachtler reasoned, he could have never made a knowing decision. "Although we understand and respect his mother's despair, as we respect the beliefs of those who oppose transfusions on religious grounds, a court should not in the circumstances of this case allow an incompetent patient to bleed to death because someone, even someone as close as a parent or sibling, feels that it is best for the one with the disease," the court said.[16]

Later, Wachtler recalled *Storar* as, internally, the most difficult of the right-to-die cases. "What would happen if this mother just said, 'I don't want this burden anymore. I can't live with this burden'? What if the child had a disease that could be cured with penicillin? Could we sanction that? Isn't that murder?"[17]

Yet the court took a different approach in a case where, essentially, the issue wasn't whether the plug should be pulled, but whether it should be inserted in the first place.

In 1983, the unanimous court, in a strongly worded but unsigned opinion, upheld a Long Island couple's right to withhold corrective surgery from their seventeen-day-old daughter. The case involved a child born with spina bifida (exposed spine) and hydrocephalus (water on the brain). Without surgery, doctors said she would die within two years. With surgery, she could live a painful existence—severely retarded and bedridden—for over twenty years. A lawyer in Albany who challenged the parents' right to refuse treatment faced an unusually severe grilling in court from Wachtler, who demanded to know why a stranger should be allowed to intervene "like a medical vigilante squad, to walk around looking for what he feels is lacking." The court dismissed the petition, declaring that allowing a total stranger to initiate such proceedings "would catapult him into the very heart of a family circle, there to challenge the most private and most precious responsibility vested in the parents for the care and nurture of their children—and at the very least to force the parents to incur the not inconsiderable expenses of extended litigation."[18]

Even then, the case wasn't over. The federal secretary of health brought an action in federal court to obtain the hospital records, ostensibly to determine if the hospital was discriminating against a disabled infant in violation of the Rehabilitation Act of 1973. The government lost.

But it wasn't until 1988 that the New York court, and Wachtler, got another chance to address the right to die. The case involved 77-year-old Mary O'Connor, a stroke-debilitated patient at the Westchester County Medical Center who was totally incapable of caring for herself. Although conscious, responsive to some questions, reactive to pain, and able to obey some simple commands, she could not take food orally. When the hospital sought to replace the intravenous feeding with a nasogastric feeding tube, her two daughters refused to consent. They said that their mother, while caring for dying relatives and friends, had repeated that if she were in that position and unable to care for herself, she would not want to be sustained by artificial means. Even though there was no dispute that Mrs. O'Connor had clearly expressed her wishes, the divided court in the *Matter of Westchester County Medical Center on Behalf of Mary O'Connor* v. *Hall*[19] found a lack of "clear and convincing evidence," essentially adopting the position of the Missouri court in the *Cruzan* case.

"This is a demanding standard, the most rigorous burden of proof in civil cases," Wachtler wrote for the court. "It is appropriate here because if an error occurs, it should be made on the side of life."[20] Wachtler's decision imposed on judges the burden of not only determining whether patients had expressed a wish to die, but whether their desire was reasoned and settled and "makes a change of heart unlikely"—a clause that directly brings to mind the incident with his mother. "The persistence of the individual's statements, the seriousness with which those statements were made and the inferences, if any, that may be drawn from the surrounding circumstances are among the facts which should be considered," the court instructed.

Simons led the dissent, joined by Judge Alexander. "Judges," they argued, "the persons least qualified by training, experience or affinity have overridden Mrs. O'Connor's wishes, negated her long-held values on life and death and imposed on her and her family their ideas of what her best interests require."[21]

The ruling was counter to those of many other states, where courts had affirmed the right of patients' families to decide whether to continue life-sustaining measures. Wachtler, however, offered a rationale. "Her comments—that she would never want to lose her dignity before she passed away, that nature should be allowed to take its course, that it is 'monstrous' to use life-support machinery—are in fact no different than those that many might make after witnessing an agonizing death," he argued. "Similarly, her statements to the effect that she would not want to be a burden to anyone are the type of statements that older people frequently, almost invariably, make. If such statements were routinely held to be clear and convincing proof of general intent to decline all medical treatment once incompetency sets in, few nursing home patients would ever receive life-sustaining treatment in the future."[22]

Wachtler later remarked that he was "mindful of the fact that New York is out of step with almost every other state in not applying the doctrine of substituted judgment," but suggested that that task was up to the legislature, not the courts. In *O'Connor*, he specifically invited the legislature to allow living wills that spelled out the type of treatment a person would, or would not, want.

"I would be the first to concede that the courts are unsuited and ill-equipped to deal with this problem," Wachtler said in an oft-repeated speech on the topic.

> The courts do not possess the particular competence necessary to reach the ultimate decision which often depends not only on medical data, but also on theological tenets and perceptions of human values which defy classification and calibration. It has been said that the judicial process, dealing as it does with one case at a time, is exposed to too narrow a slice of reality to properly form policy. The legislatures, on the other hand, are well suited to balance the interests involved in determining whether to permit termination of care. They have the plenary power to make laws for the protection of the patient as well as the doctor; they are empowered to define homicide and grant statutory immunity from criminal and civil liability; they can devise a plan for medical procedures to determine when death occurs; and they can present clear guidelines which provide a sufficient range of moral autonomy and procedural safeguards to allow the tragic choice to be made.[23]

The New York legislature, however, was terribly slow to address the issues, and even by the late 1990s had resolved little.

"And so we are confronted with scenes such as were witnessed . . . when the father of a 21-year-old brain dead man went to a New York court seeking a judge's permission to let his son die," Wachtler said. "At the court hearing, an assistant district attorney asked the doctor why, if he was so certain that the patient was dead, he did not sign a death certificate. The doctor responded: 'Because of people like you, who would call me a murderer for turning off life support on someone I know is already dead.'"[24]

Two years later, in 1990, the court again was forced to address a matter ignored by the legislature, striking a chord for self-determination when it held in the *Matter of Fosmire* v. *Nicoleau*[25] that a 35-year-old Jehovah's Witness should not have been forced to undergo a blood transfusion following a Cesarean delivery. The hospital had argued that the forced procedure was legally warranted to avoid denying the child of the mother. "The state does not prohibit parents from engaging in dangerous activities because there is a risk that their children will be left orphans," Wachtler wrote for the court. "Although the state will not permit a parent to abandon a child, the state has never gone so far as to intervene in every personal decision a parent makes which may jeopardize the family unit or the parental relationship."[26]

Wachtler, unable to come to firm grips with the issue judicially, again and again pleaded for help from the legislature. But the legislative branch seemed no more comfortable with the issue than the judiciary, leaving the issue perpetually muddled.

"The *Storar* case, the *Brother Fox* case, the *Quinlan* case—all of these represent only facets in a kaleidoscope of situations that involve the futility of treatment and the implications which follow the termination of treatment," Wachtler lamented.

The legislatures alone have the power and the ability to statutorily mitigate the uncertainties and generate adequate legal measures to permit a dignified death. . . . Legislation will not eliminate all need to resort to the courts. There will always be questions of interpretation and constitutional rights. But legislation should be able to provide answers in most cases and, in others, provide the courts and potential litigants with a clear statement of public policy to inform the choice. No one can eliminate the agony of a personal loss of a friend or family member. But in most cases we can eliminate the agony and expense of litigation involving life-and-death decisions.[27]

Notes

1. Wachtler's archives.
2. Ibid.
3. *Becker* v. *Schwartz*, 46 NY2d 401 (1978), 386 NE2d 807.
4. Interview with Wachtler on August 20, 1997.
5. *Becker*, p. 420.
6. *Schloendorff* v. *Society of New York Hospital*, 211 NY 125 (1914).
7. Wachtler's archives, draft speech.
8. Ibid.
9. *Union Pacific Railway Co.* v. *Botsford*, 141 US 250 (1891).
10. *Cruzan* v. *Director, Missouri Dept. of Health*, 497 US 261 (1990).
11. Interview with Wachtler on August 20, 1997.
12. *People* v. *Eulo*, 63 NY2d 341 (1984), 472 NE2d 286.
13. Wachtler's archives, draft speech.
14. *Matter of Storar*, 52 NY 363 (1981); 420 NE2d 64.
15. Wachtler's archives.

16. *Storar.*

17. Interview with Wachtler on August 20, 1997.

18. *Matter of Weber* v. *Stony Brook Hospital,* 60 NY2d 208, 213 (1983); 456 NE2d 1186.

19. *Matter of Westchester County Medical Center on Behalf of Mary O'Connor* v. *Hall,* 725 NY2d 517 (1988); 531 NE2d 607.

20. Ibid., p. 531.

21. Ibid., p. 552.

22. Ibid., p. 532.

23. Wachtler's archives.

24. Ibid.

25. *Matter of Fosmire* v. *Nicoleau,* 75 NY2d 218 (1990); 551 NE2d 77.

26. Ibid., p. 230.

27. Wachtler's archives.

CHAPTER 11

Errant Knights
and Activism

To insiders and longtime court observers, the *Scott* and *Keta*[1] cases were, in retrospect, a clear sign that Wachtler was losing his grip. Wachtler's court, so often in unanimous agreement, so rarely engaging in public bickering, was airing its dirty laundry for all to see, and it was doing so on an issue where the chief had once been firm: independence. What could be going on? No one guessed that the chief judge was preoccupied with sending dirty letters to his former mistress.

The consolidated cases were each decided by a 4-3 vote, with Wachtler in the minority. Wachtler's inability to build a majority consensus is revealing, but far more revealing is the fact that the majority "opinion" yielded four free-wheeling, separate opinions in which the judges engaged in a bruising debate over judicial federalism—essentially, whether the state constitution should provide broader protections than required under the U.S. Constitution, as interpreted by the Supreme Court. At the moment of truth, Wachtler was distracted; his campaign of harassment directed at Joy Silverman had reached a new, and ultimately catastrophic, level. Wachtler was beginning to send obscene and threatening letters to Joy and her daughter just as the court suffered an institutional identity crisis. Preoccupied by his private scheme, Wachtler was unable to rein in his judges, to forge a consensus, to carry the majority, and—most seriously—to prevent a testy and very public display of judicial backbiting.

"This is when I started slipping," Wachtler later observed after observing a videotape of the oral arguments archived by Albany Law School. "And the slippage is noticed not so much in my performance on the bench, but in my failure to control the court. This shows a court functioning without any leadership, with all the vitriol in the decision. I would have found that intolerable had I been [stable] at the time."[2]

Scott involved a man who was convicted of marijuana possession after authorities found numerous plants growing on his 165-acre parcel in Chenango County. Police learned of the marijuana field, and orchestrated a warrantless search, after they were tipped off by a hunter who had ignored several "no trespassing" signs and tracked a wounded animal onto the property. Defense attorney Terence L. Kindlon of Albany made a shrewd tactical decision, basing his entire argument on the state constitution and quite purposely avoiding mention of the federal constitution. The U.S. Supreme Court had ruled in 1984 that owners of "open fields" were not shielded from such searches under the Fourth Amendment.[3]

Keta dealt with a search of an auto-dismantling business, a so-called chop shop, in Queens that was the target of a New York City police probe. Authorities entering the property to conduct an administrative inspection, as opposed to a search, began snooping around without a warrant and found parts of stolen cars. In 1987, the U.S. Supreme Court specifically allowed such searches.[4] But the Court of Appeals, with Wachtler in the minority, found the searches illegal under Article 1 Section 12 of the New York State Constitution. The Fourth Amendment and its New York counterpart, which both address unreasonable searches, are worded identically. Yet the Court of Appeals, directly snubbing the Supreme Court, found broader rights for New Yorkers.

It was precisely the type of issue that Wachtler, in his early years on the court, would have embraced. Toward the end, however, Wachtler was losing control and respect. Unable to focus on what he was doing, and becoming preoccupied by both Joy and his flirtation with the gubernatorial race, Wachtler was no longer the esteemed leader of the other judges, and the *Scott/Keta* case was the result of a court which had lost both its captain and its rudder.

"When Sol Wachtler was elevated to Chief Judge in January 1985, it seemed that the court's independent tradition would continue," observed court scholar Vincent M. Bonventre of Albany Law School in a June 1992 article.

> In Wachtler's first few years, the Court of Appeals rejected "conservative" Supreme Court decisions in the areas of free expression, search and seizure, and equal protection. The Court also struck out on its own, without rulings to reject or follow, in such decisions as restricting random drug testing and involuntary medication. Justice William Brennan . . . called the Court of Appeals the "acknowledged leader" in protecting individual liberties through state constitutional law. But recently there has been little such leadership.[5]

That Wachtler disagreed with his court's position in *Scott/ Keta* is not altogether surprising. He had always had a pragmatic vein, had always been reluctant to let off obvious criminals on what could be construed as technicalities, and had been elected to the court largely on a law-and-order platform. What is surprising is that he allowed—or, more accurately, failed to prevent—the public clash among his judges.

"The court's declaration of independence from the Supreme Law of the Land . . . propels the court across a jurisprudential Rubicon into a kind of Articles of Confederation time warp," declared Judge Bellacosa, author of the dissent and one of Wachtler's few truly close allies on the court at a time when he was losing control. "The United States Supreme Court rulings should be given greater respect."[6]

Wachtler signed off on the dissent, not even bothering to soften Bellacosa's divisive rhetoric, and provoking an exceedingly rare chiding from Associate Judge Kaye. Kaye, a strong-willed yet reserved and cautious jurist, reminded her colleagues that the state court's refusal to follow the Supreme Court in lockstep is a "perfectly respectable and legitimate thing to do."[7]

While his judges were debating that issue, the chief was too busy writing anonymous and obscene notes and plotting a battle against Mario Cuomo to take an active role in any of the four writings produced by the *Scott/Keta* appeals.

The underlying principle, which Wachtler had always found compelling, is that the U.S. Supreme Court sets the basement level of rights, as guaranteed under the federal constitution, while the Court of Appeals sets the ceiling level. No state may offer its citizens narrower protections than the U.S. Constitution, as interpreted by the Supreme Court, requires. It may, however, offer broader protections, and the New York Court of Appeals has traditionally done so.

"As the Supreme Court retreats from the field, or holds the

line on individual rights, state courts and litigants seeking solutions to new problems are turning with greater frequency to the state constitutions, which for many years lay dormant in the shadow of the federal Bill of Rights," Wachtler said in various speeches in the late 1980s. "This is not, as some have suggested, a way of evading the edicts of a conservative Supreme Court. It is a resumption of a role which the state constitutions were originally designed to fulfill, as the primary guardians of the rights of all individuals within their borders. New York has been an active participant in this movement."[8]

Under the federal constitution, police have to simply advise a suspect of the right to counsel before proceeding with questioning. In New York, once an attorney is involved in a case police cannot question the suspect without the lawyer present; if they do, the evidence is suppressed. Similarly, under federal law a suspect in custody does not have a right to have an attorney present at a lineup. Under the New York Constitution he does. The state constitution also offers far broader free speech protections to its citizens, protecting both mainstream artists and pornographers to a far greater degree than the federal constitution.

When it so chooses, the Court of Appeals can simply overrule the Supreme Court, as it did rather loudly in *Scott/ Keta,* and essentially snub the highest court in the land. Its traditional habit of doing so has rankled many, including Chief Justice William Rehnquist, who, in 1987, observed that while the Court of Appeals is "free to do as it chooses, [it] . . . ought to have some basis for what it's doing."[9]

Independence, however, was hardly a new concept for the Court of Appeals; it was one that was articulated decades earlier. Long before the Supreme Court, the Court of Appeals repudiated the *Dred Scott* decision upholding slavery, enforced the privilege against self-incrimination, and firmly supported the free expression of religion.[10]

In the early 1940s, Chief Judge Irving Lehman reaffirmed the court's independent stance: "Parenthetically, we may point out that in determining the scope and effect of their guarantees of fundamental rights of the individual in the Constitution of the State of New York, this Court is bound to exercise its independent judgment and is not bound by a decision of the Supreme Court of the United States limiting the scope of similar guarantees in the Constitution of the United States."[11]

In New York, the "dual protection" principle—the concept that citizens are protected by two constitutions, federal and state—has special meaning. Alexander Hamilton, James Madison, and John Jay all preached dual protectionism to New Yorkers in 1787 in a successful effort to get them to ratify the U.S. Constitution. It worked; by a scant three votes, New Yorkers ratified the federal constitution. Also, New York has had a bill of rights, written by Jay, since 1777 that guarantees everything from free speech to equal protection.

Regardless of that tradition, the Court of Appeals has wrestled repeatedly with the question of when to yield to the Supreme Court and when to flex its judicial muscle, and Wachtler's tenure as chief left the issue, if anything, more uncertain.

When Wachtler took over as chief in 1985, it appeared that he would maintain the court's independent tradition. In the early years, the court rejected several "conservative" or rights-limiting decisions by the Supreme Court and struck out on its own to find new rights not before contemplated by either the judges in Albany or the justices in Washington. It followed the lead of Justice Brennan, who, in a seminal 1977 article,[12] called for a new federalism as an antidote to backpedaling by the Supreme Court and Nixonian pressures.

The judicial activism/restraint debate dates back at least a century. At the end of the nineteenth century, James Bradley Thayer, dean of the Harvard Law School and an influential advocate of the judicial restraint philosophy, had substantial impact on Harvard Law School graduates like Oliver Wendell Holmes (who wanted to limit judicial review to acts of the state governments) and Felix Frankfurter. Thayer explained his philosophy in an 1893 *Harvard Law Review* article titled "The Origin and Scope of the American Doctrine of Constitutional Law," in which he expressed the fear that if judges interfered too much in the work of legislators, the citizenry would lose confidence in the courts. The debate continues to this day.*

Richard Nixon wanted judges who were "strict constructionists," i.e., jurists who would interpret the Constitution, not view themselves as instruments of social change. Brennan countered that if Nixon's appointees wouldn't force social change, the state courts could, and should. "The spotlight is often focused upon the decisions of the United States Supreme Court," Brennan wrote.

> Too often, I think, that focus tends to divert attention from the vital role of the state courts to the administration of justice. Actually the composite work of the courts for the fifty states has greater significance in measuring how well America attains the ideal of equal justice under law for all. It is important to stress that the Supreme Court of the United States has power to review only those decisions of state courts that rest on federal law. I suppose the state courts of all levels must annually hand down literally millions of decisions that do not rest on federal law, yet deter-

---

*Philosophically, the debate is between the *legal realists,* who view the legal process as essentially political with little or no objective basis and influenced heavily by the attitudes and instincts of the presiding judge, and the *logical positivists,* who view the law formulaically and reduce knowledge to a series of linguistic manipulations. Wachtler wasn't particularly comfortable with either camp, and sought to adopt his own interpretation.

mine vital issues of life, liberty, and property of countless human beings in the nation. . . . The overwhelming number of trial decisions upon which depend life, liberty, and property thus are decisions of state courts.[13]

Wachtler initially embraced that stance and seemed eager to stake new ground, albeit cautiously. He was too much of a politician to fail to realize that real recognition of the court comes in the political, not the legal, realm. And he was too much of a judge to fail to realize that the court was part of the state power structure. Through its power to veto legislation, a court has enormous power, yet it is not subject to popular control, particularly since the Court of Appeals is now an appointive bench. Wachtler, a man with a foot in both worlds, was naturally engaged in a perpetual personal struggle between the philosophies of restraint and activism, legal realism and logical positivism.

"We do not believe that a court should decide more than the actual case before it," Wachtler said once, articulating the judicial philosophy of his court, or what he perceived and hoped that philosophy was. "We feel the courts should go from case to case in developing the common law and not consider themselves a group of self-starters or freewheeling interlopers roaming the countryside as 'knights-errant' determined to separate good from evil and right from wrong for all time."[14]

The "knights-errant" remark referred to Benjamin Cardozo's observation in 1921 that a judge "is not a knight-errant roaming at will in pursuit of his own ideal of beauty or of goodness." Cardozo generally favored restraint, but along with his successors—Breitel, Cooke, Wachtler and, probably the most independent-minded chief of the century, Kaye—helped perpetuate the state court's independent tradition.

Judges and other legal scholars continue to debate the nature of the Constitution and the way in which it is to be applied to modern problems. Advocates of "original intent" (such as Chief Justice Rehnquist, Judge Robert Bork, and Edwin Meese) maintain that the aim of the framers is expressed exclusively in the Constitution, and nothing should interfere with a literal, "strict construction" interpretation. At the other end of the spectrum are judges, like Wachtler, who view the Constitution largely as a procedural document, delineating the manner in which the judiciary is to resolve disputes involving such difficult topics as slavery and abortion, neither of which was originally addressed in the Constitution.

Wachtler was well aware that if "original intent" were the only guidepost to judicial decision making, "the public schools of Brooklyn would still be segregated"; he struggled constantly, and unsuccessfully, to resolve the issue in his own mind. Wachtler generally agreed with Justice Brennan's famous comment on original intent: "Indeed, if it were possible to find answers to all constitutional questions by reference to historical practices, we would not need judges. Courts could be staffed by professional historians who would be instructed to compile a comprehensive master list of life in 1791."[15]

Wachtler's view, in various speeches, echoes Brennan's sentiments:

We had to decide if fish had the right to breathe in the Hudson River. We had to decide that the Grand Central Terminal should stand, and that the blue laws should fall. We had to tell Taiwan that they could romp and play on Quemoy and Matsu, but they couldn't come to the Olympics at Lake Placid. We had to tell a parent of an infirm young child that that child had a right to live. And we told a terminally ill elderly patient that he had a right to die. We said that a man could be found guilty of raping his wife, that an obese woman could not be fired simply because she was obese if she could do the work assigned to her.[16]

Those are all pragmatic questions, but with little or no guideposts from the past, how are judges who are supposedly wedded to "original intent" supposed to consider such issues?

Wachtler was well aware that until the Nazis came along before World War II, simple obedience to the law was presumptively the right thing to do, and applying that law was the right course for a judge. The horrors of Naziism required judges and philosophers to distinguish between laws and justice. But how? "I confess my inability to know precisely how our Founding Fathers would have decided cases involving issues of telephonic eavesdropping, or Hudson River pollution," Wachtler offers. "I can't imagine how they would have viewed the rights of an unconscious patient to be removed from a life-support system. I don't think that our Founding Fathers intended for us to interpret the Constitution divorced, somehow, from contemporary understanding and morality."[17]

Under our political system the majority rules. But the founders understood all too well that the majority could tyrannize the minority. For instance, 51 percent could vote to enslave the remaining 49 percent. The court and Constitution are designed to prevent this type of tyranny. The Constitution they drafted, however, does not provide an absolute answer to every legal question, nor was it meant to. The framers knew their foresight, as impressive as it was, was limited, and added the peculiar Ninth Amendment: "The enumeration in the Constitution of certain rights, shall not be construed to deny or disparage others retained by the people." Read narrowly, the amendment is meaningless. Read expansively, it is a bottomless pit from which judges can declare an endless range of new rights that are neither stated nor implied by either the Constitution or the legislature.

"The framers were not so arrogant as to presume that they were able to articulate for all time the entire range of rights that were fundamental and guaranteed by the laws of nature," Wachtler wrote in a draft of a law review article in 1991.

> It is for that reason that the Ninth Amendment, however enigmatic, took form and became a statement of the framers' profound belief that fundamental rights were fundamental because they were a function of the natural order and not because they were memorialized in the Constitution and elevated to popular consent into the law of the land. . . . How can we ensure that the judges are identifying rights that are truly fundamental and not simply exercising judicial power in such a way as to bring about their personal conception of the common good?[18]

Even by 1991, Wachtler never came to anything more than an uneasy solution; but in July 1985, U.S. Attorney General Edwin Meese, with a vitriolic assault on the judiciary, forced him to address the issue head on.

Meese called "bizarre" a Supreme Court ruling that overturned an Alabama law permitting moments of silence for prayer or meditation in public schools, called for a return to a "jurisprudence of Original Intention," and characterized as "intellectual snobbery" any attempt by the judiciary to waver from deciding cases purely on the motives of the framers. "It has been and will continue to be the policy of this administration to press for a jurisprudence of Original Intention," President Reagan's top law enforcement official told the American Bar Association. "In the cases we file and those we join as amicus, we will endeavor to resurrect the original meaning of constitutional provisions and statutes as the only reliable guidepost for judgment."

Wachtler was incensed.

"I don't think for a moment that our Founding Fathers intended for us to interpret the Constitution according to their divined intent, divorced somehow, from contemporary understanding," Wachtler said.

> As Thomas Jefferson phrased it, in a free society "nothing is unchangeable but the inherent and unchangeable rights of man." And John Marshall, a member of the Virginia ratifying convention, and later Chief Justice of the United States, spoke to this very point when he said that the Constitution was intended to "endure for ages to come and be adapted to the crisis of human affairs." That Constitution, written in ninety days, has survived for two hundred years; that Constitution, written with a quill pen, has survived to this era of the microchip, precisely because we have recognized that the framers of the Constitution were not so arrogant as to suppose that they could anticipate the future.[20]

Viewing Meese's diatribe as an open offensive against judicial independence, Wachtler responded publicly at the Chautauqua Institution on July 3, 1985. "There can be no words less in need of annotation than those so proudly proclaimed by our Founding Fathers that 'All Men Are Created Equal,' " Wachtler said. "But even though they wrote those words with a heart full of love and enduring faith, they never once meant to include women or members of the black race. It was the courts through each generation from *Dred Scott* to *Plessy* v. *Ferguson* to *Brown* v. *Board of Education* which gave those words, 'All Men Are Created Equal,' a meaning and significance all their own."[21]

Although engaged in a perpetual struggle between the philosophies of restraint and activism—a perhaps healthy struggle—Wachtler admired the vision of the Warren court, *in the context of its historical time frame.* When the Warren court saw something that needed to be done—like desegregating schools, protecting the rights of the accused, or keeping church and state separate—it took an activist role in removing the obstructions. The same confidence in judicial independence occasionally encouraged Wachtler to spread his wings and shape the limits of majority rule.

"This nation has survived because we have recognized our obligation to adapt the law to the 'crises of human affairs,' " Wachtler said. " So long as we remain constant to that obligation, so long as we recognize that we bear the burden not to appease the majority, but to protect the rights of the individual, so long as we are willing to defend in our courts those basic freedoms which are cherished by all of our citizens— even if that protection is unpopular—then we would have done our part in seeing to it that America will survive."[22]

After his first few years as chief, Wachtler and his court had, without stating so, seemingly adopted a general philosophical approach based on traditional concepts of individual liberties as expressed in the state or federal constitution or inferred by the Ninth Amendment. "I have always felt that the best way to induce legislative action is to encourage it by decisional law and not discourage it by allowing the courts to assume a legislative role," Wachtler said.[23]

In interpreting statutes and limiting the power of the majority, the court, in Wachtler's view, must be aware of the need for predictability and certainty, even if it causes injustice in the particular case under consideration.

Notwithstanding the result in *Scott/Keta*, the obvious internal strife undermined the court's aura of predictability and certainty, and would continue to haunt the court for years. Wachtler, regrettably, was unable to participate.

Notes

1. *People* v. *Scott* and *People* v. *Keta*, 79 NY2d 474 (1992), 593 NE2d 1328.

2. Interview with Wachtler on August 19, 1997.

3. *Oliver* v. *United States*, 466 U.S. 170 (1984).

4. *New York* v. *Burger*, 482 U.S. 691 (1987).

5. Vincent Martin Bonventre, "Tilting the Scales of Justice," *Empire State Report*, June 1992, p. 21.

6. *Scott/Keta*, p. 506.

7. Ibid.

8. Wachtler's archives.

9. John Caher, "Dispute over State Constitutional Law Splits Court," Albany *Times Union*, April 6, 1992, p. A-1.

10. Bonventre, "Tilting the Scales of Justice," p. 22.

11. *People* v. *Barber*, 289 NY 378 (1943).

12. *Harvard Law Review* 90 (1977): 489.

13. William J. Brennan Jr., "Justice Nathan L. Jacobs—Tributes from His Colleagues," *Rutgers Law Review* 28 (1974): 209–10.

14. Wachtler's archives.

15. William J. Brennan, "Constitutional Adjudication and the Death Penalty: A View from the Court," Oliver Wendell Holmes Lecture, Harvard Law School, September 5, 1986, p. 21.

16. Wachtler's archives.

17. Ibid.

18. Ibid.

19. Ibid.

20. Ibid.

21. Ibid.

22. Ibid.

23. Ibid.

PART III

The Mystery

CHAPTER 12

Mental Illness

"There was no 'snap,' " U.S. Attorney Michael Chertoff sneered. "Wachtler's acts weren't the product of a severe mental illness. They were the product of anger. Here was a man who, by God's grace, had the things everybody dreams about—position, honor, an intellectually challenging job—and yet when he was scorned in one area, he simply couldn't let go. A snap? Mental illness? This was a man capable of going up on the bench and conducting lucid, erudite oral arguments. He wasn't a man who was staying home in a bathrobe or going around like a screaming banshee."[1] Previously, Chertoff said he wouldn't buy the argument that Wachtler was mentally ill absent evidence that he had a "tumor the size of a basketball."

Although Chertoff did raise a legitimate issue on the efficacy of the mental disease defense and a fair question on how

273

Wachtler could have functioned on the bench if he was indeed a manic-depressive, as the judge's psychiatrists claimed, the prosecutor's remarks infuriated mental health experts, regardless of whether Wachtler did or did not suffer from a psychiatric disease or defect, and it enraged Joan as well. "I am a licensed certified social worker who has been practicing in mental health for sixteen years," Joan Wachtler wrote in a letter to the editor of the *New York Times*.

> Michael Chertoff's characterization of a manic-depressive as someone 'staying home in a bathrobe or going around like a screaming banshee' destroys the progress made by the medical-psychiatric community and the entire mental health profession in educating the public about mental illness.
>
> Mr. Chertoff with this stereotyped negative bias has made a retrograde contribution to the mental health movement, setting it back many decades to a time before the advent of clinical assessment, diagnosis and treatment with psychotherapy and medication. He has redrawn the archaic picture of any person with a mental illness as an unproductive citizen—an out-of-control raving maniac.[2]

Suspicious that Sol was suffering from some sort of imbalance, Joan noted his odd behavior in her diary and nagged him to seek help. But he adamantly refused to seek professional psychiatric assistance.

The misperception that mental illness, particularly depression, is a sign of weakness rather than a health problem is widespread, and it creates a stigma that prevents many people—Wachtler included—from seeking help. Wachtler, well aware of how news leaks of Thomas Eagleton's psychiatric woes derailed his vice-presidential bid in 1972 and of how it became a major issue in the campaign of Michael

Dukakis in 1988, was more afraid of the stigma than the disease. The chief judge seeing a psychiatrist? Inconceivable.

Wachtler's response, or lack of it, was typical. Although some 10 million Americans suffer from a severe longterm mental illness (and, according to the National Institute of Mental Health, approximately 40 million adults in the United States suffer from some form of mental disorder in any one year), a great many suffer in silence, fearing ostracism. The National Alliance for the Mentally Ill, one of the major advocacy organizations, did a survey in 1990 revealing that 71 percent of those responding viewed mental illness as a sign of emotional weakness. Fully one-third thought it resulted from sinful behavior. Roughly 40 percent concluded that mental illness was brought on by the inflicted and that the patients could wish it away at will.[3]

A survey conducted in 1991 for the National Mental Health Association showed that one in six adults would not even tell their spouse if they were undergoing treatment for depression. Another study by the Institute for Social Research at the University of Michigan showed in 1994 that the majority of people with psychiatric disorders go without professional help, partly because of the stigma involved and partly because their families, and often their physicians, fail to recognize the problem.

"I am ashamed that as a professional person who assesses mental illness daily, I did not recognize the early signs," Joan said in her letter to the court, acknowledging that her husband was behaving oddly. "I could not imagine Sol Wachtler as being anything less than a wonder of energy. I had only thought about his behavior as it related to me."[4]

Despite advances in recent years, mental illness remains something of a scientific mystery and a legal nightmare. Always uneasy with questions of science, particularly the unresolved questions, the law seeks objectivity in a subjective field. No scientist can definitely draw a line between criminal behavior that is *caused* by mental illness and that which is merely *exacerbated* by a psychiatric or psychological affliction. Yet that is what the court must strive to do in determining whether a person should be held responsible for her or his behavior. The general standard is arbitrary and centers around two questions: Does the suspect know right from wrong and can he or she appreciate the nature and consequences of his actions? With that standard, someone who genuinely thinks she or he is the Great Pumpkin can be held criminally responsible if he or she knows that society frowns on axe murders and understands that people beaten over the head with hatchets often die. Also under that standard, a John W. Hinckley, who shot President Reagan to impress an actress, is deemed insane while a Jeffrey Dahmer, who dismembered roughly a dozen people and even ate parts of them, is not.

As a judge, Wachtler was leery of the psychiatric defense and far more inclined to err on the side of caution. In a 1979 case, for instance, he led the dissent when the court released from a mental institution a police officer who shot and killed a fifteen-year-old boy. The officer was found not guilty of murder because of mental disease or defect. Wachtler opposed his release. "Our primary concern must be to protect the public from those who, for psychological reasons, have caused and are likely to cause serious harm to others," he wrote for the dissent in *People* v. *Torsney*.[5]

Regardless, Chertoff had a legitimate concern that Wachtler would attempt to use an insanity defense—which the judge briefly considered—to evade justice or mitigate his crimes, and insisted that the defendant undergo examination by mental health experts hired by the government. So, during the first few months after his arrest, Wachtler underwent a battery of psychiatric tests and evaluations—some by Chertoff's experts, some by his own—that predictably and understandably led to different conclusions. However, while the psychiatrists and psychologists differed in their diagnosis and debated the degree of Wachtler's affliction, they uniformly agreed that he was disturbed, behaving aberrantly and suffering at least to some degree from a mental disease or defect.

"At the time I committed my criminal acts, I may not have appreciated the extent of my wrongdoing—and my judgment, while in a manic state, may be have been dreadfully impaired—but I was not legally insane," Wachtler said in his diary. "My capacity was diminished, but I knew that what I was doing was wrong and, therefore, under the applicable federal standard, I was responsible for my conduct."

Wachtler's capacity was undeniably diminished by his abuse of medication. Included in the toxic brew were:

- **Tenuate.** A central nervous system stimulant to combat fatigue. Wachtler was prescribed the amphetamine-like drug after complaining of a lack of energy. The manufacturer warns that chronic use could cause personality changes, including manic-like behavior similar to schizophrenia, and recommends only short-term use.[6] Wachtler, according to records from his pharmacy, took 1,440 tablets over a sixteen-month period between February 1991 and November 1992.
- **Pamelor.** This antidepressant that acts on the central nervous system was prescribed for Wachtler by a physician who warned him against taking any other drugs and who was unaware that he was taking Tenuate. Pamelor, according to the PDR, can launch a manic stage and its use must be closely monitored when used in conjunction with drugs like Tenuate.[7]

- **Halcion.** A sedative prescribed after Wachtler complained of trouble sleeping had been banned in Great Britain and severely limited in the United States because of the side effects, which include mania. The manufacturer recommends only short-term use, such as three doses a day for seven to ten days.[8] Wachtler had 240 doses in the eight months prior to his arrest.
- **Celestone.** A corticosteroid, Celestone was prescribed as an elixir to treat Wachtler's headaches. The PDR warns of "psychic derangements," including euphoria, insomnia, mood swings, personality changes, and severe depression that have been attributed to corticosteroid use.[9]

Wachtler was on a Tenuate high when he first started harassing Silverman and concocting schemes to drive her back to him for help. With the introduction of Pamelor and Halcion, "David Purdy," the imaginary Texas detective who was hunting Mrs. Silverman, took on a life of his own, with his unique appearance and personality. Wachtler became "David Purdy," going so far as to don a cowboy hat and string tie and mumble through lips drawn over his teeth. He bloused his shirt so it would appear that he had a big belly and, amazingly, walked all over Manhattan in that costume, eventually appearing at Silverman's apartment and leaving a threatening note with the doorman.

Within hours after his arrest and confinement in the Payne-Whitney Clinic of New York Hospital—Cornell Medical Center, Wachtler was examined at length by Frank T. Miller, a psychiatrist. Miller first met with Wachtler on November 23, 1992, and found the judge "pressured, loquacious, tangential and circumstantial . . . expansive and grandiose."[10]

"For approximately forty-five minutes, Mr. Wachtler imitated the 'David Purdy' character," Miller said in his report.

He was so enamored by his creation that he insisted upon demonstrating Purdy's walk, talk, mannerisms, and gestures. Since Purdy was toothless, Mr. Wachtler instructed me to pay particular attention to the way he positioned his jaw and lips to conceal his teeth. When I was not able to interrupt this monologue, I asked two other physicians to join us in the hope that their presence in the room would calm him. To my dismay, their presence only served to intensify his display and I asked them to leave. Although the situation was sobering and grim, he was not able to appreciate or grasp it. He had very limited insight and his judgment was poor, even though his higher intellectual functioning was intact.[11]

Miller's diagnosis was that Wachtler suffered a major mental illness from the summer of 1991 through 1992 and that his illness led to the bizarre conduct. He diagnosed the problem as a bipolar disorder—or manic depression—that was exacerbated by Pamelor, Tenuate, Halcion, and Celestone.

During the manic periods, Miller said, a patient "believes that he is an actor on a stage and the world is his audience. He believes that the thoughts, feelings, and behaviors exhibited during the manic episode will be interpreted in this light—viewed as an astonishing performance, to be appreciated for its inventiveness, its cleverness, but not to be taken seriously or acted upon." During the depressed periods, the patient is devoid of hope and energy.

Despite Chertoff's insistence that Wachtler couldn't have functioned as a judge if he were mentally ill, the medical evidence is to the contrary. David P. Klein, a psychiatrist in New York City, said: "It has been argued that Judge Wachtler's functioning indicated that he could not have been severely ill. This view represents a stereotyped misunderstanding of mental illness. Patients may have relatively intact cognitive functions and still be extraordinarily severely impaired, to the point of requiring supervision."[12]

Miller said it is entirely consistent that Wachtler could, for a time, pull off his official duties. But he said the chief was perilously close to collapse when he was arrested.

During those last months, Wachtler was indeed acting peculiarly, and his friends and staff were alarmed by his behavior. His attention span was nil. His work product was substandard.* He stopped preparing for cases, and essentially winged it from the bench. Once, he summoned a secretary to his home to take dictation and appeared with a hooded sweatshirt, explaining that part of his head had been shaved for an operation. The following day, he appeared with a full head of hair. Another time, without any prompting, he suddenly started mimicking Ralph Marino, the majority leader of the New York State Senate and one of the most powerful players in the Capitol. "Duh, I got to go back and tawk to my pee-pull," Wachtler clowned in imitation of Marino. "When you are the chief judge, your acts are assumed to be totally rational," Wachtler said later, with considerable regret.

According to Miller, manias like Wachtler's "often coalesce around an issue central to the patient's life, for example a love interest." But he said the judge's scheme was designed to *invite* detection and rejects Chertoff's notion that Wachtler was motivated primarily by jealousy.[13] "Mr. Wachtler has no

---

*Some unsuccessful appellants during this period later asked the court for a rehearing, arguing that the chief judge had been incompetent when the panel decided their cases. The court refused to reconsider any decisions.

history of exhibiting extreme jealous behavior and while a moderate jealousy may have played a role in October of 1991, the increasingly bizarre conduct which took place in 1992 was different in kind," Miller said. "Neither jealousy nor romance was the dominant theme, nor were they even a significant factor in his conduct."[14]

On Wachtler's second day in the hospital, he was visited by another psychiatrist, Sanford "Sandy" Solomon, who was brought in by Wachtler's physician, Dr. Geraldine Lanman. What Solomon found was "what appeared to be a very old and frail man, cowering and weeping in the corner of a chair, repeating, between sobs, how sorry he was to have brought shame on his family and his court."[15]

Robert L. Spitzer, professor of psychiatry at Columbia University, concluded after examining Wachtler that "had Judge Wachtler not suffered from a severe major depression he never would have engaged in the behavior that ultimately led to his arrest."[16]

But a psychiatrist hired by Chertoff, Steven S. Simring of Tenafly, New Jersey, said Wachtler was more lovesick than mentally ill. In a July 13, 1993, letter to the prosecutor, Simring acknowledged that Wachtler "probably had periods of depression over the last several years," but he "found no objective evidence for a history of psychotic symptoms or cognitive disturbance."[17]

Simring wasn't impressed by his colleagues' findings. "The bottom line seems to be, if I may paraphrase, 'With all these drugs he was taking and all of these bizarre things he did, it is obvious that he must have been out of his mind,'" Simring said in his report.

If Sol Wachtler had any malady when he committed the crimes, that malady was lovesickness. . . . This is no small matter because individuals who have been spurned by the objects of their love can develop any number of symptoms which look like depression, including loss of appetite, crying and loss of interest in the outside world. It is certainly not uncommon for people to commit suicide after the failure of an important love relationship. The point is that Sol Wachtler's symptoms were not caused by some mysterious mental illness that was visited upon him, or by the injudicious use of psychotropic medication. Sol Wachtler's behavior during the period from October 1991 to November 1992 was directly related to his grief at the loss of his relationship with the woman who was so important to him.

Sol Wachtler was brilliant and sophisticated in affairs of the mind, but he was exceedingly naive in the realm of emotions. If the same acts of harassing the woman who had spurned him had been committed by a teenage boy, they would have probably been regarded as the excesses of youthful love, even if they broke the law. These acts are bizarre only in the context of the actor, a famous judge who should have had better things to do than to change his voice and wear disguises.[18]

Simring continued: "I do not think that anyone can be unmoved by the misfortune that befell Sol Wachtler. The many testimonials on his behalf are convincing proof that he had been a good man who led a life of dedication to work and public service. Perhaps the problem was that Sol Wachtler was too dedicated, too much involved in taking care of his responsibilities toward others, while neglecting his own emotional needs."[19]

Wachtler's daughter, Alison Braunstein, would agree with at least the latter part of Simring's report. "I have come to believe that people who are unselfish their whole lives and spend their lives for the betterment of those around them, forget their own well-being," Braunstein wrote in a letter to the court. "People depend on them, and one day the burden has nowhere to go. Their shoulders just give out."[20]

Joan Wachtler put much of the blame on herself. "The qualities which were once so attractive to me became the downfall of our relationship," she said in a letter to the court. "He cared, and cared for too many of, his ideals, and it was my perception that I was no longer a consideration. . . . The rules of the marriage had changed. . . . I was angry and hurt."[21]

Simring suggested that Wachtler's *annus horribilis* was essentially an exacerbated lost weekend.

"It seems to me that, in an odd way, Sol Wachtler derived considerable pleasure from his secret life, even though it caused him a great deal of anxiety," Simring said.

He had always put duty and dedication to work above his personal needs and he had rarely, if ever, done anything "wild" or irresponsible . . . Sol Wachtler spent many years in a loveless marriage, accepting it for what it was, essentially denying that he had any emotional needs of his own. When Joy Silverman came along, he was starved for her affection and the passion that she stirred in him. Their affair was more than a brief flirtation; it lasted almost four years. It would have gone on much longer, perhaps, had Sol Wachtler made the decision to leave his wife and marry Joy. He hesitated and she found another lover. . . . Judge Wachtler's love for Joy Silverman eventually became quite obsessive, particularly after she told him she wasn't coming back.[22]

Louis B. Schlesinger, a Maplewood, New Jersey, psychologist hired by the prosecution, found Wachtler "somewhat compulsive, with a need for order, control and a lot of attention to detail. . . . Narcissist features are much more subtle, but still evident. The judge is not an overtly self-centered or egocentric person, but it is very likely that he has a strong need for attention and recognition beyond the normal range."[23]

Schlesinger explained that such people are particularly vulnerable when their "sense of self is threatened or injured." He diagnosed Wachtler as a basically sound person with a personality disorder compounded by compulsive and narcissistic traits. "We are dealing with a 62-year-old male of superior intellect who is currently experiencing depression (of moderate intensity) with accompanying anxiety, inner tension and with the likelihood for periodic episodes of agitation. Mr. Wachtler's current depression is undoubtably due in large part, but perhaps not entirely, to the extreme predicament in which he finds himself."[24]

Many researchers have recognized a link between mental illness and genius and creativity and there have been suggestions that Wachtler falls into the group that includes: writers Ernest Hemingway, Virginia Woolf, and Sylvia Plath; artist Vincent van Gogh; preacher Mary Baker Eddy, who founded the Christian Science religion; General Douglas MacArthur; singer Elvis Presley; musicians Kurt Cobain and Cole Porter; and inventor Alexander Graham Bell. In a 1995 book, Dr. Arnold Ludwig, professor of psychiatry at the University of Kentucky College of Medicine and recipient of the Hofheimer Prize from the American Psychiatric Association, found a definite relationship between mental illness and genius.

Ludwig found a "psychological unease" common to the intellectual and creative elites: "Members of the upper elite are inclined to be restless, discontented, impatient and driven people whose success does not necessarily satisfy them for long."[25]

Regardless of the cause, there is little doubt that Wachtler suffered from at least some degree of manic depression, a disorder so common* that the National Depressive and Manic-Depressive Association, with sixty-one chapters throughout the United States and Canada, and the National Institute of Mental Health, lists warning signs. The signs of depression include:

- Sadness, anxiety, a heightened sense of hopelessness, and an "empty" mood
- Loss of energy and motivation (At times, Wachtler would rent a motel room and remain there, alone, for days.)
- A sense of impending doom (Wachtler was convinced he was dying.)
- Reduced feelings of pleasure
- Low self-esteem
- Guilt (Wachtler clearly felt guilty about betraying his family and neglecting his court.)
- Sleep disturbance
- Diminished ability to concentrate (According to clerks and aides Wachtler was unusually distracted.)
- Recurring thoughts of death
- Persistent physical symptoms, such as headaches, that fail to respond to conventional treatment.

The signs of mania include:

- Rapid and unpredictable mood changes
- Extreme irritability

---

*Wachtler's grandmother, who may have been a manic-depressive, committed suicide, something he didn't know until after his arrest. Apparently, the suicide was considered a family secret. When Wachtler had been told by his mother that his grandmother died of a "broken heart," he assumed she meant heart attack.

- High energy level (At times Wachtler was able to function with little or no sleep.)
- Hyperactivity
- Distractibility, with attention focusing on unimportant or irrelevant matters
- Grandiosity
- Poor judgment.

Kay Redfield Jamison, an eminent psychologist at Johns Hopkins who revealed her own battles with manic-depressive illness in 1995, eloquently describes the symptoms:

> There is a particular kind of pain, elation, loneliness and terror involved in this kind of madness. When you're high, it's tremendous. The ideas and feelings are fast and frequent like shooting stars, and you follow them until you find better and brighter ones. Shyness goes, the right words and gestures are suddenly there, the power to captivate others a felt certainty. There are interests found in uninteresting people. Sensuality is persuasive and the desire to seduce and be seduced irresistible. Feelings of ease, intensity, power, well-being, financial omnipotence and euphoria pervade one's marrow. But, somewhere, this changes. The fast ideas are far too fast, and there are far too many; overwhelming confusion replaces clarity. Memory goes. Humor and absorption on friends' faces are replaced by fear and concern. Everything previously moving with the grain is now against—you are irritable, angry, frightened, uncontrollable, and enmeshed totally in the blackest caves of the mind. You never knew those caves were there. It will never end, for madness carves its own reality.[26]

What Jamison describes is precisely what Wachtler claims he lived. "People should learn that mental illness is not something that can be tampered with," Wachtler told a national audience on the April 2, 1997, edition of *Larry King Live*. "Mental illness is something that should be recognized and treated. Anyone who is bipolar can fall off the edge. If it happened to me, it can happen to anyone."

After his incarceration and release, Wachtler continued to see a psychiatrist twice a week and take medication, under the strict control of a physician.

Notes

1. Comment outside federal court in Trenton, N.J., on March 31, 1993, as reported by Linda Wolfe in *Double Life: The Shattering Affair between Chief Judge Sol Wachtler and Socialite Joy Silverman* (New York: Pocket Books, 1994), p. 242.

2. *New York Times*, April 4, 1993.

3. Enid Peschel and Richard Peschel, "Time to Treat Mentally Ill as Medically Ill," *Houston Chronicle*, March 12, 1990, p. 11.

4. Joan Wachtler's undated letter to the court, approximately May 1, 1993.

5. *People* v. *Torsney*, 47 NY2d 667, 686 (1979), 394 NE2d 262.

6. *Physician's Desk Reference*, 44th ed. (Montvale, N.J.: Medical Economics Books, 1994).

7. Ibid.

8. Ibid.

9. Ibid.

10. Dr. Miller's report is part of the court record.

11. Ibid.

12. Dr. Klein's report is part of the court record.

13. Miller report.

14. Ibid.

15. Dr. Solomon's report is part of the court record.

16. Dr. Spitzer's report is part of the court record.

17. Dr. Simring's report is part of the court record.

18. Simring report.

19. Ibid.

20. Alison Wachtler Braunstein letter to the court, April 26, 1993.

21. Joan Wachtler undated letter to the court, approximately May 1, 1993.

22. Simring report.

23. Dr. Schlesinger's report is part of the court record.

24. Ibid.

25. Arnold M. Ludwig, *The Price of Greatness* (New York: The Guilford Press, 1995).

26. Kay Redfield Jamison, *An Unquiet Mind* (New York: Alfred A. Knopf, 1995), p. 67. Reprinted with permission of the author.

CHAPTER 13

An Abuse of Power?

Any woman who has ever tried to enforce an order of protection against a harassing or stalking ex-lover knows that Joy Silverman got special treatment, despite the government's claims to the contrary. The director of the FBI does not normally intervene in such cases, nor does the agency routinely assign dozens of agents to tail a man making prank phone calls and sending dirty letters.

But that was just the start of a suspiciously aberrational case.

When author Norman Mailer stabbed and seriously wounded his wife,[1] he was sent to the same psychiatric center as Wachtler, the Payne-Whitney psychiatric unit, but he was free to roam the halls while the judge was confined to a room and guarded around the clock. Senator Robert Packwood of Oregon allegedly abused several women and effectively sold out his constituents, but he was permitted to retire from the senate in 1995 without any criminal prosecution—and with his annual pension of nearly $90,000 intact. Mark Putnam, the FBI agent who murdered his pregnant girlfriend in Kentucky,[2] was allowed to turn in his badge to two colleagues at a preselected location. Wachtler was pulled over on a crowded highway in broad daylight and forced to resign via telephone while shackled and guarded by armed marshals. Even former football star O. J. Simpson, charged with a double and particularly brutal homicide, and mobster John Gotti, accused of murder, were allowed to surrender on their own terms. Gotti got bail, but Wachtler was denied immediate release and instead was chained to a hospital bed in the psychiatric ward at Long Island Jewish Hospital.

In September of 1996, New York Judge Lorraine Miller was caught after sending sixty harassing letters to newspapers, businesses, and individuals about her former boyfriend, a fellow judge, and his new wife. Some of the mailings included confidential information on his wife's prior marriage obtained through confidential court records. Miller wasn't followed by the FBI. She wasn't arrested. She wasn't prosecuted. She wasn't even fired. Lorraine Miller was censured, or wrist-slapped, by the New York State Commission on Judicial Conduct.[3] The commission, which is responsible for monitoring judicial conduct in New York State, noted that Miller was "motivated by the anguish over her break-up with Judge [S. Barrett] Hickman. She now regrets it and agrees she will not engage in similar or other harassing conduct toward the Hickmans."[4] Further, the commission found that Miller, during her time of anguish, had improperly allowed a murder defendant to plead guilty without telling his lawyer that the deliberating jury had reached a verdict.[5]

Wachtler—whose conduct when the FBI first learned that it

was he who was "stalking"* Joy Silverman was really not much different than Miller's—was not shown such compassion.

Certainly, Joy had every right and every reason to fear for her safety and that of her daughter. Certainly she had every right and reason to be angry with Wachtler when she learned he was her tormentor. Certainly she had every right and reason to approach the director of the FBI, just as a less prominent victim might go to the local constable. Surely, Wachtler wasn't entitled to lenient treatment because of his stature or his contributions to the public and society. Nor, however, was he deserving of unusually harsh retribution from Silverman and her friends in Washington's political hierarchy. But a simple examination of the facts, and circumstantial evidence, suggests an extraordinary use, and perhaps misuses, of government power in bringing Wachtler to justice. Among the factors that raise concerns among Wachtler and his supporters, as well as objective observers, are:

- The use of eighty (or forty, depending on whom you believe) FBI agents to trail Wachtler at a time when the

---

*Wachtler adamantly insists he was not a "stalker," arguing that he never physically harassed Silverman. However, under a broad definition he most certainly did stalk Joy Silverman, although from a distance. Stalking is a particularly common crime, affecting 1.3 million American men and women annually (Patricia Tjaden, "The Crime of Stalking," Center for Policy Research, Denver, as reporter in *U.S. News & World Report*, November 24, 1997, p. 43). One of every twelve women claims to have been a victim of some sort of stalking, ranging from annoying, repeated telephone calls to overt threats. The culprits are rarely prosecuted and, when they are, it is almost never with the ferocity exhibited in the Wachtler case. Perhaps that is an indication that authorities have, for too long, paid short shrift to complaints from women. Perhaps from that perspective, the Wachtler prosecution could be viewed as pioneering. In any case, fundamental fairness requires that people who commit similar crimes should receive similar punishment.

Justice Department knew the mastermind of the World Trade Center bombing was in New Jersey—U.S. Attorney Chertoff's own jurisdiction—and considered him dangerous, but later claimed that it lacked sufficient resources to tail the suspect.*

- The fact that Wachtler's most egregious behavior, by far, and the conduct that led to his incarceration occurred during the last few weeks, when authorities knew who was harassing Joy Silverman.[6] If Wachtler had been stopped earlier, his offense would have been no more serious than Judge Miller's.

- Transcripts of the tapes showing that Silverman, with the FBI present, goaded Wachtler and encouraged him to make specific threats (although he never really did) as his behavior became increasingly bizarre. All the telephone calls that supposedly terrified and traumatized Silverman were made after the FBI was in the picture. Many of them were made after the identity of the perpetrator had been confirmed.

- Despite veiled attempts by both Joy Silverman and the FBI to encourage Wachtler to do something really foolish, like threaten physical violence or actually take money, he never did. He stopped short—maybe because he was shrewd, maybe because he was incapable of going that far—of making a physical threat. He never picked up the so-called extortion money and, in fact, was heading in the opposite direction from where it was stashed when arrested by the FBI. In the end, the

---

*In contrast, in 1980, when two men broke into the Isabella Stewart Gardner Museum in Boston, assaulted and bound two guards, and made off with $300 million in artwork, the FBI assigned only thirty agents. As of this writing, the crime remains unsolved. Steve Lopez, "The Giant Art Caper," *Time* magazine, November 17, 1997, p. 74.

government agreed that Wachtler had no intention of taking the money (which was promptly retrieved by authorities).

- The timing of a *New Yorker* article that appeared shortly after the arrest suggests that it was either the product of a high-level leak or that the writer was actually in the command room as the FBI was closing in on Wachtler and preparing to take him down. The article was very pro-Chertoff, very prejudicial, and it contained details that only an insider to a supposedly confidential investigation could know. It was written by Lucinda Franks, wife of longtime Wachtler adversary Robert Morgenthau, the Manhattan district attorney.

- The case was prosecuted in New Jersey, even though all the conduct that Wachtler pleaded guilty to took place in New York. Chertoff has said, alternately, that his office handled it to prevent the New York "old boy network" from aiding Wachtler or tipping him off—which certainly suggests that officials knew who the culprit was from the moment the FBI got involved, several weeks before the arrest and prior to any felonious conduct—and because some of the early letters were mailed from New Jersey. Assuming authorities knew that Wachtler was the perpetrator, that raises the question of why he wasn't immediately confronted and stopped.

- Chertoff's efforts to force Wachtler out of his position as Silverman's trustee, even though there were no allegations that he had violated the trust. A prosecutor for the government normally does not act as civil advocate for a victim.

- Chertoff's insistence that Wachtler plead to a charge that would result in a prison term and rule out the possibility of a home confinement or probation. Initially Chertoff had indicated that Wachtler would be allowed to resign and plead to something minor. Between then and the time that Chertoff decided to come down hard, no new information was developed that accounts for the prosecutor's change of heart.

- The sudden order that Wachtler report to Camp Butner, a comparatively unpleasant facility in North Carolina, for his imprisonment when the previous plan, and the judge's recommendation, was for assignment to a prison camp in Florida.
- The peculiar stabbing incident at Butner and the extremely unusual public pronouncement by an FBI agent that authorities thought the wound was self-inflicted. The FBI eventually backed off that theory.

Chertoff surely knew he had a big fish on the line, and he clearly intended to stuff, mount, and flaunt it for all it was worth. As a Republican appointee, Chertoff's job was already in jeopardy with a new Democratic administration in the White House (and in fact he was replaced under Clinton) when he was presented with a high-profile case. Chertoff had no responsibility to protect Wachtler from himself, no obligation to stop his quarry while the scheme was still in the misdemeanor realm. And Chertoff has a reputation as a hard-nosed, ruthless, bullying—but straight arrow—prosecutor with a take-no-captives mindset. In comparison, Albany County's district attorney, Sol Greenberg, said that if he had been in charge of the Wachtler investigation he would have simply called up the chief judge and said, "Hey, Sol, cut the crap!" and put an end to it before it got out of hand.

Chertoff, however, insists that the severity of Wachtler's

crime warranted an aggressive prosecution. "The nature of the crime is, essentially, an extortion, a demand for money under the threat of kidnapping a fourteen-year-old girl," Chertoff said. "Now that is an act of violence. . . . It is in my view a serious crime. It caused an enormous amount of pain and suffering to innocent people. And it was wrong."[7]

Chertoff also rejects the notion, promoted by Wachtler's supporters, that the government nurtured and encouraged a spiraling flow of criminal activity that could have been stopped early. "What actually happened was the time that elapsed was time that was spent trying to explore all the possibilities," Chertoff said.

> Until we had a recorded call from a telephone booth where we had a recording that was incriminating and we had a surveillance of him at the phone booth and we had a fingerprint from the handset—and all that came in—we were not in a position to make sure we had the right person. That occurred about three or four days before the arrest.
>
> The second piece that was open was we didn't know if he was working with anybody. One of the letters came from El Paso, or someplace in Texas, at a time when we had him coming from Nevada back to New York. We had to ask ourselves, 'Is there someone else in league with Wachtler and carrying out this scheme?' We had to make sure that we didn't miss somebody who was part of the conspiracy. As it turned out, ultimately the explanation for that letter being mailed [from Texas] is he conned some stewardess into dropping that letter in a mailbox in Texas. We were not able to exclude the possibility of a co-conspirator until we actually followed him on the day of the money [drop]. Only then could we determine if someone else was going to pick up the money. To say that we "let it run out" is a total and complete falsehood. Anybody who says that is

either totally ignorant of the facts or is simply interested in pursuing an agenda.[8]

Regardless, Chertoff's handling of the case raised eyebrows across the criminal justice spectrum.

John Dunne, a former Republican state senator in New York, was working in Justice as an assistant attorney general in the civil rights division while the department was investigating Wachtler. Although Dunne had nothing to do with the Wachtler prosecution, as an insider, he said: "I'm inclined to agree that it was overkill. I could never understand the extraordinary use of resources to affect his arrest."[9]

Dunne knows Chertoff slightly. "He is a *real* prosecutor, one tough guy. He will use all the resources available to a prosecutor. I have only high professional regard for him. He is a very diligent, forceful prosecutor." Even then, the ferociousness of the prosecution was extraordinary and, to Dunne and others, surprising.[10]

The harshness of the Wachtler indictment prompted outrage from celebrity defense attorney William Kunstler, who died in mid-1995, and his partner, Ronald L. Kuby. In an *Amsterdam News* Op-Ed piece, Kunstler, who had been somewhat critical of the chief judge, and Kuby condemned "Wachtler's precipitous highway arrest . . . and the imposition of humiliating conditions of pretrial release, including virtual confinement to his Long Island home and the wearing of an electronic monitoring device."[11]

Kunstler and Kuby pointed out the disparity between Wachtler's treatment and the way Judy G. Russell, former special assistant U.S. attorney in the same office that Chertoff later headed, was dealt with in 1987. Russell, while prosecuting a pair of young Sikhs targeted for extradition back to India, sent a series of threatening anonymous letters to herself and a judge. The letters, explicitly warning that Russell and the magistrate were in danger from the Sikh community, resulted in extraordinary protections for the prosecutor and the judge, and extraordinary restraints on the suspects. Until the following year, when the hoax was uncovered, every court appearance was accompanied by rooftop sharp-shooters. Russell, who was never arrested and instead was allowed to voluntarily surrender to a psychiatric hospital for a fifty-day evaluation, was eventually adjudicated not guilty by reason of insanity.

"The contrast between the Russell case and that of Mr. Wachtler is obvious," Kunstler and Kuby wrote. "Mr. Chertoff . . . well knows how to exploit a high-visibility pros-ecution that has fallen his way. He is determined to turn what is patently a mental aberration into a show trial tailored to advance his own career."[12]

Herbert Hoelter, director of the National Center on Insti-tutions and Alternatives in Alexandria, Virginia, a private, non-profit organization that advocates for prisoners, said: "Chertoff hated Wachtler." Hoelter was hired by Wachtler's attorneys to put together sentencing arguments and review appropriate facilities. "The sentencing and everything was approached with a venom I don't usually see. It was justice run amok. There were forces beyond normal that were affecting this case."[13]

In the federal system, sentences are calculated on a grid that is supposed to take into account the convict's prior record, if any, and the seriousness of the most recent crime. Those numbers are factored into an equation that results in an offense level. Judges have only limited discretion in devi-ating from the sentences recommended for each level of offense. For instance, if a convict ends up at Offense Level 13, the judge must impose a prison sentence. But if the offense level is at Level 12, a split sentence of probation and minimal jail time is allowed. Chertoff insisted that Wachtler plead to at least a Level 13, which he did. Judge Anne Thompson had to impose a sentence of between twelve and eighteen months; she gave Wachtler fifteen months and recommended that the time be spent in a Florida prison camp, Saufley Field. Chertoff agreed that he would not challenge the placement.

But at the last moment, Wachtler was ordered instead to Butner, the place where they sent John Hinckley after he shot President Reagan in 1981 and the prison where the spy Jonathan Pollard, who sold U.S. secrets to Israel, was incarcerated. Camps are minimum security. Butner, an administrative facility with no official security rating, is run as a medium- to high-level prison. Movement is controlled. Prisoners march in crowds. Only a few "white collar criminals" are sprinkled among the common street thugs at Butner. Hoelter and Wachtler were astonished.

"In 99 percent of the cases in which we work, if a defendant qualifies for a minimum-security federal prison camp, that is where they go," Hoelter said. "Somewhere along the way, there was a hitch. It always seemed to me that there was a larger agenda to this. He [Wachtler] was just being treated differently. We have worked with a lot of high-profile cases over the years, including Leona Helmsley. In my experience, this was the most arbitrarily handled of any."[14]

"When Wachtler got transferred to Rochester, it was like a lightning bolt out of the sky," Hoelter continued.

> Why in the world would he go to Rochester? Rochester has a longterm medical and psychiatric ward, but it is usually used for people who are bouncing off the walls. There was no legitimate correctional reason for Sol Wachtler to serve a sentence in Rochester, Minnesota. None. . . . They

could say he was psychologically fragile and they were concerned about the stabbing, but I don't think there is any evidence that supports any of that. If you look at the psychological record, a good year after the offense had happened, this was a guy who had been distressed, but was stabilized.[15]

In fact, the psychiatric diagnosis at Rochester concluded that Wachtler, despite having a history of depression and abuse of prescription medications, was "not viewed as actively mentally ill [and] not an appropriate referral for inpatient mental health treatment."

Hoelter assumed, without evidence, that someone was pulling strings for some unknown reason. "My initial assumption in this case was that the government got involved, despite the plea agreement," he said. "My theory would be that there was a continued and strong presence of people guiding the case through the federal prison system. The proof is in the pudding. . . . The Bureau of Prisons tries hard not to treat people differently. They really do. If you have a very, very strong governmental influence, things happen. And it is not by accident."[16]

The inarguably harsh and unusual treatment of Wachtler cannot be explained solely by the fact that the victim of his harassment was on a first-name basis with the director of the FBI. Something else, it appears, was driving the prosecution.

Perhaps Chertoff, according to one theory, was embarrassed over letting terrorists slip through his hands while his forces were busy chasing Wachtler.

On September 1, 1992, an international Iraqi terrorist named Ramzi Ahmed Yousef arrived in New York City via Pakistan International Airlines Flight 703 from Karachi. Yousef used a phony name, but his lack of a visa attracted attention. After claiming political asylum, Yousef was finger-printed, photographed, and released, and his file was turned over to immigration officials in Chertoff's district.[17]

According to federal records, Yousef promptly went to the Jersey City, New Jersey, apartment building that housed terrorists Omar Abdel Rahman, Abdo Mohammed Haggag, and Siddig Ibrahim Siddig Ali. Rahman had advocated the assassination of Egyptian President Mubarak, and the Egyptian government warned authorities under Chertoff's command that the terrorist was in his territory and dangerous. The Newark office of the FBI, while dozens of its agents were following Wachtler around the country, apparently did not have sufficient personnel to surveil the terrorists.[18]

On February 26, 1993, after months of conspiring under Chertoff's nose, the terrorists bombed the World Trade Center in Manhattan, leaving six people dead and over a thousand injured. To justify the time and expense of the Wachtler surveillance, particularly in light of the big fish he missed while pursuing a minnow, Chertoff had to come down hard on the judge, or so goes the theory from the Wachtler camp.

In addition to the Chertoff embarrassment angle, some Wachtler partisans weave an intriguing Machiavellian theory that leads to U.S. Senator Alfonse M. D'Amato. The fact that D'Amato benefitted more than anyone else from Wachtler's demise fueled speculation and the rumor that the senator was somehow involved, despite a total lack of anything more than circumstantial evidence.

In New York, D'Amato scandals are so routine[19] that, over time, they have almost become devoid of newsworthiness. Despite the scandals, D'Amato's power was never more evident, never more absolute, never more unquestionable than in the mid-1990s—when Sol Wachtler was finally out of the picture.

D'Amato and Wachtler had been antagonists since the

days when they were clubhouse pols with the Nassau County Republican organization in the early 1960s. Wachtler was the fair-haired boy, the one blessed with intelligence, eloquence, and good looks. D'Amato by contrast was a hardscrabble politician with a reputation as a crude shakedown artist. He could get money, and lots of it, particularly from the building trades, and over the years had erected a power base of people who owed him for their own political successes or government contracts. But Wachtler was different. He didn't need D'Amato and he didn't owe him anything. Wachtler was always a step ahead.

When Wachtler was supervisor of North Hempstead, Long Island, D'Amato was a lowly councilman in Hempstead. By the time D'Amato became supervisor, Wachtler was a state Supreme Court justice. When D'Amato grew beyond local politics and became a U.S. senator, Wachtler had already been on the Court of Appeals for eight years; he was clearly on track to become chief judge; and was wined and dined by the party's political elite, people who viewed the jurist as a perennial favorite son for governor, even president. D'Amato, as a Republican from the same Long Island organization, was simply lost in Wachtler's shadow, like a little brother who never quite measures up, or the black sheep in an otherwise dignified family.

"There was very bad blood between Wachtler and D'Amato," confirmed one high-ranking figure in New York state government and politics. "They are polar extremes. Wachtler was intelligent, urbane, articulate, and honest. D'Amato was a buffoon . . . and a machine politician. Wachtler looked down on him with contempt, as not the kind of person who should be in politics."[20]

D'Amato's history, as chronicled in various media, is littered with instances that call into question his ethics:

- As a Nassau County official in the 1970s, D'Amato was investigated in connection with a scandal in which county employees were forced to kick back 1 percent of their salaries to the Republican machine. In 1975, D'Amato told a federal grand jury that he was completely unaware of the fund-raising scheme. Ten years later, after the statute of limitations had run out, a letter emerged that proved he had known about the maneuver as early as 1971.[21]
- While serving as Hempstead supervisor, D'Amato deposited huge sums of town tax money—$8 million by some estimates—in a local bank account that earned no interest. The same bank gave D'Amato an $80,00 campaign loan at a rate 8 points below prime.[22]
- The Abscam congressional bribery sting also yielded information on D'Amato. One of the convicts, Alfred Carpentier, told FBI agents posing as Arabs that he could buy then Hempstead Supervisor D'Amato. "The guy is on the take," Carpentier told the FBI. "If you want to give him something, we'll weigh that when the time comes. You make your analysis based on what he's giving us."[23]
- As a United States senator, D'Amato was at the center of the Wedtech scandal (the secret takeover of minority-owned military contractors eligible for a series of no-bid Pentagon contracts). At trial, Wedtech's former vice chairman, Mario Moreno, testified that the firm gave at least $30,000 in illegal contributions to D'Amato "in exchange for favors we expected to get." Wedtech had secured a $55 million contract to build Navy platoons, even though it had no experience in the market. D'Amato said at the trial that he was ignorant of any illegal activities involving Wedtech. No charges were brought against him.[24]
- In 1991, the Senate Ethics Committee criticized

D'Amato for letting his brother, Armand, use his Senate office for personal business. Armand D'Amato had lobbied for Unisys Corporation, a New York-based defense contractor who had been paid $120,500 to secure his brother's support to obtain a $100 million contract to manufacture a missile guidance system that the Navy deemed obsolete. Armand D'Amato was convicted of fraud, but the conviction was overturned. Alfonse D'Amato was required to return illegal campaign contributions from Unisys and the Senate Ethics Committee found that he "conducted the business of his office in an improper and inappropriate manner."[25]

The ethics probe was hindered by the fact that more than two dozen of the subpoenaed witnesses invoked their Fifth Amendment right against self-incrimination and refused to testify. At the conclusion of the investigation, the panel noted that a further probe of D'Amato's affairs would "jeopardize ongoing criminal investigations or put contemplated prosecutions at risk."[26]

- Between 1981 and 1986, when D'Amato had direct oversight of the investment banking firms and brokerage houses, he raised at least $500,000 from those firms.[27]

- In 1996, lobbyists complained that D'Amato was essentially shaking them down. One lobbyist reported that he told a D'Amato aide that his client's business hadn't been concluded and the assistant responded: "Well, we haven't seen a contribution from them."[28]

- D'Amato has also been linked on several occasions to the mob. In 1983, for instance. he was the only character witness at the triad of Philip Basile. Basile was convicted of conspiring with the Luchese crime family in a no-show job scheme. D'Amato called Basile "an honest, truthful, hardworking man, a man of integrity."[29]

Even assuming D'Amato had nothing to do with the Wachtler prosecution, he struck political paydirt on November 7, 1992, when the FBI took down the judge.

Nothing would have been worse for D'Amato's political/ power aspirations than to have Rudolph Giuliani in the New York City mayor's office and Wachtler in the governor's mansion. Giuliani won his race, but Wachtler blew his chance, and the main benefactor was Alfonse M. D'Amato. With Wachtler out of the picture, D'Amato and his protégé, state GOP chairman Bill Powers, handpicked the candidate, an obscure state senator named George E. Pataki, who fell into the vacuum created by Sol's downfall, knocked off Mario Cuomo, and returned the governor's mansion to Republican control for the first time in twenty years. As *de facto* head of the state Republican party, D'Amato suddenly had control of government in one of the country's largest and most influential states. And, as such, he had access to the money bags of New York investors and businesses—coincidentally, the same sources of Wachtler's gubernatorial support before the downfall.

By 1995, D'Amato was one of the most influential senators in Washington by virtue of his simultaneous hold on three prominent positions: chairman of the Senate Banking Committee undertaking an investigation of President Clinton, head of the Republican organization that raises money for Republican senatorial candidates, and chief of Senator Bob Dole's presidential steering committee. He owes the latter two positions to the downfall of Wachtler.

The senator's checkered ethical history, combined with circumstantial evidence suggesting D'Amato had the means, motive, and opportunity, lends support to the conclusion that he could and would facilitate Wachtler's (self-)destruction:

- D'Amato has a history of trying to undermine Wachtler. When Wachtler was being touted as chief judge, D'Amato made remarks at least twice which seemed aimed to derail the effort. One was at the Aqueduct Race Track on Long Island, where a judge heard D'Amato bad-mouthing Wachtler. Another occasion was in Rochester, where Mike Gabrielli reported that D'Amato was attempting to undermine the appointment.[30]
- When Supreme Court Justice William J. Brennan Jr. suddenly announced his retirement in 1990, D'Amato promoted U.S. Circuit Judge Roger J. Miner rather than Wachtler, who was from his own county and was chief judge. Later, D'Amato advanced Wachtler's name, as something of a grudging afterthought.[31]
- D'Amato has known Joy Silverman for many years. Acquaintances of both say they used to meet for lunch regularly at a restaurant in Astoria.[32] Joy and her former husband, Jeffrey Silverman, have long bankrolled D'Amato campaigns, according to federal campaign records. After Wachtler's conviction, D'Amato occasionally appeared publicly with Silverman when she promoted antistalking legislation around the country.
- D'Amato was Joy Silverman's prime supporter, according to federal records, when she was up for the ambassadorship of Barbados. He gave a glowing speech about her credentials, although she had none, on September 28, 1989, in oral testimony before the Committee on Foreign Relations. A day before her hearing, the state department submitted forms on her political contributions and showed that the Silvermans had donated hundreds of thousands of dollars to Republican political causes, many of them dear to D'Amato.

- Silverman was also very close to Larry Bathgate, a major Republican fund-raiser, a D'Amato crony, and chairman of the National Republican Finance Committee. Bathgate got Chertoff his job as U.S. attorney in New Jersey. Bathgate also set Silverman up with his personal attorney, David Samson, the man who replaced Wachtler as her lover.[33]
- After losing his post as U.S. attorney in New Jersey, Michael Chertoff got a new job—special counsel to the Senate Banking Committee for the Whitewater investigation. And he got the job through D'Amato.

"Certainly, it was in Al's best interest [to do in Wachtler]," said one source with strong connections to the D'Amato camp.[34] The source said D'Amato loyalists were almost giddy with delight at Wachtler's demise. "With Wachtler as governor and Giuliani as mayor, Al is dogshit. . . . It was necessary to destroy Sol. . . . It was very strange that D'Amato would reach to a New Jersey U.S. attorney to become his chief counsel [for Whitewater]. Any lawyer would have given their right arm for that and he didn't pick anybody from New York. . . . There is no question in my mind that there was a payback [to Chertoff]."

Nevertheless, the same source, a longtime friend of Joy Silverman's, doubts D'Amato had any direct influence on the case and views the political windfall as just that. "Joy, you have to understand, is very well connected. Joy certainly wanted to hurt Sol, and had every right to. I can't blame her. But she was very close to D'Amato's people. Bottom line: Joy wants Wachtler to suffer. She is close to D'Amato people, who want him to suffer for other reasons. . . . Chertoff knew what pleased D'Amato. He didn't need any prodding."[35]

Chertoff, however, found the entire conspiracy theory asi-

nine and offensive: "I had never spoken to, had any communication of any kind, with Alfonse D'Amato until years after
this event," Chertoff insisted.

> My only contact with Al D'Amato was watching him on
> television or reading about him in the newspaper. He had
> zero to do with this case. Until 1994, in June 1994, when I
> was contacted at the end of the month about the possibility
> of going to work on Whitewater, I had never directly or
> indirectly in any form or fashion had any contact with
> Alfonse D'Amato. . . . It's ludicrous. Look what the man
> [Wachtler] did for a year and a half. How did anybody
> make him do this? It is ludicrous on its face. Secondly, it is
> plainly and completely false. . . . There is only one person
> who caused this prosecution to occur, and that is Sol
> Wachtler.[36]

D'Amato himself denies having anything to do with the
case. "Absurd, and more absurd."[37]

James Fox, who was head of the FBI in New York when
Wachtler got nailed, denied even that Joy Silverman received
special treatment. He claimed—incredibly—that any woman
with a similar complaint would have received the same response from law-enforcement people, an argument that a
former top official at the U.S. Department of Justice called
ridiculous.

"Joy Silverman, of course, first reported to [FBI director]
Bill Sessions, who referred it to the Newark office," Fox
said.[37] Regardless, he said the investigation was handled with
absolute secrecy.

"The day he was arrested, nobody outside the FBI knew he
would be arrested," Fox said. "I would bet a month's salary
that not D'Amato—not anybody in politics—knew. Once we

got the complaint and the investigation started, miraculously, it went on for quite a while, and it did not leak."[38]

Fox admitted, however, that Joy could have leaked news of the investigation to Zenia Mucha—a friend who was a close confidante to D'Amato and who later became Governor Pataki's communications director—and others. "If she wanted to, she could have leaked it. But even she did not know the extent of the investigation. These things so often leak. . . . We made the decision early on that there was no reason to treat him differently. A lot of my friends said, 'You must have realized he was sick. Why not get him help?' That's not what the FBI does. It tries to arrest criminals."[39]

Sessions's replacement, Louis Freeh, has been overheard to say the Wachtler prosecution was grossly overhanded. Another very high-ranking federal law-enforcement official confided: "The contact with Sessions was extraordinary and bizarre."[40] The official, who knows Chertoff well and respects him as a top-flight prosecutor, said that once the case had been assigned out of Washington it was ripe for overtreatment. Nobody, he offered, wants to offend his boss, or for that matter the president of the United States.

Michael Quinlan, former head of the Bureau of Prisons, said there could be absolutely sound penological reasons for the way the Wachtler case was handled and for his initial placement at Butner rather than a prison camp. He's skeptical of any claims of outside influence. "If I had been director, the bureau never would have put him in a camp until we could have our own mental health professionals evaluate him," Quinlan said. "After that evaluation, if everything seemed to be okay and he seemed stable for a minimum-security setting, that is where he would have gone. Minimum-security facilities are not places for people potentially in need of emergency medical intervention."[41]

A major Long Island Republican political official who has, at various times, been very close to both D'Amato and Wachtler, said the Chertoff appointment was the culmination of a "very strange fact pattern."[42] According to him, everyone in Nassau County politics grew suspicious when D'Amato hired Chertoff.

"Sol was the fairhaired boy, and he was in the way," the politician said. "There's no doubt that Al would not be the force that he now is in New York politics if Sol had run for governor. And there's no question that if Sol had run, he would have won."[43]

Francis Purcell, former Hempstead presiding supervisor, former assemblyman, and Republican strategist on Long Island, has always been bothered by the Wachtler case.

"I thought the whole thing could have been handled differently," Purcell said. "Sol was wrong, but we all make mistakes in life. It was very heavy-handed. . . . Sol Wachtler was on the way to be governor. Three days before Sol was picked up, I had lunch with him and told him he'd be an excellent candidate. He said he was very definitely considering it. I'm sure there were people who didn't want to see him go too far, too fast."[44]

Even Norman Sheresky, the divorce lawyer who represented Silverman and who, a year before the arrest, told Wachtler that he was on to him, said the prosecution was heavy handed. "Somebody was pushing it."[45]

"Until Wachtler went over the bend, he was going to be the Republican gubernatorial candidate," said a Long Island political strategist. "If Al wanted Wachtler out of the picture, this would have been the way to do it. Alfonse *made* the governor. He couldn't have made Wachtler."[46]

Notes

1. Al Cohen, "Sad, Sad, Sour Episodes," *Newsday*, January 23, 1992, p. 8.

2. "Ex-FBI Agent Admits He Killed Pregnant Informer," *Chicago Tribune*, June 13, 1990, p. 14.

3. Michele Salcedo, "Lovelorn Justice," *Newsday*, September 26, 1996, p. A7.

4. Ibid.

5. Ibid.

6. Jim Mulvaney, "Wachtler a Suspect from the Start," *Newsday*, March 24, 1993, p. 17.

7. Interview with Michael Chertoff on December 1, 1997.

8. Ibid.

9. Interview with John Dunne on May 22, 1995, with the author serving in his capacity as a reporter for the Albany *Times Union*.

10. Ibid.

11. William Kunstler and Ronald L. Kuby, "The U.S. v. Sol Wachtler, The U.S. v. Judy G. Russell: A Study in Contrasts," *Amsterdam News*, New York City, February 27, 1993, p. 19.

12. Ibid.

13. Interview with Herbert Hoelter on May 22, 1995, with the author serving in his capacity as a reporter for the Albany *Times Union*.

14. Ibid.

15. Ibid.

16. Ibid.

17. Laurie L. Merrill, "September Trial Set in Blast," *New Jersey Record*, April 12, 1993, p. A3.

18. Patricia Cohen, David Kocleylewski, and Kevin McCay, "Tapes Reveal What Feds Knew," *Newsday*, October 29, 1993, p. 5.

19. Dennis Bernstein, "The Corrupt Career of Alfonse D'Amato: King Alfonse," http://www.ny-politics.com/eony/features.

20. Interview with confidential source on May 22, 1995.

21. Paul Vitello, "A Troubling Pattern, Al," *Newsday*, June 20, 1996, p. 8.

22. The *Village Voice*, in a series published October 8-14, 1990, and cited as part of "Alfonse D'Amato's Ethical Sampler," a World Wide Web site maintained by Back to Business, an organization of Democrats.

23. *New York Times*, November 11, 1981, as cited in the "Alfonse D'Amato Ethical Sampler."

24. Bernstein, "The Corrupt Career of Alfonse D'Amato."

25. Helen Dewar, "Ethics Panel Criticizes D'Amato for Letting Brother Use Office," *Washington Post*, August 3, 1991, p. A2.

26. Bernstein, "The Corrupt Career of Alfonse D'Amato."

27. *Wall Street Journal*, September 25, 1986, as cited in the "Alfonse D'Amato Ethical Sampler."

28. Elizabeth Schwinn, "D'Amato Dominates Capitol Money Chase," Washington bureau of the Albany *Times Union*, May 28, 1995, p. Al.

29. *New York Times*, October 27, 1991, as cited in the "Alfonse D'Amato Ethical Sampler." Further, in 1991, the former head of the Luchese family, Alphonso D'Arco, testified that D'Amato had contact with a number of crime figures, including Luchese operatives like Basile, Danny Cutaia, Frank Manzo, and Paul Vario, and Colombo boss Victor Orena. See Sidney Schanberg, "Is the Mob a D'Amato Constituency?" *Newsday*, July 10, 1992, p. 47.

30. Interview with a confidential source, April 1995.

31. Ibid.

32. Ibid.

33. Linda Wolfe, *Double Life: The Shattering Affair between Chief Judge Sol Wachtler and Socialite Joy Silverman* (New York: Pocket Books, 1994), p. 153.

34. Interview with a confidential source, May 22, 1995.

35. Interview with Chertoff on December 1, 1997.

36. As relayed by his spokesman, Harvey Valentine, on November 8, 1995, with the author serving in his capacity as a reporter for the Albany *Times Union*.

37. Interview with James Fox, May 1995, with the author serving in his capacity as a reporter for the Albany *Times Union*.

38. Ibid.

39. Ibid.

40. Interview with a confidential source on May 23, 1995.

41. Interview with Michael Quinlan on May 23, 1995, with the author serving in his capacity as a reporter for the Albany *Times Union*.

42. Interview with a confidential source on May 22, 1995.

43. Ibid.

44. Interview with Francis Purcell, May 1995, with the author serving in his capacity as a reporter for the Albany *Times Union*.

45. Interview with Norman Sheresky, May 1995, with the author serving in his capacity as a reporter for the Albany *Times Union*.

46. Interview with a confidential source on May 24, 1995.

CHAPTER 14

Redemption

"**M**ario Cuomo asked me what I want more than anything else. I said: Redemption," Wachtler stated.
"The one thing I would like very much to do is to redeem my
reputation. It is the only thing I have to give my kids. No
matter what I do, no matter what, the first column of my
obituary will be of my crime and punishment. I would like to
try to leave something better than that to my kids and grandchildren. That's what I would like to do . . . to try to regain
my reputation as best I can, and then just fade away."[1]

Sol Wachtler, the judge and the man, is extraordinarily
talented but tragically flawed, a person who cracked along a
fault line. In short, he is a *human being*, with all that entails
and implies.

"When you are a judge of the Court of Appeals, you think
you are a very important person," said Wachtler. "When you

313

go to a bar association function, they all defer to you. When you leave the scene, you realize you are not as important as you thought."[2]

Clearly, in light of his life's work and characteristics, Judge Wachtler's behavior during that strange period of 1991–92 was aberrational. On the other hand, the personality traits that contributed to his demise where always there. They were just exacerbated, exaggerated, and caricatured during his time of crisis. Take his love of pranks and gadgets and the mischievous playfulness, add the influence of stress, drugs, and jealousy—and innocent interpersonal games become devious. He took the wrong path and before he knew what had hit him, his career was ruined and his reputation destroyed.

Wachtler's legacy can be found not only in his judicial opinions and law review articles, but also in his basic approach to jurisprudence and, above all, his personality. "There was a certain *greatness* that surrounded him," said Sal Ferlazzo, who had clerked for another judge at the court in the early 1980s. "I think in time the greatness will again shine brightly. His contributions to the court and to justice will, in twenty or thirty years, when everyone forgets his frailties, be judged with great distinction."[3]

Wachtler may not have been the greatest judge of New York's highest court, but he was in many regards the most influential.

"I think [Wachtler's] jurisprudence was somewhat erratic," said court analyst Vincent Bonventre. "I don't think he was in the same league as some of the more scholarly judges on the court, like Hancock and Kaye. But having said that, you can't take away from the fact that this man . . . had such an incredibly endearing and disarming personality, in addition to being very, very bright and energetic, [and] that he was able to get an awful lot done."[4]

Indeed. Wachtler served on the court for nearly twenty years and wrote more than five hundred opinions, including 183 during his seven years as chief judge. Governors come and go and today's headlines quickly become a footnote to history, but Wachtler's impact on the law, jurisprudence, society, and the court is lasting.

As chief judge, Wachtler was a reformer, combining the best of his political and judicial talents. He established the Permanent Judicial Commission on Justice for Children, which focused on the needs of poor and disabled children and transformed the Family Court system into a clearing-house and outreach center, matching needy people with health, education, mental health, and social service programs. Wachtler's commissions on minorities and women helped eradicate racial and gender bias—the reality as well as the perception—and his work force diversity program increased the employment and advancement possibilities for minorities and women.

"Sol was an extraordinary elected official," Hazel Dukes, stalwart of the NAACP and admirer of Wachtler from his town supervisor days in the 1960s, wrote to the sentencing court. "His depth of understanding the needs of people and inclusion was remarkable."[5]

Wachtler pressured lawyers to meet their professional obligation—in some cases, kicking and screaming—to assist the poor, dramatically increasing the availability of legal services for the needy. Jay Carlisle, a law professor at Pace Law School, wrote in a letter to the court that, "Judge Wachtler has done more than any other person in New York to encourage *pro bono* service. . . . Judge Wachtler's *pro bono* leadership has resulted in an unprecedented increase in free legal services to tens of thousands of New York citizens."[6] Alexander Forger, former president of the New York State

Bar Association, said Wachtler pursued the *pro bono* issue, even though it made him unpopular with lawyers. "There was no need for him to take on such a volatile and inflammatory issue, but nonetheless he did so out of the conviction that it was the right thing to do."[7]

One of Wachtler's great disappointments was the inability to restructure New York's byzantine, eleven-tiered court system. For political reasons, he was never able to win the concessions necessary to simplify a system rooted in colonial times. But he was able to physically reconstruct courts and revolutionize case management with the Individual Assignment System.

"He has great strength," Judge Bellacosa said just before Wachtler's arrest. "He is a self-assured, strong person. How do you know that? It's in the battles he has fought and the fact he has not shied away from them. Whether it's arguing with Mayor [Ed] Koch or [Manhattan District Attorney] Bob Morgenthau on case assignment or standing up for his responsibilities against the governor."[8]

Mario Cuomo said: "He was wrong. He was convicted. He paid his price. That does not erase the decisions he rendered, the way he ran the court or the way he lived the rest of his life."[9]

Wachtler paid for his sins, and then some, but when the dust had settled his stumble seemed just that—a stumble, in a lifetime of good works. By early 1995, Wachtler was busy with his own reincarnation. He began to appear in public, joined his former colleagues at an annual tribute to the Court of Appeals by the Albany County Bar Association, and slowly worked his way back into polite society. He began lecturing at Pace University School of Law, met with politicians to offer his newly refined views on crime and punishment, and openly discussed his crime and mental illness. He attended the court's 150th anniversary celebration on September 8, 1997.

In mid-1995, while still on probation, Wachtler formed a company called CADRE to promote a concept he has favored since his earliest days on the Court of Appeals—alternative dispute resolution. The company, Comprehensive Alternative Dispute Resolution Enterprise Inc., was started to resolve business disputes that cannot be handled efficiently in the regular courts. It was conceived during Wachtler's incarceration when several dear friends—Robert Tisch, former postmaster general and chief executive officer of Loew's Corp.; Fred Wilpon, the owner of the New York Mets and his son's father-in-law; John Rosenwald of Bear Stearns; and Judge Bellacosa—came up with an idea to utilize the ex-judge's talents when he resumed his life. Wachtler draws no salary (his years of public service entitle him to an annual pension of $68,400) and he has promised to turn over all profits to groups providing legal services to the poor.

In April 1997, Random House published Wachtler's prison diaries, *After the Madness: A Judge's Own Prison Memoir,* and he hit the publicity circuit, appearing on news shows like *Dateline* and talk shows like *Oprah* and *Larry King Live.* Suddenly, Wachtler was back in the public eye, addressing things that matter—like crime and punishment, and help for the mentally ill—and doing so with eloquence and rationality. The six-figure advance and royalties all were put into CADRE. Wachtler was doing everything imaginable to atone for his crime, to earn his redemption. Yet it proved elusive. Wachtler remained a target for easy criticism, cheap political opportunism, and sensationalism. Seemingly every newspaper article referred to him as the "disgraced former chief judge," and focused on his sins rather than his contributions. Victims' rights groups protested Wachtler's appearances on nationally televised talk shows. The New York attorney general, Dennis C. Vacco, crassly compared Wachtler to a mafia hit man who was peddling his own book. Feminists continued to haunt his few public appearances, exploiting Wachtler's notoriety for their cause while utterly ignoring his contributions and denying him any measure of redemption.

After inviting Wachtler on her show, aired April 3, 1997, Oprah Winfrey was lobbied by groups close to Silverman and by professional "victims" looking for a carcass and uninterested in the judge's long commitment to human rights. David Beatty, acting executive director of the National Victim Center, a group with which Silverman is affiliated, distributed an alert via the Internet asking advocates to protest Wachtler's public appearances.[10]

"It appears clear that where he plans to profit most is in the market of public opinion—he plans to rehabilitate his standing in the community by engendering sympathy through shifting blame and by attempting to demonstrate his commitment to good works and good citizenship (like so many jail house converts before him)," Beatty wrote.

The National Victim Center will keep you informed of talk shows and other media programs on which Sol Wachtler is scheduled to appear. As you learn which shows are planning to feature this convicted offender, let them know your views about giving stalkers and other criminals national platforms from which they can promote themselves and re-victimize their victims. . . .

We recently sent out an alert when we first heard, much to our shock and disappointment, that the *Oprah Winfrey Show* had booked Sol Wachtler. When my efforts failed to persuade the show's producers not to provide this man, convicted of crimes against women and children, a national forum from which he might repair his reputation by excusing his crime, we asked leading advocates across the nation to let their views be known. Although we could not claim total victory, we did meet with some success. After being deluged with letters and phone calls from advocates across the country, the *Oprah Winfrey Show* had to disconnect its fax lines!

Beatty followed that up with a further electronic posting on April 1, 1997: "We just got word that *Larry King Live* will be featuring Sol Wachtler tomorrow, Wednesday, April 2nd, on CNN at 9:00 P.M. EST. . . . Let's . . . try to jam those call-in lines. . . ."[11]

Even supportive feminists, like Laura "X" in California, had difficulty with Wachtler and were reluctant to lionize— no matter how great his accomplishments—a man who had harassed a woman. Yet "X," in the final analysis, urged her sisters to consider the whole story and evaluate the man *in toto* before passing judgment. Whatever his sins, Wachtler did, after all, write *Liberta*, and continues to believe in its premise: that women are constitutionally owed basic dignity. If anyone is due a redemption, "X" reasons, it is Wachtler.

"That decision [*Liberta*] was what we carried around in our pocket to give us courage and to give us power," "X" said.

It is clear from that decision that someone in authority believes that women don't deserve this kind of treatment. It took a great person to do that. The sense that somebody really cared was very important. When somebody in authority listens to you, it makes a difference. . . . I don't like anything he did [to Silverman and her daughter], but I want very much to remember the whole person. It seems to me that I am a benefit of the good that he has done, and it would be wrong to now pretend it never happened.[12]

Joan Wachtler knows she can never forget the humiliation Sol brought to himself, her, and their marriage. Yet the marriage continues.

"People ask me why I stay," Joan said. "I am heartbroken. I am still angry. Sol's not perfect. He has his failings. But he is basically someone who is good, and tries very hard to be good. You know, I don't care if the world doesn't love me. But he cares very deeply."[13]

So, Wachtler trudges on in a seemingly endless quest for redemption, like Ralph Branca, the sensational Brooklyn Dodgers hurler known only for throwing the pitch that lost the 1951 playoff (Bobby Thompson hit a home run to win the game for the New York Giants) and frustrated that his life would seemingly be defined by a single incident.

"I've become philosophical about these things," Wachtler said. "In my book I wrote about the importance to me of public image. My God, it was my whole life—having people like me! I have now resigned myself to the fact that because of what I did, there are a lot of people who will never like me, and people who will use what happened to me to further themselves. That is troublesome, but it is a kind of political opportunism I can understand."[14]

To go into seclusion, however, to refuse to use his intelligence and abilities to advance important causes would, in Wachtler's mind, be sinful. And he already has enough sins for which to atone. "I was given more opportunities, more privileges than almost anyone, given the chance to sit on one of the greatest courts in the world, the opportunity to be chief judge of that court, and I betrayed it," Wachtler told the national audience, refusing to be dragged into to a he-said-she-said debate. "I am thoroughly ashamed. But for me to say there is no redemption, that I might as well just end my life now and not do something decent with my life . . . would be to betray my opportunity a second time."[15]

Nevertheless, the peaks of power and public respect shall, it seems, remain forever elusive for Sol Wachtler. Yet he remains the king of the most important mountain of all: the husband of a betrayed woman who, despite her enduring anger, remains married to the kindest, sincerest man she has ever known; the father of four children who care little about landmark decisions and cherish the man who was always there to guide and nurture, as he now guides and nurtures his grandchildren. On their mountain, he reigns supreme.

At this writing, Sol Wachtler is teaching a popular course at Touro Law Center, managing CADRE, and suffering through a recurring nightmare. In it, Judge Wachtler is in the robing room with the other judges, who are happy to see him and congenial. When the court session is about to start, they begin filing into the courtroom, Wachtler last in line. Just as he is about to step over the threshold, Chief Judge Kaye turns to him and says, "I'm sorry, Sol, you can't come," and shuts the door.

Notes

1. John Caher, "Wachtler Tries to Leave Kids His Good Name," Albany *Times Union*, February 19, 1995, p. B-1.

2. Interview with Wachtler on August 15, 1997.

3. Interview with Salvator Ferlazzo on September 3, 1997.

4. John Caher, "Wachtler Leaves a Mixed Legacy after 20 Years," Albany *Times Union*, January 31, 1993, p. A-1.

5. Hazel Dukes's letter to the sentencing court, May 12, 1993.

(Dukes incurred legal troubles herself in late 1997 when she admitted stealing from an employee, according to an Associated Press transmission of November 7, 1997).

6. Joy Carlisle's letter to the sentencing court, April 26, 1993.

7. Alexander Forger's letter to the sentencing court, April 29, 1993.

8. Charles Anzalone, "The Judge Takes a Stand," *Buffalo Magazine*, September 6, 1992, p. 14.

9. Interview with Mario Cuomo on November 10, 1997.

10. David Beatty, e-mail transmission of April 1, 1997, to leaders of "the victims' movement."

11. Ibid.

12. Interview with Laura "X" on August 20, 1997.

13. Interview with Joan Wachtler on September 26, 1997.

14. Interview with Wachtler on August 5, 1997.

15. *Oprah*, April 3, 1997.

Wachtler's Key Opinions

Arbitration

Matter of Weinrott, 32 NY2d 190 (1973)

In one of his first cases as a Court of Appeals judge, Wachtler wrote an opinion providing the arbitration process with legal strength and legitimacy.

"A broad arbitration agreement reflects a general desire by the parties to have all issues decided speedily and finally by the arbitrators. If, in the case at bar, we hold that the arbitration agreement did not contemplate the submission of fraud in the inducement to the arbitrators we would be opting for the 'specifically unenumerated' approach since it is difficult to construct any generic wording which would have a broader sweep than the provision used in this case."

Criminal Procedure

Wilkinson v. *Skinner,* 34 NY2d 53 (1974)

Twenty years before he had any personal experience with solitary confinement, Wachtler expressed little sympathy for an inmate locked in dungeon-like conditions for five days. The majority, through Wachtler, said prisoners cannot be punished arbitrarily and established, for the first time, that those who are can obtain money damages. But the judges gave wide latitude to corrections officials and Wachtler's decision even suggested that if a lower court finds damages are warranted, it should "keep in mind that the wrongs, if any, were committed by officials performing the most dangerous of jobs where occasional lapses of judgment are understandable if not excusable."

Wachtler adopted what he clearly viewed as a pragmatic solution, adhering to a standard he would increasingly rely upon, and set forth a strong statement of his jurisprudential approach.

"It is apparent that [Wilkinson] seeks to have this court lay down some generic and far-reaching guidelines for conduct of detention officials and the conditions of prisoners. We do not believe that is our role. We would but observe that a prison cannot be run by unbridled ukase; by the same token we recognize that it cannot be run as a fledgling democracy. We may disagree with many of the actions taken by detention officials. But it is not up to this court to choose from conflicting penal sociological theories. Even detention officials' activities which are universally condemned will not be terminated by this court if they do not transgress some law or pertinent rule or regulation. The role of the courts is not to put a stop to practices that are unwise, only to practices that are unconstitutional or illegal."

People v. *DeBour,* 40 NY2d 210 (1976)

This unique decision by Wachtler established an extraordinary four-tiered shield that seeks to protect innocent citizens from intrusive police while still affording law enforcement the leeway to perform its function. At the first level, a police officer needs only some "objective credible belief" before approaching a citizen to request information. The citizen has every right to ignore the officer and walk away, and doing so does not in itself warrant a more intrusive response from the officer. At the second level, police may "interfere" with a person to the extent needed to obtain information, but not to the degree of a forcible seizure, and only when there is a "founded suspicion that criminal activity is afoot." The third level level of encounter, in which an officer stops, briefly questions, and frisks the suspect for weapons, requires a reasonable and articulable suspicion of criminal activity. Finally, the fourth level, an arrest, requires "probable cause" to believe that a crime has been committed by the suspect.

With the approach mandated under *DeBour,* the Court of Appeals, through Wachtler, erected a far higher protective barrier than is required under the U.S. Constitution and provided police with an unusually explicit set of guidelines in performing their duty. (The court revisited and refined this ruling in a 1992 opinion written by Wachtler, *People* v. *Hollman,* 79 NY2d 181. See below.)

"This case raises the fundamental issue of whether or not a police officer, in the absence of any concrete indication of criminality, may approach a private citizen on the street for the purpose of requesting information. We hold that he may. The basis for this inquiry need not rest on any indication of criminal activity on the part of the person of whom the inquiry is made but there must be some articulable reason sufficient to justify the police action which was undertaken."

People v. *Torsney,* 47 NY2d 667,686 (1979)

The case involved a police officer who shot and killed a fifteen-year-old boy on Thanksgiving Day 1976, only to be found not responsible by reason of mental disease or defect. Following his acquittal on murder charges, the officer was remanded to a secure mental institution. However, within months he petitioned for his release, arguing that he did not have an identifiable mental illness and was not a danger to himself or others.

In a 4-3 decision, the court said the state could not involuntarily confine those whose mental illness was neither diagnosable nor treatable. Wachtler led the dissent, with an increasingly pragmatic view of criminal justice.

"The court holds today that a man committed to a psychiatric institution because he shot and killed a young boy should be released despite expert testimony that under similar circumstances he would be prone to act again with the same uncontrolled violence. I cannot agree with such a result."

People v. *Benjamin,* 51 NY2d 257 (1980)

In a revisit to the *DeBour* issue (see above), the Wachtler-led court reinstated the conviction of man caught with a concealed weapon. The case illustrated the difficulty judges were having, and would continue to have, in applying the *DeBour* standard.

On the night of October 27, 1977, William Loran, a veteran Queens police officer, got an anonymous tip that there were guns at a specific street location. Loran and his partner went to that location and found a crowd of people, including a man who, when he saw the officers, stepped back and reached toward his back waistband with both hands. Loran ordered the suspect to the ground, conducted a search, and found an illegal weapon. The suspect was convicted, but the conviction was overthrown as resulting from an improper search.

No, Wachtler wrote for his unanimous court, that is not the result they had in mind in *DeBour.* Declaring that an anonymous radio tip alone would not, under *DeBour,* authorize the search, Wachtler's court found that officers can, and must, observe the situation at the scene and take necessary actions for their own safety.

"It is quite apparent to an experienced police officer, and indeed it may almost be considered common knowledge, that a handgun is often carried in the waistband. It is equally apparent that law-abiding persons do not normally step back while reaching to the rear of the waistband, with both hands, to where such a weapon might be carried. Although such action may be consistent with innocuous or innocent behavior, it would be unrealistic to require Officer Loran, who had been told that gunmen might be present, to assume the risk that the defendant's conduct was in fact innocuous or innocent."

People v. *Bartolomeo,* 53 NY2d 225 (1981)

The court said that a suspect represented by an attorney on a pending charge could not, in the absence of an attorney, be questioned on a new charge, even if he agreed to the query. Wachtler dissented and in 1991, when he was chief judge, the court overturned the decision in *People* v. *Bing* (76 NY2d 333), terming "unworkable" the standard erected in *Bartolomeo.*

"A defendant who commits a crime while out on bail should not be immune from questioning by police with respect to his latest criminal acts. Such a rule would be beneficial to the repeat offender and an obstacle to law enforcement. . . . It is the common criminal, not the one-time offender, who nearly always will manage to have at least one serious charge pending, so that the attorney in the picture can provide him with virtual immunity from questioning in a subsequent investigation. I had thought it clear that although our courts are sometimes required to let the guilty go free, this is not because the Constitution serves only the miscreant, but rather because our constitutional protections apply evenly to us all. By its analysis, I believe the majority has turned this basic principle completely around by providing what is in effect a dispensation for the persistent offender."

People v. Hughes, 59 NY2d 523 (1983)

Long before the hysteria over so-called repressed memory syndrome and hypnotically induced recollections, the Court of Appeals was called upon to address the admissibility of hypnosis in the context of a Syracuse rape case. In a landmark decision written by Wachtler, the court granted the defendant a new trial and set forth procedures judges should follow when confronted with hypnotic testimony.

"Because of the unique and sometimes unfathomable consequences of hypnosis, the People should assume the burden of demonstrating by clear and convincing proof that the testimony of the witness as to his or her prehypnotic recollection will be reliable and that there has been no substantial impairment of the defendant's right of cross-examination. If the witness is held to be competent to testify, the defendant, of course, has the option at trial of introducing proof with respect to the hypnotic procedures followed as well as expert testimony concerning the potential effect of the hypnosis on the witness's recollections. And since there is general agreement in the scientific community that a witness who has been hypnotized usually acquires some measure of confidence in events recalled under hypnosis, the court should charge the jury to that effect if the defendant requests it. In our view these measures represent a reasonable accommodation between the legitimate uses of hypnosis and the defendant's right of confrontation."

People v. Liberta, 64 NY2d 152 (1984)

Wachtler wrote the opinion that, for the first time in New York state, found that a man could be held criminally liable for the rape of his wife. Previously, a husband in New York could be convicted of marital rape only if the couple were legally separated. Wachtler described rape as a "degrading, violent act which violates the bodily integrity of the victim" and found "no rational basis for distinguishing between marital rape and nonmarital rape." New York's marital exemption to the rape statute dated to seventeenth-century England when women were viewed as the property of their husbands.

"A marriage license should not be viewed as a license for a husband to forcibly rape his wife with impunity. . . . A married woman has the same right to control her own body as an unmarried woman."

People v. Bernhard Goetz, 68 NY2d 96 (1986)

Wachtler's opinion in this case, involving the so-called "subway vigilante" who made national news after he shot four menacing black youths in a Manhattan subway, reversed two lower courts and allowed Goetz's prosecution for attempted murder. The case redefined the law of self-defense. Wachtler wrote that deadly force is justified only when an individual "reasonably believes" that violence is necessary.

"To completely exonerate such an individual, no matter how aberrational or bizarre his thought patterns, would allow citizens to set their own standards for the permissible use of force. It would also allow a legally competent defendant suffering from delusions to kill or perform acts of violence with impunity, contrary to fundamental principles of justice and criminal law."

People v. *Ronnie Banks* and *People* v. *John Taylor*, 75 NY2d 277 (1990)

For the first time, the court considered whether "rape trauma syndrome" could be used by the prosecution to explain the hesitation of a sexual assault victim to come forward and testify about the attack and the assailant. Wachtler wrote the unanimous opinion in which the court said that under some circumstances and subject to limitations, evidence of rape trauma syndrome is admissible.

"Because cultural myths still affect common understanding of rape and rape victims and because experts have been studying the effects of rape upon its victims only since the 1970s, we believe that patterns of response among rape victims are not within the ordinary understanding of the lay juror."

People v. *Bonaparte*, 78 NY2d 26 (1991)

During jury deliberations, a judge had ordered a court officer to notify jurors that they would be sequestered for the evening. On appeal, the conviction was overturned because the judge had, according to the appellate court, improperly delegated a judicial function. Wachtler found the result hypertechnical and absurd, and wrote an opinion reinstating the conviction.

"The better practice, and the one that should be followed in the future, would be for the court, in the presence of the defendants and his counsel, to notify the jurors that they are going to be sequestered for the evening and to instruct them as to their duties and obligations during this period, including their duty to refrain from discussing the case among themselves or with others."

People v. *Erick Jackson*, 78 NY2d 641 (1991)

The sharply divided court, speaking through Wachtler, backtracked somewhat from its previous stance on a right-to-counsel issue. Historically, New York has recognized a far stronger right to counsel than is required by the U.S. Constitution and other states. In the precedential case, the 1961 matter of *People* v. *Rosario* (9 NY2d 286), the court adopted a rule that any prior statements of a prosecution witness must be turned over to the defense before trial. Over the years, the court generally strengthened that requirement—until this case—holding that any failure to reveal such evidence would automatically result in a reversal. In *Jackson*, the Wachtler court reconsidered and declared that a *Rosario* violation is not automatic ground for a reversal. Instead, the defendant must prove to a "reasonable possibility" that his case was prejudiced by the violation.

"To prevail . . . a defendant must do more than demonstrate that the conduct at issue was improper. . . . To assume prejudice without requiring the defendant to demonstrate actual prejudice would eviscerate the language [of the statute] and the concern of finality underlying that language."

People v. Hollman, 79 NY2d 181 (1992)

Sixteen years after his landmark decision in *People* v. *DeBour* (see above), Wachtler and the court revisited the limits on permissible police-citizen encounters. In this decision, written by Wachtler, the panel clarified the difference between a simple request for information (the lowest level of encounter) and an inquiry (the second level). It also said that the four-part test, while not required under the U.S. Constitution, should continue to be applied as a matter of state common law.

"We recognize that the tone of police-initiated encounters with civilians can be subtle and ever-shifting, that words and gestures are susceptible to many varying interpretations, and that suspicions can grow based on intangibles evident only to the eyes of a trained police officer. Despite our sensitivity to the rapidity with which suspicion can escalate, however, we must place limits on the power of police to pick out targets and subject them to invasive questioning based on nothing more than the objective and credible reason required for a request for information."

(See also *People* v. *Manfred Ohrenstein*, 77 NY2d 238, 1990, under "Government Administration")

Estates

Matter of Snide, 52 NY2d 193 (1981)

The Court of Appeals had long been ahead of the pack in estate litigation, ruling, for instance, in 1889 that a killer could not inherit from his victim. In that case, and its progeny, the court affirmed its commitment to what is known as the "statute of wills." Wachtler wrote an important opinion in this series, a ruling that upheld the intent of a will that had been confused because of a lawyer's mistake.

"Under such facts it would indeed be ironic—if not per-verse—to state that because what has occurred is so obvious, and what was intended so clear, we must act to nullify rather than sustain this testamentary scheme."

Family Relations

Ninesling v. *Nassau County,* 46 NY2d 302 (1978)

The court ruled that a two-year-old boy, who had spent virtually his entire life with foster parents, could be removed from their home and returned to the mother who had never bothered to visit him. Wachtler dissented.

"To completely sever his relationship with his foster parents at this stage, under these circumstances, borders on the inhumane.... The majority ... has overlooked the unique predicament of this two-year-old-boy by wrenching him away from the only parents he has ever known."

Matter of Pamela P. v. Frank S., 59 NY2d 1 (1983)

The court was called upon to resolve a child-support dispute involving Frank Serpico, the legendary New York City cop who blew the whistle on his corrupt colleagues (and was later played by Al Pacino in the Hollywood movie). Serpico fathered a child with a woman who had purposely deceived him with regard to her use of contraception, and sought to avoid paying support. However, the Court of Appeals, through Wachtler, stressed that child support is for the child and that the mother's deceit is irrelevant. "In determining the parents' obligations to support their child, the statute mandates considerations of two factors—the needs of the child for support and education and the financial ability of the parents to contribute to that support. The statute does not require, nor, we believe, does it permit, consideration of the 'fault' or wrongful conduct of one of the parents in causing the child's conception."

Avitzur v. Avitzur, 58 NY2d 108 (1983)

The court split 4-3 on whether a Jewish man could be compelled to submit his marital problem to a religious council, as he had promised his wife. Although the minority was concerned about state interference in a church matter, Wachtler and the majority found that a *keubah*, a Jewish marriage agreement, is an enforceable civil contract. The decision had broad implications for all religious-oriented contracts.

"The relief sought by the plaintiff in this action is simply to compel defendant to perform a secular obligation to which he contractually bound himself. In this regard, no doctrinal issue need be passed upon, no implementation of religious duty is contemplated, and no interference with religious authority will result."

(Also see marital rape case of *People* v. *Liberta*, 64 NY2d 152, 1984, above.)

Free Speech

Chapadeau v. *Utica Observer-Dispatch,* 38 NY2d 196 (1975)

In an opinion by Wachtler, the court made it harder for private persons to sustain a libel action when the media are pursuing a story of significant public interest. Although a newspaper account of a schoolteacher's arrest was partly wrong, Wachtler said the *Observer-Dispatch* had taken reasonable steps to ensure accuracy and could not be sued for libel.

"It becomes abundantly clear that the challenged communication falls within the sphere of legitimate public concern. Chapadeau's occupation, one highly influential with the youth of the community, coupled with the oft-cited menace of heroin addiction makes further expatiation unnecessary."

People v. *Remeny,* 40 NY2d 527 (1976)

Wachtler wrote the decision which said, for the first time, that First Amendment protections prohibited New York City from preventing all distributions of commercial handbills.

"The city, of course, has a legitimate interest in seeing that the exercise of the [free speech] right does not contribute to the litter on the streets or otherwise violate the law. . . . Although we sympathize with the city's desire to eliminate litter from the streets, we have concluded that the ordinance . . . is unconstitutional."

Gannett v. DePasquale, 43 NY2d 370 (1977)

In a case involving a closed-door pretrial hearing in a murder case, Wachtler wrote a decision which said the press could be excluded from some proceedings. But he expressed discomfort with that prospect, and the decision strove to strike a balance between the interests of the press and the rights of the accused.

"Suspicion enshrouds whatever determination is not freely aired in a forum open to public inspection, scrutiny and, sometimes, scorn. The public has a right to know that the constitution protects equally each person accused of a crime, and has the right to scrutinize the effectiveness of police agencies in coping with criminal activity."

Matter of Curle v. Benjamin Ward, 40 NY2d 1049 (1979)

The question in this case was whether the commissioner of corrections had a right to prohibit prison guards from joining the Ku Klux Klan and demanding to know whether the officers were members of the secret society. The court ruled against the commissioner in a decision from which Wachtler dissented.

"It has long been recognized that the constitutional guarantees of freedom of speech and assembly necessarily imply like protections for the freedom of association. . . . On the other hand, it is true . . . that our commitment to liberty must sometimes yield to the exigencies of maintaining an orderly society. . . . If the threat to the prison system is shown to be grave and immediate, it would be irresponsible and indeed indefensible to await catastrophe as a necessary antecedent to preventative action. The First Amendment does not require such a result, and the conscience will not allow it."

Westchester Rockland Newspapers v. *Leggett,* 48 NY2d 430 (1979)

In what Wachtler termed "a sequel to *Gannett Co.* v. *DePasquale*" (see above, 43 NY2d 370, 1977), the court ruled that lower tribunals had wrongly closed a mental competency hearing for a man suspected of several sexual assaults. Writing for the court, Wachtler called upon the judiciary to strike a balance between the sometimes conflicting rights of free press and fair trial.

"The public, of course, is not only concerned with seeing that the accused is fairly treated. The public also has an interest in seeing that there is justice for the accuser—the police and prosecutors who must enforce the law, and the victims of crime who suffer when the law is not enforced with vigor and impartiality."

Beach v. *Shanley,* 62 NY2d 241 (1984)

The court found that the state shield law protected a television reporter from disclosing the identity of the person who leaked a confidential grand jury report calling for the ouster of the Rensselaer County sheriff. Wachtler wrote a concurrence, urging the court to find not only a statutory protection for reporters, but a constitutional protection as well.

"The ability of the press to gather information is deterred if the press can be compelled to disclose their sources to the government. Similarly, publishers and reporters will be reluctant to publish what they have learned if they can be jailed, fined, or otherwise held in contempt for refusing to disclose the source of their information to state investigators."

A few years later, when Wachtler was chief, the court found such a constitutional right.

Shad Alliance v. Smith Haven Mall, 66 NY2d 496 (1985)

A divided court found no free-speech right entitling people to hand out leaflets in a private shopping mall. Wachtler, in his first year as chief judge, dissented.

"In the past, those who had ideas they wished to communicate had the unquestioned right to disseminate those ideas in the open marketplace. Now that the marketplace has a roof over it, and is called a mall, we should not abridge that right."

Arcara v. Cloud Books, 65 NY2d 324 (1985), 503 NE2d 492 (1986)

This free-speech case, which dealt with the question of whether an otherwise valid nuisance statute could be used to close down an adult bookstore, came before the court twice and became a defining moment for the Wachtler court. Wachtler's initial opinion, barring prosecution of the bookstore on First Amendment grounds, was reversed by the U.S.

Supreme Court. Then Wachtler's court revisited the issue, declared the use of the statute a violation of the New York State constitution, and, effectively, snubbed its nose at the highest court in the land.

"Freedom of expression in books, movies, and the arts generally is one of those areas where there is great diversity among the states. . . . New York has a long history and tradition of fostering freedom of expression, often tolerating and supporting works which in other states would be found offensive to the community. Thus, the minimal national standards established by the Supreme Court . . . cannot be considered dispositive in determining the scope of this state's constitutional guarantee of freedom of expression."

Government Administration

Hellerstein v. Town of Islip, 37 NY2d 1 (1975)

This politically explosive decision shot down the 200-year-old practice in New York of taxing real property on a fractional assessment. Wachtler wrote for the court that localities in New York could no longer tax its citizens and business on an arbitrary scale.

"The practice has time on its side and nothing else."

People v. Abrahams, 40 NY2d 277 (1976)

The court, through Wachtler, struck down the so-called Sunday Blue Laws, which prohibited the sale of merchandise on the Sabbath. The law stemmed from the Old Testament directive to rest on the seventh day; the case from a pharmacist who was prosecuted for selling a ceramic bank on a Sunday. Wachtler called the law "a classic example of an eighteenth-century statute which has never been modernized and is unable to function in a twentieth-century world." (One of judges who would later join Wachtler on the Court of Appeals, Stewart F. Hancock Jr., got around the Sunday Blue Laws as a trial judge by declaring Christmas trees vegetables, thus authorizing their sale on the Sabbath).

O'Connor v. City of New York, 58 NY2d 184 (1983)

In a major municipal liability case involving the city of New York, the court upheld by a narrow 4-3 margin a long-standing rule that immunized cities against legal action unless they had a "special relationship" with the victim. The court said that New York City was not liable for a 1970 gas explosion that killed twelve people, even though the city building inspector had approved the defective gas line that caused the tragedy. Wachtler dissented.

"This judiciously created caste system represents an indefensible exception to the basic principle of negligence law that a plaintiff is entitled to compensation when he has been injured by the defendant's failure to observe standards of reasonable care under the circumstances. In addition, efforts to decide tort liability by placing, or attempting to fit litigants into rigid categories, breeds exceptions and often produces incongruous, unfair and arbitrary results."

DeLong v. *Erie County,* 60 NY2d 296 (1983)

Wachtler wrote the majority decision which said that Erie County was liable for the death of a woman whose call to a 911 emergency number was mishandled. Police responded to the wrong address and the woman, who called to report that a burglar was in her home, was murdered.

"In this case the decision had been made by the municipalities to provide a special emergency service which was intended and proclaimed to be more effective than normal police services. Those seeking emergency assistance were advised not to attempt to call the general number for the local police, which ironically might have avoided the tragedy in this case, but were encouraged to dial the 911 number to obtain a quicker response."

People v. *Manfred Ohrenstein,* 77 NY2d 238 (1990)

The court, in a 6-1 decision by Wachtler, said the minority leader of the state senate could not be prosecuted for assigning public employees to work on political campaigns because "at the time the defendants acted, their conduct was not prohibited in any manner . . . nor was there any rule or regulation defining the duties of legislative assistants or limiting the nature or extent of their permissible political activities." Prior to the decision, the legislature adopted a resolution prohibiting such conduct in the future.

Denise R. v. *Lavine,* 39 NY2d 279 (1976)

The court split 4-3 on this case involving a sex-change operation and whether a genetic male was properly denied public
medical assistance for the sexual conversion. Wachtler, writing for the majority, threw the case out. "The court cannot
assume the role of either social agency or legislative body."

Human Rights/Discrimination

NOW v. *State Division of Human Rights,* 34 NY2d 416 (1974)

The National Association for Women had sued the Gannett
newspaper company for publishing separate help-wanted
advertisements for men and women. Even though Gannett
had ceased its practice of running "help wanted—male" and
"help wanted—female" ads before the matter got to the
Court of Appeals, the court through Wachtler opted to comment and decided that the company had fostered a discriminatory practice.

"It may well be that more women are interested in secretarial jobs than are men. Or that more men are interested in
accounting jobs than women. However, it is often the case
that a person or organization acting in a manner which genuinely intends to be descriptive becomes in effect prescriptive. A policy purporting to reflect a statistical phenomenon
actually becomes a self-fulfilling prophecy which helps to
generate the very presumptive foundation for its existence."

Batavia Lodge v. *State Division of Human Rights,* 35 NY2d 143 (1974)

Wachtler wrote an opinion which reinstated awards of $250 to black people who were denied service at a Moose Lodge bar after they had been invited to a fashion show at the facility.

"The unlawful discrimination in this case was blatant and intolerable. . . . It is evident that such conduct perpetrated in a place used as a public accommodation cannot be tolerated."

Imperial Diner v. *State Division of Human Rights,* 52 NY2d 72 (1980)

In this case, a waitress subjected to ethnic obscenities by her boss was awarded $500 by the state Human Rights Division, but the award was overturned on appeal. The Court of Appeals, in an opinion by Wachtler, reinstated the award.

"The employer's contempt for complainant and his other female employees of her religion or creed was proclaimed crudely and openly, not only to her but to all within hearing. This type of vilification is humiliating, not only when it is done wholesale, but also, and perhaps especially, when it is directed at a lone individual in an isolated incident."

McDermott v. *Xerox,* 65 NY2d 213 (1985)

Wachtler wrote an opinion which said the Xerox Corporation's refusal to hire an obese woman was unlawful discrimination against the handicapped.

"The statute protects all persons with disabilities and not just those with hopeless conditions. . . . We have found nothing in the statute or its legislative history indicating a legislative intent to permit employers to refuse to hire persons who are able to do the job simply because they have a possibly treatable condition of excessive weight."

New York State Club Association v. City of New York, 69 NY2d 211 (1987)

Wachtler wrote the opinion which said that women and minorities could not be excluded from some men's clubs. Seven years earlier, he had resigned from an exclusive club in Albany because it would not admit women.

"Although plaintiff's constituent members have a right to free speech and association, they lack the right to *practice* invidious discrimination against women and minorities in the distribution of important business advantages and privileges."

Patchogue-Medford Congress of Teachers v. Board of Education, 70 NY2d 57 (1987)

In a unanimous opinion written by Wachtler, the court shot down mandatory drug testing of probationary teachers.

"By restricting the government to reasonable searches, the state and federal constitutions recognize that there comes a point at which seizures intended to serve the public interest, however effective, may undermine the public's interest in maintaining the privacy, dignity and security of its members."

Jews for Jesus v. *Jewish Community Relations Council,* 79 NY2d 227 (1992)

After the council circulated a document criticizing Jews for Jesus and urging that it be denied access to certain facilities, the group sued under New York's Human Rights Law. Wachtler, writing for the court, said that the memo was not in violation of the law because it never got beyond the proposal stage and did not incite or directly intend to incite discrimination.

"Defendant's conduct here, asking associates to ask others to engage in prohibited conduct, is too far removed from the potential unlawful conduct to be considered incitement."

Product Liability

Hymowitz v. *Lilly & Co.,* 55 NY2d 571 (1989)

In a decision that attracted national attention, Wachtler cleverly established a "market share" liability standard for victims of DES—diethylstilbestrol—a synthetic estrogen product. The drug tended to harm the daughters of women who ingested it, but the damage typically did not show up for twenty years or more, well after the statute of limitations had run. The legislature passed a bill allowing the victims to sue, but the bill was potentially impotent since the plaintiffs could almost never testify as to what brand of DES their mother had ingested a generation before. Wachtler's decision, which held the manufacturers liable in proportion to their market share, put teeth in the law.

"It would be inconsistent with the reasonable expectations of a modern society to say to these plaintiffs that because of the insidious nature of an injury that long remains dormant, and because so many manufacturers, each behind a curtain, contributed to the devastation, the cost of injury should be borne by the innocent and not the wrongdoers."

Enright v. *Eli Lilly and Co.,* 77 NY2d 377 (1991)

In this ground-breaking case, the majority, through Wachtler, backtracked from New York's traditionally strict products liability posture and held that the granddaughter of a woman who had ingested DES could not sue the manufacturer. The woman claimed that her injuries resulted from a premature birth, which resulted from her mother's in utero exposure to DES. Wachtler, writing for the split court, said the link was too tenuous to permit such a lawsuit.

"For all we know, the rippling effects of DES exposure may extend for generations. It is our duty to confine liability within manageable limits. Limiting liability to those who ingested the drug or were exposed to it *in utero* serves this purpose."

Right-to-Die

Becker v. *Schwartz,* 46 NY2d 401 (1978)

In a peculiar twist to the "right-to-die" debate, the court considered whether a doctor could be sued for failing to inform expectant parents that their child would be born severely handicapped. The "wrongful life" case involved a couple with a Down's Syndrome baby. They claimed they would have aborted the fetus had they known of the disability, and sued the doctor for their own emotional damage, for the cost of raising a handicapped child and for the injuries to a child they said should not have been born. The court allowed them to sue for child-rearing costs, but Wachtler dissented, fretting that such a ruling would pressure doctors to recommend abortions.

"A doctor exposed to liability of this magnitude will undoubtedly, in marginal cases, be inclined to practice 'defensive medicine' by advising abortion rather than run the risk of having to pay for the lifetime care of the child if it is born with a handicap. Thus the majority's decision will involve human costs as well, in those cases where otherwise healthy children will be unnecessarily aborted as the only alternative to the threat of pecuniary liability."

Matter of Storar, 52 NY2d 363 (1981)

Wachtler wrote an opinion that said the mother of a profoundly retarded 52-year-old man dying of cancer could not deny him a life-prolonging blood transfusion.

"Although we understand and respect his mother's despair, as we respect the beliefs of those who oppose transfusion on religious grounds, a court should not in the circumstances of this case allow an incompetent patient to bleed to death because someone, even someone as close as a parent or sibling, feels that this is best for someone with an incurable disease."

Matter of O'Connor, 72 NY2d 517 (1988)

Wachtler established New York's unusually stringent standard for right-to-die cases in this matter involving an elderly woman in Westchester County and a hospital that wanted to insert a nasogastric feeding tube over the objections of the patient's children, who said she would not want to be kept alive by artificial means. Writing for a divided court on an issue that continues to bother the panel, Wachtler said life-sustaining treatment could not be denied a patient absent "clear and convincing" proof that the patient would object to such treatment. This was the last in a triumvirate of cases, all written by Wachtler, in which the court gradually rejected the "substituted judgment" doctrine that had been adopted by other states. (See *Matter of Storar* and *Matter of Eichner* v. *Dillon*, 52 NY2d 363, 1981.)

"There always exists the possibility that, despite his or her clear expression in the past, the patient has since changed his or her mind. . . . In addition, there exists the danger that the statements were made without the reflection and resolve that would be brought to bear on the issue if the patient were presently capable of making the decision."

Matter of Fosmire v. Nicoleau, 75 NY2d 218 (1990)

Wachtler wrote the majority opinion in a case that decided a Jehovah's Witness should not have been forced to undergo a blood transfusion following a Cesarean delivery. The hospital had argued that the forced procedure was legally warranted to avoid denying the child of a mother.

"The state does not prohibit parents from engaging in dangerous activities because there is a risk that their children will be left orphans."

Sportsmanship

Mercury Bay Boating Club v. *San Diego Yacht Club*, 76 NY2d 256 (1990)

In the twenty-seventh America's Cup challenge, yachtsman Dennis Connor utilized an inherently faster catamaran to ensure victory over New Zealand's Mercury Bay crew in the September 1988 race. Mercury Bay challenged the race in court, contending that San Diego violated the Deed of Gift that had generally established the ground rules for the previously friendly competition. The court said there was nothing in the Deed of Gift to ensure a fair contest, and therefore Connor must win despite his poor sportsmanship. Wachtler, in a concurrence, bemoaned the fact that his court was even called upon to address such a dispute.

"This case has little or no significance for the law, but it has caught the public eye like few cases in the court's history. Much of the reason for this attention, apparently, is the supposition that at stake here are grand principles—sportsmanship and tradition—pitted against the greed, commercialism and zealotry that threatens to vulgarize sport. In the end, however, the outcome is dictated by elemental legal principles."

Stolen Property

Guggenheim Foundation v. *Lubell,* 77 NY2d 311 (1991)

This peculiar case involved a 1912 Marc Chagall watercolor that had been stolen from the Guggenheim Museum in the late 1960s. Rachel Lubel and her husband purchased the painting from a well-known Madison Avenue gallery and openly displayed it in their Fifth Avenue home, just a few blocks from the museum, for over twenty years. They exhibited the artwork twice. In the mid-1980s, the museum learned that the Lubels had the painting and sued to compel its return or, alternatively, to force the Lubels to pay $200,000 to keep the art. The question before the court, whether a good-faith buyer of a stolen painting who purchases from a reputable dealer can be forced to return it to the original owner, boiled down to a statute-of-limitations problem. Wachtler wrote that the statute of limitations did not start to run until the museum demanded the return of the artwork.

"New York enjoys a worldwide reputation as a preeminent cultural center. To place the burden of locating stolen artwork on the true owners and to foreclose the rights of that owner to recover its property if the burden is not met would, we believe, encourage illicit trafficking in stolen art."

Timeline

- **April 29, 1930:** Sol Wachtler born in Brooklyn, New York, to Philip and Faye Wachtler.
- **June 1947:** Meets Joan Carol Wolosoff, a high school junior.
- **September 1947:** Enrolls at Washington and Lee University.
- **February 1951:** Sol and Joan elope.
- **May 6, 1954:** First child, Lauren, born.
- **July 19, 1956:** Daughter Marjorie born.
- **November 17, 1958:** Daughter Alison born.
- **1960:** Father, Philip Wachtler, dies of nephritis at the age of fifty-seven.
- **May 21, 1961:** Son, Philip, born.
- **1963:** Elected to a four-year term as North Hempstead town councilman.
- **1965:** Appointed North Hempstead town supervisor after incumbent resigns. Wins election that November.

- **1967:** Wachtler runs for Nassau County executive and loses to incumbent Eugene Nickerson. As a reward for running in a race he didn't want to run in, Governor Nelson Rockefeller gives Wachtler a Supreme Court judgeship.
- **1968:** Takes the bench as a state Supreme Court justice.
- **1972:** Wins election to Court of Appeals.
- **1973:** Writes major decision legitimizing the arbitration process.
- **1974:** Authors key decision shielding New Yorkers, to a much greater degree than required under the federal constitution, from intrusive police searches and seizures.
- **1974:** Writes an opinion prohibiting a large newspaper chain from running separate "help wanted" advertisements for men and women.
- **1974:** Forces a fraternal club to pay a fine for refusing to serve an African American couple at its bar.
- **1975:** Holds public school teachers to a higher standard than other citizens when pursuing a libel case against a newspaper.
- **1976:** Strikes down on free-speech grounds a New York City law banning distribution of commercial handbills.
- **1977:** Allows prosecutors to bar the public, in limited circumstances, from some pretrial matters in criminal cases.
- **1978:** Dissents when the court decides to wrest a two-year-old boy from his foster parents and return him to a mother who had never bothered to visit the child.
- **1981:** Dissents when the court issues a liberal ruling limiting police interrogations of suspects represented by an attorney on an unrelated charge.
- **1981:** Orders officials to provide a blood transfusion to a retarded, cancer-stricken 52-year-old man, despite the wishes of the man's mother.

- **1984:** Rules that a reporter cannot be forced to reveal the source of a secret grand jury report calling for the removal of a public official.
- **1984:** Writes landmark decision stating, for the first time, that a man can be held liable for the rape of his wife.
- **1985:** Holds that the Xerox Corporation cannot refuse a woman a job simply because she is obese.
- **1985:** Appointed by Governor Mario M. Cuomo chief judge of the Court of Appeals.
- **1985:** Dissents from an opinion in which the court fails to recognize a free-speech right to distribute leaflets in a private shopping mall.
- **1986:** Oversteps the U.S. Supreme Court and finds that the New York constitution's free-speech clause shields a pornographic bookstore, even though it would not be protected under the federal constitution.
- **1986:** Writes the opinion allowing authorities to prosecute so-called subway vigilante Bernhard Goetz for attempted murder.
- **1987:** Authors opinion barring some private clubs from discriminating against minorities and women.
- **1987:** Shoots down mandatory drug testing of probationary teachers.
- **1988:** Establishes an unusually high standard in right-to-die cases, ensuring that patients can be denied life-sustaining treatment only when there is "clear and convincing proof" that the patient would choose death over life.
- **1990:** Authors decision that allows prosecutors to introduce evidence of "rape trauma syndrome" to explain why a sexual assault victim does not immediately report the crime.
- **1990:** Writes the decision in which the court lets off the minority leader of the state senate, who assigned public employees to work on political campaigns.

- **October 1991:** Wachtler breaks up with mistress Joy Silverman and starts making hang-up calls.
- **January 8, 1992:** Wachtler has the court's deputy clerk, Stuart Cohen, perform research on David Samson, Silverman's new beau.
- **March 28, 1992:** Wachtler learns from a *New York Times* article that Samson is representing a corporation trying to win approval for a toxic waste incinerator.
- **April 1992:** Joy Silverman and her fourteen-year-old daughter, Jessica, start getting notes and cards mailed from New Jersey.
- **May 27, 1992:** Wachtler obtains from Leonard A. Weiss, presiding justice of the Appellate Division, Third Department, a copy of David Samson's confidential bar admissions records.
- **June 13, 1992:** Wachtler devises the character of "David Purdy," a seedy Texas investigator hired to undermine Samson and the incinerator project.
- **June 16, 1992:** Having misgivings about Purdy, Wachtler creates a second character, "Theresa O'Connor," a church-going New Jersey woman who had hired Purdy but was leery of his unsavory tactics.
- **June 16, 1992:** Wachtler sends Jessica Silverman an obscene greeting card with a condom inside. Her mother gets a note threatening that explicit tapes and photographs of Jessica are "for sale."
- **July 2, 1992:** Silverman's divorce lawyer, Norman Sheresky, approaches Wachtler and tells him that Joy knows it is he who is sending the letters.
- **August 28, 1992:** A handwritten missive is delivered to Silverman's door. It includes a threat to return in the fall and to "tell you then what it will cost to get me out of your life."

- **September 1992:** Silverman goes to Washington to meet with FBI Director William Sessions, who refers the case to the bureau's criminal investigation division in Newark, because some of the letters were mailed in New Jersey. Agents move into Silverman's apartment, install tracing equipment, and begin monitoring calls.
- **September 18, 1992:** The FBI begins tailing Wachtler.
- **October 3, 1992:** The FBI traces a threatening call to Silverman from the mobile phone in Wachtler's state-issued car.
- **October 7, 1992:** Wachtler, as "David Purdy," calls Silverman from a hospital where he is being treated for a bad back: "You're gonna get a letter from me and you better listen to every word of it and do what it tell you to do or you're not gonna see your daughter again, you hear me? I'm a sick and desperate man. I need the money."
- **November 7, 1992:** Wachtler is stopped by FBI agents and charged with extortion.
- **March 31, 1993:** Wachtler signs a plea agreement admitting he transmitted an interstate threat to kidnap Jessica Silverman. The government said in the plea agreement that: "The defendant's intent was not financial or economic gain and there is no evidence that the defendant took any steps to take physical possession of the money. The gravamen of his offense was one of threatening communications to harass. . . . There is no evidence that Sol Wachtler intended to carry out his threats."
- **July 20, 1993:** Wachtler resigns from the bar.
- **September 28, 1993:** Begins serving prison term at Federal Correctional Institution at Butner, North Carolina.
- **November 21, 1993:** Stabbed at Butner while resting on his cot.
- **December 1993:** Transferred to Federal Medical Center at Rochester, Minnesota.

- **August 29, 1994:** Released to a Brooklyn halfway house.
- **October 26, 1994:** Released from custody.
- **October 1995:** Forms a dispute resolution business, CADRE.
- **April 1997:** Random House publishes his prison memoir, *After the Madness.*
- **September 1997:** Begins teaching at Touro Law School.
- **1998:** Writing a novel centering on themes of ethnic tolerance and justice, teaching at Touro, running CADRE, and praying for redemption.

APPENDIX C

Speeches

Death Penalty/October 2, 1982

The death penalty is the chicken soup of politics. It is an old folk remedy which had fallen victim to "modern" theories but which is now making a dramatic comeback. Nobody knows if it truly does what its proponents claim, but as any fancier of old-fashioned remedies can tell you, like chicken soup, "it can't hurt."

But whether we are for or against the death penalty, we will all agree that it certainly is tailor made for a political campaign. It provides a brief, tough message with overwhelming public support. The only negative is that it does not enable the politicians to play their favorite game of one-upmanship. When arguing about the economy, one candidate can claim he will reduce taxes more than the other. But what do you say to

357

one-up someone on the death penalty? You can't very well call for life imprisonment after the death penalty.

We'll probably see a return of the death penalty—and the initial enthusiasm will be great. The public may even swarm to watch the first executions on cable television. But after a few months we'll all be back to watching reruns of *Gilligan's Island* and complaining that it still isn't safe to go to the corner drug store without an armed escort. It's all chicken soup. At its best, it does no harm unless the public starts to believe that enacting the death penalty will cure the cancer of crime. . . .

Again, the fact of the matter is that despite all the political rhetoric, convictions in this state are still being obtained where they should be. . . . That's not to say that our court system is untroubled—the opposite is true. But our trouble is not the lack of a "death penalty" or the "soft on crime" judges. Although these issues have voter appeal, they don't contribute much to the resolution of the real problems which stem from the lack of public understanding necessary to make the justice system work better. . . .

The public should know of the inefficiency and confusion caused by our antiquated multi-layered court structure. It should be told that jail is a precious correctional commodity to be used sparingly and only for serious crimes. It should be informed of the fact that the principal job of the courts is not to stop crime, but rather to administer justice.

I could not imagine a better time for the communication of these ideas than in the midst of political campaigns. It is then that the attention of the public is called to candidates and their ideas. It is then, through the offering and debate of imaginative proposals, that the public could be made aware of the fact that as the twentieth century draws to a close, our judicial system is perfect for 1850.

But I'm afraid that this period of revelation is not at hand. Perhaps when it is all over we can look to those who have been elected to communicate the complexities of our judicial system and the need for reform to our citizenry. Until then, I'm afraid that we have to be content with chicken soup

Law and Order/1981

A few years ago it seemed fashionable in some circles to discuss the so-called law-and-order issue as a code phrase for arch conservatism, and even for racism. When it became so harshly apparent that the problem was deeper and more comprehensive, and that it was more than mere demagoguery, the language changed. Men in political life declared solemnly that "law and order is not a partisan issue."

They were correct: Law and order is not a partisan issue, or it ought not to be, and neither is it simply a code phrase for other ills or ideologies. It has become a code phrase for civilization. When law and order breaks down, civilization itself threatens to break down. . . .

And so the public looks desperately for answers. It searches for some group out there at whose doorstep it can lay the blame. Tragically, it is the courts which have provided the most convenient target and scapegoat. It might be bureaucratically comforting to say that if the courts did their job, the war on crime would be won. But to do so would be misleading. The courts do not cause crime and the courts do not prevent it. And even if the courts were properly funded and permitted to function at maximum efficiency, it would still make only a small impact on crime prevention because they are simply at the wrong end of the criminal cycle. The courts' principal job is not to stop crime, but rather to administer justice. . . .

We do not provide criminal defendants with constitutional protections for their benefit alone. We do it for ourselves as well. Every time we protect the rights of a stranger, we reaffirm the sanctity and safety of our own constitutional rights. We reaffirm that if the day comes that we, or those dear to us, need the protection of law, the protection will be there. . . .

Of course, we recognize that prison is resorted to because of the failure of the criminal to respond to probation and the lack of any better alternative. Moreover, since we do not know the causes of crime we do not know very much about the rehabilitation of criminals. We have found that you cannot tell much about how a man will behave free by studying how he behaves in a cage. And we do know that prisons do not rehabilitate—they are more likely to be hotbeds of advanced criminal technology and homosexuality. That is not to say, of course, that society can afford to give up and abandon its responsibility. We must do a better job and continue to be as creative as possible in educating and training the inmates in our local and state facilities as much for their benefit as for ours.

I might note, parenthetically and in defense of the experts in this field, that the single greatest factor disrupting rehabilitation programs, in or out of prisons, has been the change in the composition of the known criminal population in background, drug abuse, and social alienation. Before the criminologist could solve the problems of the group he was beginning to understand, that group has been largely changed.

And much has been said about the disparity of sentences and the consequent and adverse effects this has had on the rehabilitation of prisoners and the image of the criminal justice system. Some legislators have called for the fixing of mandatory sentences for specified crimes. I think this is an unrealistic solution. Obviously, the same crime, meaning the legal category of crime, does not call for the same penal sanction. There is a vast difference between a man who steals powdered milk to feed his family and someone who steals powdered milk to cut heroin. . . .

But what of the persistent violent felony offender, the person who is responsible for destroying our civilization? In the days of medieval torture and public executions and during the age of the pillory and chain gangs, we believed that public punishment would be a deterrent. It wasn't. . . .

As drastic and dramatic a solution as this might appear to be, it must be recognized that as long as these career criminals are allowed to remain on the streets, we will have violent crime. Efforts at rehabilitating these people have not worked and the fear of prison does not deter them. Many of them are as much at home in jails as they are in the neighborhood which they terrorize.

What of the violent juvenile? I have always felt that we cannot, in the name of restoring civilization, be so uncivilized as to think in terms of incapacitating teenagers. On the other hand, we must recognize that a rape or mugging, or the fear of being raped or mugged by a fourteen-year-old, is no less traumatic, and murder at his hands no less final, than if the same crime were committed by an adult. These violent juveniles must be taken off the streets and taken away from the environment which has twisted them and which they, in turn, pollute. Rehabilitation programs such as counterparts of the civil conservation corps and job training enterprises can be considered with ultimate release an objective, but their violence must be dealt with by immediately removing them from society. . . .

The challenge of our day is not whether we should be hard on crime—or soft on crime—but whether we shall be effective in our battle against it. The resolution of that challenge requires hard choices and courage. We cannot delay. Time moves quickly and while the present may seem eternal, all too soon future generations will be here to appraise us. When they do, they will hopefully conclude that we did as much as we could to restore civilization.

Right to Die
(Various Times, Places in Early 1980s)

We have heard much in recent years of the right to die with dignity, considered by many to be the ultimate right of privacy. But dying has never been an entirely private matter. Even in the Middle Ages there are woodcuts showing deathbed scenes with a doctor, priest and lawyer in attendance to provide for physical, spiritual and legal needs of the patient. Today, in many cases that picture would have to include a judge. The judge would be there to determine whether too much or too little is being done to prolong the life of a patient who, because of illness or general mental incompetence, is unable to personally determine the course of treatment.

Many consider the court's presence in these matters offensive. But this is not a role which the judiciary has assumed for itself. It has been thrust upon the courts by advances in medical treatment which can extend the lives of the terminally ill beyond medical and legal precedent. As a result, family members and doctors called upon to provide for a person who is both terminally ill and incompetent frequently come to court to determine in advance whether a decision to administer, withhold or discontinue a particular medical treatment may subject them to civil or criminal liability.

A case reported several years ago in the newspapers illustrates the problem. There, the father of a 21-year-old brain-dead man went to a New York court seeking a judge's permission to disconnect his son's body from life-support machines. At the court hearing an assistant district attorney asked the doctor why, if he was so certain that the patient was dead, he did not sign a death certificate. The doctor responded: "Because of people like you, who would call me a murderer for turning off life support on someone I know is already dead."

The fact is that in this area medical technology has outdistanced law and poses a challenge to our traditional, ethical and legal standards. People who are terminally ill rarely die at home because the availability of medical services and facilities has shifted the place of dying to health care institutions. This has the effect of transferring control over treatment away from the patient and his family to the provider of health care. In most instances, there is an accommodation with respect to treatment—but what of the case where a terminally ill patient wishes to forego treatment for any number of reasons such as pain and suffering, financial concerns or religious beliefs? Does the public have a right to interfere? Whose life is it anyway?

There are strong arguments against allowing a patient to refuse lifesaving treatment. For example, it would be no defense in an ordinary homicide prosecution to say that the decedent wanted to die. Similarly, society has an interest in the life of the individual and so our laws condemn euthanasia as well as "mercy killings." It is argued that if an individual has no right to consent to his own death in a euthanasia situation, then he would have no right to prohibit lifesaving medical treatment.

On the other hand, in New York, as in many other states, there is no law which prohibits a patient from declining necessary medical treatment or a doctor from honoring the patient's decision even if the treatment may be beneficial or even necessary to preserve the patient's life. We have identified the patient's right to determine the course of his own medical treatment as paramount to what might otherwise be the doctor's obligation to provide needed medical care. As Judge Cardozo of our Court stated: "Every person of adult years and sound mind has a right to determine what should be done with his own body; and a surgeon who performs an operation without his patient's consent commits an assault for which he is liable in damages."[1] It follows that a state which imposes civil liability on a doctor if he violates the patient's right to decline treatment cannot also hold him criminally responsible if he respects that right.

At the heart of this right to resist lifesaving medical treatment are considerations of personal choice and individual autonomy. But when the patient is incompetent or unconscious, this can lead to agonizing choices for family members, treating physicians, and the courts. For one thing, an unconscious person would presumably retain the right to be free of bodily invasion of government monitoring even if he could no longer sense those things. Therefore, where a patient has, while competent, or conscious, stated preferences as to the course of treatment—or withholding of treatment—self-determination is promoted by implementing the patient's wishes. . . .

Litigation in these cases has served to expose the problems and deficiencies of existing law. We know now that it is not a single problem with a single solution but a number of problems requiring a number of solutions, some of which are still debatable. We also know that the courts are unsuited and ill-equipped to serve as the sole forum or even the primary one for the resolution of the many problems generated by advances in medical technology. It is an area in which the legislature can and must play an important role.

The courts cannot provide answers for all, most or even the more common problems. They can only decide the cases before them. Oddly, many of those who originally criticized the courts for making what they considered an unwarranted intrusion into the sickroom now criticize the courts for not going far enough to settle the law in cases that have not yet reached the courts. Obviously what is needed is a broad body of law which can provide clear guidelines for the public and medical professionals, not only in the cases that have arisen but in those which are likely to arise in the future. Only the legislature has the authority and the capacity to promulgate such rules. . . . The legislatures of most states have responded by adopting laws specifically designed to eliminate the need for litigation in these cases. . . . The New York legislature has not been one of the leaders in enacting statutes of this type, and it has been slow to follow the lead of others, if, indeed, that is what it intends to do. . . .

Choosing appropriate care for a terminal patient unable to choose for himself always involves a difficult and painful decision for the patient's family and physicians. This decision should not be made more difficult and agonizing by uncertainty concerning the legal consequences, or by requiring them to resort to litigation. These are not just the problems of private litigants. They are the problems of us all. They raise fundamental questions concerning our social and ethical values that should be considered initially by the representative branch of government where all views can be aired and hopefully accommodated.

Legislation will not eliminate all need to resort to the courts. There will always be questions of interpretation and constitutional rights. But legislation should be able to provide answers in most cases and, in others, provide the courts and potential litigants with a clear statement of public policy to inform the choice. No one can eliminate the agony of a personal loss of a friend or family member. But in most cases we can eliminate the agony and expense of litigation involving life-and-death decisions.

Grand Jury (Versions of This Speech Were Delivered throughout the Late 1980s)

Consider how today's grand jury functions. Information comes to a district attorney concerning the commission of a crime. Witnesses are interviewed and evidence is gathered. The prosecutor concludes that sufficient proof exists to charge an individual with a crime. Now, with mind made up, the district attorney goes to the grand jury to obtain an indictment. The stamp of approval will be sought. The same witnesses, already interviewed, and the same evidence, already gathered, will now be presented to the grand jury. The legal adviser to the grand jury will be the same district attorney. The prosecutor alone will decide what they will hear. The defense has no right to present its case, or cross-examine, or have counsel present. It is, by design, a one-sided affair.

Is it any wonder that nearly everyone experienced with the criminal law readily concedes that the grand jury almost invariably does what the prosecutor wants? Is it really necessary to expend the time and the energy to assemble twenty-three jurors, court officers, police, witnesses and prosecutors—merely to have them confirm—as they almost invariably do—a conclusion already reached by the only legal adviser they will hear?

Another drawback of the grand jury system is the misunderstanding it generates. The public often equates an indictment with guilt, either because it is ignorant of the difference between grand and petit juries, or because, notwithstanding the constitutional presumption of innocence, it assumes that where there is smoke in the form of an indictment, there must be fire in the form of guilt.

In this nation we hold few rights more dear than the right to be free from unreasonable searches and seizures. We protect that right by authorizing search warrants only when a judicial officer determines that probable cause exists. We can readily adopt that procedure for the prosecution of felonies. Why not permit a felony prosecution upon a judicial determination that the available evidence—submitted by affidavits of the same persons we now require to appear before the grand jury—constitutes probable cause to believe that the felony charged has been committed by the defendant? That determination, like the issuance of a search warrant, will be subject to judicial review and will be open, unlike grand jury proceedings, to public scrutiny and we will have saved the enormous expenditure of time, money and personnel now required to submit every felony charge to a grand jury. Police officers, who must now spend untold hours waiting to testify before grand juries, can put their time to better use deterring crime on the streets.

I am not in favor of abolishing the grand jury entirely. As an investigative body, it has served us long and well. Cases will remain—of organized crime or corruption by public officials—or in which it is essential to test questionable witnesses—for prosecutions to proceed by grand jury indictment. Such cases will be in the minority. When they appear, however, the district attorney or the court ought to have the option to direct prosecution through the grand jury.

Judicial Activism (Versions of This Speech Were Delivered Various Times during the Late 1980s)

I cannot think of words less in need of annotation than the truth so proudly declared self-evident in our Independence Declaration that: "All men are created equal." Yet, it is all too clear that while our founders wrote those words with hearts full of devotion to freedom and justice for mankind, they never once meant to include members of the black race, or women. . . .

And this nation has survived because there has been, in this state and country, a recognition of our obligation to enact laws and to adapt the law to the "crises of human affairs." There is a need for judicial respect for the prerogatives of the executive and legislative branches under our separation doctrine. There is a place for judicial restraint. But the protection of such things as individual and privacy freedoms is a uniquely judicial obligation and responsibility. Judicial restraint should not be confused with judicial abdication. . . .

Those responsible for our justice system, the courts and lawyers, were given the responsibility of maintaining our constitutional ideals of justice, and their success—our success—will be measured, not in what we do to appease the majority, but what we do to protect the rights of the individual. . . .

. . . So long as we are willing to defend in our courts those basic freedoms which are cherished by all of our citizens—even if that protection is unpopular. Then we would have done our part in seeing to it that the future of our Constitution is secure.

Time moves quickly, and while the present may seem eternal, all too soon future generations will be here to appraise us as we now appraise the work of our forebears. When they do, they will hopefully conclude: This was our nation—still in its youth—and we too did our work well.

Jews and Italians (Late 1980s)

... All of my life I have had a very special relationship with the Italian people, and they have been so very good to me.

My career in government was started by Joe Carlino, who had the courage to foster the nomination of the first Jew to ever run on the Republican ticket in the 200-year history of the Town of North Hempstead. That invited a three-way primary.

Ed Speno worked harder than any political leader should be expected to when I ran for county executive.

And Joe Margiotta, despite the fact that the Conservative party refused to endorse me and he was aware of the fact that I would have an uphill fight, played a major role in my nomination and election to the court on which I now sit.

And along the way there was Scarry and Razzy and Matty and Eddie and Nettie, and the John Michael Marino Lodge in Port Washington, and so many dear and wonderful friends.

When I ran in 1972 my running mate was my dear friend Mike Gabrielli. . . . A year after I came to the Court of Appeals, a friend of mine from Nassau County with the name of Bellacosa came into my life in a very genuine way when he became the Chief Clerk of our court. He and Mike Gabrielli and I had lunch together every day for a decade. We must have consumed over a ton of garlic.

And then another Italian reached out and tapped me on the shoulder—Mario Cuomo named me Chief Judge of the Court of Appeals. Of course, I evened that score when I swore him in as Governor of the State of New York.

I appointed Joe [Bellacosa] as the Chief Administrative Judge. He became my right arm and my left arm—administering this writhing monster we call the New York State

Court System. He is one of the most remarkable administrators I have ever known and has forgotten more about how to handle a bureaucracy than Oliver North ever knew. Now he sits as a member of my court. And Mike Gabrielli has moved his law offices to Albany—and so once again there is garlic in the Court of Appeals Hall.

To all of them—and to all of you—I owe so much.

State Constitutionalism (Around 1990)

Whenever we hear of constitutional rights, we generally think of the federal constitution, especially the Bill of Rights found in the first ten amendments. We often forget that the states also have constitutions and that in the eastern states, the original thirteen colonies, these constitutions were adopted at the outbreak of the Revolution, ten years before the federal constitution. In these years of the bicentennial we are frequently reminded that these state constitutions served as the model for the federal one. But the personal guarantees in the state constitutions are of more than historical significance. They continue as important sources of individual rights, often affording greater protections than the federal Bill of Rights. This is as it was intended to be.

From the outset of the republic the founders contemplated that the states would be the primary guarantors of individual liberties. That was one of the reasons the federal constitution originally contained no Bill of Rights. The idea persisted even after the adoption of the first ten amendments which by their terms only protected individuals against encroachments by the federal government. The only protection the individual had against the actions of the states were the personal guarantees of the various state constitutions. These state guarantees were felt to be adequate protection of individuals until after the Civil War when the slaves were freed and given the status of citizens of the nation and the states in which they resided. A fear that the states might deny certain rights to the former slaves inspired the adoption of additional amendments granting all persons equal protection and due process in their dealings with the states.

After the adoption of these Civil War amendments the federal government, acting primarily through the Supreme Court, took an active role in determining what rights were binding on the states and what was the scope of those rights. As a result, most of the rights guaranteed by the Bill of Rights are now binding on the states as well as the federal government. Indeed, the Supreme Court took such an active role in defining and often expanding these basic protections that it was perceived by many, even in the legal community, as the primary, if not exclusive, guarantor of personal liberties throughout the nation. In recent years, however, the Supreme Court has expressed a renewed interest in the federal ideal, by emphasizing that its role is only to define the minimum protections and that it is up to the state courts, interpreting their own state constitutions, to decide whether these adequately meet the needs and expectations of the citizens of a particular state.

We are now experiencing a renaissance with respect to state constitutional rights. As the Supreme Court retreats from the field, or holds the line on individual rights, state courts and litigants seeking solutions to new problems are turning with greater frequency to the state constitutions which for many years lay dormant in the shadow of the federal Bill of Rights. This is not, as some have suggested, a way of evading the edicts of a conservative Supreme Court. It is a resumption of a role which the state constitutions were originally designed to fulfill, as the primary guardians of the rights of all individuals within their borders. New York has been an active participant in this movement. . . .

In this state . . . the number of cases in which the state constitution is raised is steadily increasing. In cases where the federal constitution provides no relief, or where the outcome is uncertain, or where a matter of special interest to the state is presented, the litigants and the courts are turning to the state constitution for solutions. Resolution of these cases is often difficult because, for so many years, the state constitutions were eclipsed by the federal. Nevertheless, in this state and others the problems are being solved by careful examination of the text, the available history, and the traditions and expectations of the people of the state.

In time, with experiment and experience, the states should continue to be able to develop a body of state constitutional law which meets the needs of its citizens. If a consensus is reached on a particular point it may well be adopted by the Supreme Court as the national standard. Perhaps in the future when we hear of constitutional rights we will think first of the rights guaranteed by our state constitutions.

Note

1. *Schloendorff* v. *Society of N.Y. Hosp.*, 211 NY 125, 129–30.

Comparison of U.S. and N.Y. Constitutions

New York State cannot offer its citizens lesser liberties than are required under the U.S. Constitution, but it can—and in several regards does—provide broader rights. Her are some examples:

Freedom of Religion

U.S. Constitution: "Congress shall make no law respecting an establishment of religion, or prohibiting the free exercise thereof."

N.Y. Constitution: "The free exercise and enjoyment of religion and enjoyment of religious profession and worship, without discrimination or preference, shall forever be allowed in this state to all mankind."

Freedom of Speech and Press

U.S. Constitution: "Congress shall make no law ... abridging the freedom of speech, or of the press."

N.Y. Constitution: "Every citizen may freely speak, write and publish his sentiments on all subjects, being responsible for the abuse of that right, and no law shall be passed to restrain or abridge the liberty of speech or of the press."

Workers' Rights

U.S. Constitution: Does not address.

N.Y. Constitution: "No laborer, workman or mechanic, in the employ of a contractor or subcontractor engaged in the performance of any public work, shall be permitted to work more than eight hours in any day or more than five days in any week, except in cases of extraordinary emergency."

Right to Education

U.S. Constitution: Does not address.

N.Y. Constitution: "The legislature shall provide for the maintenance and support of a system of free common schools, wherein all the children of this state may be educated."

Right to Forest Conservation

U.S. Constitution: Does not address.

N.Y. Constitution: "The lands of the state, now owned or hereafter acquired, constituting the forest preserve as now fixed by law, shall be forever kept as wild forest lands. They shall not be leased, sold or exchanged, or be taken by any corporation, public or private, nor shall the timber therein be sold, removed or destroyed."

Right to Social Welfare

U.S. Constitution: Does not address.

N.Y. Constitution: "The aid, care and support of the needy are public concerns and shall be provided by the state and by such of its subdivisions, and in such manner and by such means, as the legislature may from time to time determine."

Selected Bibliography

Alderman, Ellen, and Caroline Kennedy. *In Our Defense: The Bill of Rights in Action.* New York: Avon, 1991.

Benjamin, Gerald, and Henrik N. Dullea, eds. *Decision 1997: Constitutional Change in New York.* New York: The Rockefeller Institute Press, 1997.

Bergan, Francis. *The History of the New York Court of Appeals, 1947–1952.* New York: Columbia University Press, 1985.

Bonventre, Vincent Martin. "Tilting the Scales of Justice." *Empire State Report,* June 1992.

Bork, Robert. *The Tempting of America.* New York: Free Press, 1990.

Clark, Hunter R. *Justice Brennan: The Great Conciliator.* New York: Carroll Publishing, 1995.

Colby, Peter W., and John K. White. *New York State Today.* Albany: State University of New York Press, 1989.

Cuomo, Mario M. *Diaries of Mario M Cuomo: The Campaign for Governor.* New York: Random House, 1984.

Davis, Michael D., and Hunter R. Clark. *Thurgood Marshall: Warrior at the Bar, Rebel at the Bench.* Secaucus, N.J.: Citadel Press, 1994.

Davis, Sue. *Justice Rehnquist and the Constitution.* Princeton, N.J.: Princeton University Press, 1989.

D'Amato, Alfonse. *Power, Pasta and Politics: The World According to Senator Al D'Amato.* New York: Hyperion, 1995.

Dershowitz, Alan M. *The Best Defense.* New York: Random House, 1982.

Galie, Peter. *Ordered Liberty: A Constitutional History of New York.* New York: Fordham University Press, 1995.

Greenberg, Henry M. "Criminal Procedure," 1993–94 Survey of New York Law. *Syracuse Law Review* 45, no. 1 (1994).

Kaye, Judith S. "The Importance of State Courts: A Snapshot of the New York Court of Appeals." *Annual Survey of American Law,* New York University School of Law, 1994.

Kramer, Michael, and Sam Roberts. *I Never Wanted to be Vice-President of Anything: An Investigative Biography of Nelson Rockefeller.* New York: Basic Books Inc., 1976.

Lerner, Max. *Nine Scorpions in a Bottle.* New York: Arcade Publishing,1994.

———. *Tocqueville and American Civilization.* New York: Harper Colophon Books, 1969.

Litwak, Mark. *Courtroom Crusaders: American Lawyers Who Refused to Fit the Mold.* New York: William Morrow and Co., Inc., 1989.

Persico, Joseph E. *The Imperial Rockefeller.* New York: Simon & Schuster, 1982.

Schwartz, Bernard. *Super Chief: Earl Warren and His Supreme Court—A Judicial Biography.* New York: New York University Press, 1983.

Simon, James F. *The Center Holds: The Power Struggle Inside the Rehnquist Court.* New York: Simon & Schuster, 1995.

Wachtler, Sol. *After the Madness: A Judge's Own Prison Memoir.* New York: Random House, 1997.

Wagman, Robert J. *The First Amendment Book.* Mahwah, N.J.: Pharos Books, 1991.

Wolfe, Linda. *Double Life: The Shattering Affair between Chief Judge Sol Wachtler and Socialite Joy Silverman.* New York: Pocket Books, 1994.

Woodward, Bob, and Scott Armstrong. *The Brethren.* New York: Simon & Schuster, 1979.

Index